IAN MORTIMER

Dr Ian Mortimer is the *Sunday Times*-bestselling author of The Time Traveller's Guides to *Medieval England*, *Elizabethan England*, *Restoration Britain* and *Regency Britain*, as well as *Human Race* and four critically acclaimed medieval biographies. His novel *The Outcasts of Time* won the Winston Graham Prize in 2018.

He is a Fellow of the Royal Historical Society and a Fellow of the Society of Antiquaries. His work on the social history of medicine won the Alexander Prize in 2004 and was published by the Royal Historical Society in 2009. He lives in Moretonhampstead, on the edge of Dartmoor.

ALSO BY IAN MORTIMER

The Greatest Traitor:
The Life of Sir Roger Mortimer,
1st Earl of March,
Ruler of England, 1327–1330

The Perfect King:
The Life of Edward III,
Father of the English Nation

The Fears of Henry IV:
The Life of England's Self-made King

1415: Henry V's Year of Glory

Human Race:
Ten Centuries of Change on Earth

The Outcasts of Time

The Time Traveller's Guide to
Medieval England

The Time Traveller's Guide to
Elizabethan England

The Time Traveller's Guide to
Restoration Britain

The Time Traveller's Guide to
Regency Britain

IAN MORTIMER

Medieval Horizons

Why the Middle Ages Matter

VINTAGE

1 3 5 7 9 10 8 6 4 2

Vintage is part of the Penguin Random House group of companies
whose addresses can be found at global.penguinrandomhouse.com

First published in Vintage in 2024
First published in hardback by The Bodley Head in 2023

penguin.co.uk/vintage

Printed and bound in Great Britain by Clays Ltd, Elcograf S.p.A.

The authorised representative in the EEA is Penguin Random House Ireland,
Morrison Chambers, 32 Nassau Street, Dublin D02 YH68

A CIP catalogue record for this book is available from the British Library

ISBN 9781529920802

Penguin Random House is committed to a sustainable future
for our business, our readers and our planet. This book is made
from Forest Stewardship Council® certified paper.

This book is dedicated to Jörg Hensgen, who has now edited ten of my history books over the last twenty years. I am deeply in his debt. So are you. Although many people think that an editor's job is an easy one, it certainly isn't in my case. To rework an old metaphor: it is the editor's job to ensure that a literary camel can pass easily and smoothly through the eye of a needle. The real mark of success is when this miracle goes entirely unnoticed by the reader. So, Jörg, for all ten of your patiently worked miracles, my most sincere and heartfelt thanks.

Contents

Acknowledgements

This book has grown out of my work as a historian, in particular from four speaking engagements in 2015 and 2016. I would therefore like to thank those individuals who invited me to these events: Dr David Grummitt (Medieval Horizons), Professor Anne Curry (War), Pat Whitten and Jill Maslen (Tyndale), and Dr Aiden Gregg (Individualism). Details of the original talks are given in the first note for the relevant chapter.

I am, as usual, indebted to my agent, Georgina Capel, and her hardworking team, especially Rachel Conway and Irene Baldoni. Also to my publisher, Stuart Williams, and his team at The Bodley Head, especially my editor, Jörg Hensgen, to whom this book is dedicated. Once more, Jörg's incisive questioning and criticism have proved invaluable.

A special thank-you goes to Dr Seb Falk of the Faculty of History at the University of Cambridge, who very kindly read through an earlier draft of the book and made many helpful suggestions. All the remaining mistakes are mine, of course, but there would have been more of them had it not been for Dr Falk's attention to detail and his kind advice.

I would like to thank Louise Anson for kindly giving me permission to quote several verses from Helen Waddell's translation of the *Confession* of the Archpoet, which appear on pages 185–6.

My final and greatest debt is to my wife, Sophie, for all her support. She inspires me with her commitment to her own work and, through her companionship, gives my achievements meaning. She is the one who supplies the reassurance I need to enter the vast cathedral of recorded time and be able to marvel at it, and not be overwhelmed.

Ian Mortimer
Moretonhampstead, 4 October 2022

Introduction

Anyone looking for a literary image to sum up the Middle Ages would find it hard to beat Geoffrey Chaucer's *Canterbury Tales*, written in the 1390s. The poet describes a motley group of characters making a pilgrimage from the Tabard Inn, in Southwark, to Canterbury, each one telling an entertaining story along the way. Among them is a knight who has fought in crusades in north Africa, Spain and eastern Europe. He is accompanied by his son, a squire, adept at jousting, and a longbow-carrying servant. Also travelling in the same company are a prioress, a nun, a friar, a monk, five other priests, a merchant, a scholar from Oxford University, a sergeant-at-law, a ship's captain, a doctor of physic, a five-times married businesswoman from Bath, a reeve, a miller, a seller of pardons, a summoner who instructed people to appear in court, a manciple or provisioner for one of the Inns of Court in London, three farmers, a cook, an innkeeper, five other tradesmen and Chaucer himself. We travel with them as they ride along to the shrine of St Thomas Becket, chatting, bickering and making each other laugh – an epitome of medieval England.

We tend to forget, however, just how fleeting Chaucer's world was. We often talk about 'the Middle Ages' as if the whole period was relatively unchanging, with a fixed set of characteristics. Within 200 years, however, life had profoundly changed. Many of Chaucer's characters were antiquated. The medieval knight was an anachronism. So too was jousting. Longbows had been replaced by guns. No one went on pilgrimage in England any more. There were no prioresses or nuns here. Nor were there any monks, friars or pardoners. Priests were no longer Roman Catholic. For Elizabethans, Chaucer would have provided a rare insight into a long-forgotten world, much as Jane Austen does for us today.

Chaucer's medieval cavalcade is equally unrepresentative of Norman England. This becomes clear when we contrast *The Canterbury*

Tales with the entries in Domesday Book, the famous survey of all the property in the country compiled in 1086. There were far fewer monks and nuns in the eleventh century compared with Chaucer's time. There were fewer merchants and ships' captains too. There were no friars at all. Nor were there any pardoners, summoners or doctors of physic. There were no Oxford scholars because Oxford University did not exist; neither did the Inns of Court. Nor were there any crusades or tournaments. There were no longbows. Not many people went on pilgrimage and the few who did were serious souls who set a higher priority on seeing Jerusalem or Rome than Canterbury. Most people were agricultural workers – ploughmen, herdsmen, swineherds, dairymaids and beekeepers – and most of them were not at liberty to leave the place where they grew up. They wouldn't have been allowed to join Chaucer on his pilgrimage.

This should leave us wondering what we really mean when we use the term 'medieval'. What exactly are we referring to when that word relates to such different societies? As the comparisons just mentioned indicate, there were many Middle Ages, not just one. To describe them all in the same way is like describing seventeenth-century and twenty-first-century Europe as equally 'modern' – even though we would hardly describe the execution of witches in the seventeenth century as a 'modern' practice, quite the opposite. Such a concatenation of time periods would obviously be misleading.

Why does this matter, you may ask. First, it matters historically. The use of the word 'medieval' to describe half a millennium conceals how much daily life changed over that time. But more importantly, it suggests that everything we put in the box marked 'medieval' is separate from the modern world. As a result, we fail to realise that the way we live today is largely the result of social developments that took place between the eleventh century and the sixteenth. Many of our contemporary concepts, values and priorities originated in the Middle Ages. Many of our cultural and social practices did too, from our discovery of other continents and races to our use of surnames and our reliance on money and the written word. In short, not to know about the changes that took place in the Middle Ages means failing to understand the cluster of revolutions that shaped the character of the modern world. And that means failing to understand ourselves.

That statement might surprise you because we don't generally regard the Middle Ages as a revolutionary period. We tend to think that the most significant changes affecting our lives have been modern ones. We point to nineteenth-century inventions such as railways, photography and telephones; and to twentieth-century ones, such as TV, air and space travel, computers and the Internet. Yet although these innovations have completely altered the ways in which we do things, our main priorities as human beings have been surprisingly stable for the last four hundred years (with a few notable exceptions). They were anything but stable before that. If you look beyond the technological advances that have dazzled us since the Industrial Revolution, you will notice that the earlier centuries saw a number of social and economic pressures that profoundly affected our ancestors' thoughts and influenced their behaviour. Many of the changes that took place back then are now so deeply buried in our collective psyche that we never stop to consider them. Why do you think of yourself as an individual? Why do you need to travel? Why do you expect the state to protect you? Why do you need money? Why do we think peace is normal, not war?

This book aims to demonstrate that the Middle Ages were the formative years of the modern world by drawing attention to these fundamental questions. It will also reveal that the major obstacle preventing us from seeing the significance of these earlier changes is our obsession with technology. We are so highly focused on modern manufacturing ingenuity that many people consider the invention of the smartphone or the aeroplane far more significant than our ability to feed ourselves. To someone with a full stomach, methods of food production are nowhere near as impressive as travelling to the other side of the world and speaking to a friend back home on a phone. But to a malnourished peasant at risk of starving to death because of a poor harvest, such technology is a meaningless luxury. And in this respect, we owe a great deal to our medieval forebears. The brutal hardships through which they struggled made them introduce systems that gradually reduced the suffering and which continue to benefit us to this day.

Our interest in the ancient world is another hindrance to understanding the medieval impact. This is because we tend to know much more about the Romans than we do about, say, the people who lived in the thirteenth century. Our fascination with their domestic arrangements, their bustling markets, their systems of administration, their poetry and their love lives, makes it easy for us to think they were 'just like us'. As a result, it appears that there is a two-thousand-year continuity between the world of the emperor Augustus and our world today. We don't notice the many discontinuities that separate the Romans from the people of medieval Europe. When we read about thirteenth-century people, we imagine their daily lives to be more or less like those of the Romans before them. But if we look closely and try to reconstruct their ways of thinking, we see that medieval people were far from being the same as either Romans or us.

Consider, for example, the mirror, which I will discuss in chapter seven. The Romans had small glass mirrors: Roman ladies used them for applying makeup, just as we do. But then, with the collapse of Roman civilisation, mirrors ceased to be manufactured. We therefore differ from our early medieval ancestors in that we know what we look like and they didn't. You don't get much of a picture of yourself from a reflection in a puddle. You need either a metal-backed glass mirror or a highly polished flat piece of silver or bronze. Metal mirrors were reintroduced to Europe in the early twelfth century but remained expensive, enjoyed only by high-status individuals. Thus the reinvention of the glass mirror in Italy around 1300 allowed increasing numbers of people to see themselves as we see ourselves. Prior to that, an ordinary woman could not know how she appeared in other people's eyes. If she was lucky enough to grow old, she would never have fully appreciated how lined her face was. Not knowing what she looked like, makeup was not something that entered her life. Even more importantly, the rapid spread of mirrors led to people acquiring a new sense of self. This forced them to compare themselves to others: to change their appearance and behaviour, to make themselves more attractive, and so on. At the same time, society gradually began to turn the proverbial mirror on itself – to examine humankind for its own sake and not simply as a creature of God's making. We became aware of the human condition.

Small changes like the introduction of the mirror – which arguably led ultimately to our selfie-taking generation – hint at the complexity and depth of medieval change. I could mention many other examples of seemingly minor medieval innovations that had a profound effect on the modern world. I couldn't describe them all in this book: there were simply too many. Nor could I do justice to all the similar contemporaneous developments around the world that led to some regions developing differently from others. What I *can* do is offer a way to understand all those changes. In the first chapter, I outline how we might use the metaphorical horizon as a tool to appreciate the extent and importance of social change. The easiest way to explain what I mean by 'the metaphorical horizon' is to talk about explorers. In the eleventh century, no one in Europe had any idea of what lay to the east of Jerusalem or south of the Sahara. Very few Europeans had ever sailed across the Atlantic. But by 1600, a number of maritime expeditions had circumnavigated the globe. In other words, through looking at exploration, we can see how the horizons of Christendom gradually broadened to embrace the entire world.

This expansion of the limits of our knowledge acts as a model for many other aspects of life. Our expanding horizons were not only geographical. There was a similar expanding horizon to how far back we could remember, through the recording of more and more information. There was another expanding horizon to the proportions of the population who owned property, and another to the freedoms women enjoyed. And so on. The purpose of the first chapter is therefore to introduce the idea of the horizon as a way of perceiving social change. In the subsequent chapters, I look at some of the most important themes in history and demonstrate in more depth how the metaphor of the shifting horizon allows us to appreciate the developments that took place. How much faster could people travel in 1600 than in 1000? What proportion of their lives was spent defending themselves against violence? How many of their contemporaries did they consider their equals? How many could read – and why did it matter? I hope that, once you appreciate the concept of the metaphorical horizon, you will see medieval people in a different light – and the light in question is the light of their minds.

That date range – from 1000 to 1600 – might raise questions in your mind about my definition of 'medieval' here. On this matter, it is impossible to please everyone with a single date span. While some English political historians insist that the Middle Ages came to an end abruptly on the afternoon of 22 August 1485, when Richard III was killed at the battle of Bosworth, such hard-and-fast delineations are more misleading than helpful. The fact is that all the ages shade into one another gradually, they don't end with one man's death. Thus the word 'medieval' means different things in different contexts to different people. Most European historians agree that the Middle Ages started with the fall of Rome around 500 and ended around 1500 – normally at some point between the advent of printing in the 1450s and the Reformation, which began in 1517. However, English writers usually split the period into two phases: the early Middle Ages, which started with the collapse of Roman rule around 410 and ended with the Norman Conquest in 1066, and the later Middle Ages, which ran from 1066 to the final Dissolution of the Monasteries in 1540. Some prefer the death of Henry VII in 1509 as the terminal point; others the death of the last Catholic monarch, Mary, in 1558. It hardly needs saying that there is no right or wrong about these differences. It is far better to choose an appropriate set of dates for your subject than stick rigidly to rules devised by other people for different reasons.

In this book, my intention has been to demonstrate a number of social changes between the eleventh century and the sixteenth: hence the approximate date range from 1000 to 1600. The prime reason for starting in about 1000 is that several of the most significant developments of the Middle Ages have their roots in the eleventh century, as consequences of the Medieval Warm Period, which I discuss in chapter three. As for the terminal date, there are two prime reasons for choosing 1600. One is that the following century saw the development of statistics, mathematics, medical thinking and the scientific method, which altered our perceptions of the world and our place in it. It also saw the development of many new scientific instruments. Both the microscope and the telescope were invented about 1600, and these two inventions heralded a new wave of horizons of knowledge that were not at all medieval.

The other reason for choosing the year 1600 is down to Shakespeare, whose plays straddle the turn of the sixteenth and seventeenth centuries. We often say that Shakespeare 'speaks for us' even though he knew nothing of the cars, aeroplanes, computers or mobile phones that we believe play an important part in our lives. He shows us that the ways in which we respect each other and understand each other's emotions are comparable to how people understood each other in 1600. Despite all the technological changes and social revolutions since then, our inner lives have altered very little. Yet Shakespeare is hardly a spokesman for the people mentioned in Domesday Book; he was even further removed from them than Chaucer was. In the eleventh century, one in ten English people was a slave and at least another seven were unfree – meaning that they were bought and sold with the land on which they lived and worked. Shakespeare probably did not even know this. He would almost certainly have presumed that the majority of English people had always been able to come and go as they pleased. His plays are therefore a useful cultural benchmark for assessing how the English had come to live after six centuries of social and cultural upheaval.

Inevitably, as an English historian, most of my examples are drawn from English sources. It hardly needs spelling out that this does not imply that I believe the English led the way in all the cultural developments discussed in this book, or that other countries mattered less. In the Middle Ages, the English were on the periphery of Christendom and often were followers rather than innovators. It is rather the case that I have drawn on those aspects of the past with which I am most familiar to illustrate how the metaphorical horizon can be used to appreciate social change. A German or Italian historian might just as well explore the shifting cultural horizons of medieval Europe with an emphasis on those countries' experiences. Someone with a deep knowledge of Asian, African or American history could employ the same approach. It would be good if they did. Even if such a study revealed that the most significant cultural shocks in those regions took place in earlier or later centuries, this too would be a valuable application of the idea of the metaphorical horizon, and an important contrast in terms of understanding world history.

Finally, I cannot emphasise strongly enough that the purpose of this book is not to give you all the answers about how life altered over the course of the Middle Ages but to act as a tool that you yourself can learn to apply to past societies to gauge the extent of social change. In this respect it attempts to do for social history what Robert Hooke's *Micrographia* did for the microscopic world when that book was published in 1665. Hooke's pioneering presentation of a few subjects in magnified images – the most famous of these being an 18in-wide picture of a flea – gave his readers a new understanding of microscopic organisms. But it also demonstrated that there was much more to learn about other previously overlooked creatures that he did *not* illustrate. This book similarly shows you that many profound historical changes aren't immediately obvious. In the same way that things close to us often prevent us from seeing what is in the distance – the proverbial wood for the trees – so our present-day perceptions and obsessions with technology are the prime obstacles stopping us from seeing the dynamism of our medieval past. Obviously, the metaphorical horizon has its limitations. Like the microscope itself, it is not the right tool for every job. However, the idea is put forward in the hope that it helps you achieve a better understanding of the world in which we live – and when, as well as how, it came to be as it is today.

I

Horizons

Introducing the Metaphorical Horizon[1]

When we consider how things have changed over the centuries, we naturally think in terms of technological development. That's not surprising. All around us there are objects that make our lives very different from those of our ancestors, from TVs and kitchen appliances to cars and GPS watches. When we think about the greatest developments in human history, we normally focus on inventions. Flight, mobile phones, space travel, computers and nuclear weapons are the shining stars of such debates. Occasionally we remember something from an earlier age, such as the printing press, the gun, the compass, vaccinations or the clock. But regardless of the preferred epoch, we generally relate social change to technological invention. As a society, we worship technology. You could say that faith these days is not so much a conscious belief in a divine being as a subconscious one in technology – 'In Technology we Trust'.

This emphasis leads us to calibrate social change by referring to a timeline of technical innovations. In military history, it encourages us to interpret changing methods of warfare in terms of the successive introductions of cannon, handguns, mortars, torpedoes, aircraft, chemical weapons, tanks, bombs, radar and guided missiles. In industrial history we do much the same thing by focusing on various stages of mechanical development, from the spinning jenny in the eighteenth century to steam-powered mills in the nineteenth and automated production lines in the twentieth. Therefore, because technological change is a characteristic of relatively modern times, the further we look back, the fewer changes we see. Consequently, when we consider the Middle Ages, we assume there was little or no social change. The period appears like so many centuries of sword fighting, farming and praying. Society appears to have been largely the same, century after century.

In reality, this picture couldn't be more wrong.

What is particularly curious about this self-deception is that even professional historians endorse it. Specialists in medieval history do not try to argue in public that the fourteenth century was as important for the development of the modern world as the nineteenth or the twentieth. They know that, given the widespread faith in the power of technology, their views would quickly be dismissed and they would be regarded as being out of touch with reality. Even if they were to present the Middle Ages in terms of their genuine technological contributions, the results would emphasise the importance of more recent achievements. No medieval innovation compares with the sophistication of a mobile phone or a laser-guided missile. As a result, the reputation of the Middle Ages in the public imagination remains stuck in a muddy rut. Even the greatest scholars have not been able to change that.[2]

The specialists' dilemma in convincing the wider public of the importance of the Middle Ages is understandable. It is easy for anyone listening to a proselytising professor to conclude that he or she is biased and amplifying the case for the sake of advancing his or her career. But many generalists and public thinkers have also endorsed the idea that the Middle Ages were a time of little social change. And if a world-renowned writer looks at the last thousand years and treats the first half as relatively unimportant, who dares to disagree?

Take Yuval Noah Harari's international bestseller *Sapiens: A Brief History of Humankind*, published in English in 2014. Chapter fourteen begins like this:

Were, say, a Spanish peasant to have fallen asleep in 1000 AD and woken up 500 years later, to the din of Columbus' sailors boarding the *Niña*, *Pinta* and *Santa Maria*, the world would have seemed to him quite familiar. Despite many changes in technology, manners and political boundaries, this medieval Rip van Winkle would have felt at home. But had one of Columbus' sailors fallen into a similar slumber and woken up to the ringtone of a twenty-first-century iPhone, he would have found himself in a world strange beyond comprehension. 'Is this heaven?' he might well have asked himself. 'Or perhaps – hell?'

Harari is a professor of history at the Hebrew University of Jerusalem and a specialist in medieval warfare. It seems strange, therefore, that he chose a peasant from the place where Columbus sailed from, Palos de la Frontera, in the south-west of Spain, to serve as his example. In the year 1000, this region was under the control of the caliphate of Cordoba; it remained under Muslim rule until 1262. Harari's Muslim peasant could not have awoken in a more hostile, alien environment than that of the last days of the *Reconquista* in 1492. He would have witnessed the Christian conquest of his homeland and the expulsion, execution or forced conversion of his people. He certainly would not have 'felt at home'. Had he awoken in the twenty-first century, he might be perplexed by the ringing of a mobile phone but at least the Spanish government would not be trying to kill him on account of his religion. Harari seems happy to overlook the historical detail in favour of technological change as the common language for comparison. For someone speaking on an international stage, there is a real advantage in working with the tools that readers already have at their disposal. But in framing the comparison in this way, Harari is following his audience's presumptions, not guiding their understanding. He is passing over major social changes in the medieval period as if they were inconsequential.

I came across a second, equally striking example in a 2018 magazine article by Professor Ian Morris, author of the bestselling book *Why the West Rules – For Now*:

Take England: if we picked up a peasant from 1750 BC and dropped him or her down in 1750 AD, just before the Industrial Revolution, he or she would have quickly adjusted. Some things had certainly changed: people had switched from round houses to rectangular ones; from farmsteads to (mostly) villages, from bronze to iron, from a sun god to Jesus. The rich now wore powdered wigs and corsets. A few could now read and write, some had eyeglasses, and, in 1784, a Scotsman could fly in a balloon. Yet so much had not changed. The basic patterns of life and death, taxes and rent, sowing and ploughing, deference to lords and ladies – the visitor from 1750 BC would recognise them all. But put that peasant back in the Tardis and catapult him to this age of cars, computers, TV, literacy, skyscrapers, gender reassignment, sexual freedom, democracy, nuclear weapons . . . our peasant would have a nervous breakdown.[3]

In answer to this, 'the basic patterns of life and death' which Morris mentions only in connection with 1750 BC and 1750 AD are still with us today.

We still have to pay taxes and rent. We are still dependent on sowing and ploughing the land (even though most of us don't do it ourselves). There is as much deference to the super rich and celebrities as there was to eighteenth-century lords and ladies. As for the day-to-day differences between 1750 BC and 1750 AD, the problem is that we have no written sources illustrating what life was like in England at the outset of that 3,500-year period. Everything about it has to be inferred from archaeology. However, we do have Julius Caesar's description of the British people at the midway point, in the first century BC. He refers to our ancestors wearing animal skins, wearing their hair long, dyeing their bodies blue with woad to be more frightening in battle, wearing moustaches and 'sharing their wives between groups of ten or twelve men'. Frankly, I cannot see how a Briton of Caesar's time – let alone the Bronze Age – could have adapted more easily to the court of King George II than to putting on a pair of jeans and having a pint in a twenty-first-century pub. Indeed, there are certain modern music festivals where the long-haired, polyamorous ancient Britons would fit in quite well.

If we only ever regard benchmarks of change in terms of technological innovations, it is like looking at the world through a red lens and declaring that everything is red: you don't notice the blue or the green. In our case the lens is technology-coloured and it shows us vividly how technology has affected our lives since the eighteenth century. At the same time it conceals other important changes, such as urbanisation, epidemic diseases, and women's and workers' rights. And it completely obscures almost everything that happened in earlier centuries. Technology did not bring about the French Revolution, which was arguably the most important event of modern times. It did not bring about the Renaissance or the Black Death or the fall of the Roman Empire. In short, if you want to understand social change before 1750, technological innovation is the wrong tool for the job.

Allow me one more example of a highly regarded writer and public commentator underestimating the significance of medieval change. Professor A. C. Grayling's *The Age of Genius: The Seventeenth Century and the Birth of the Modern Mind*, published in 2016, opens with the following lines:

If you step outside on a warm clear night and look up, what do you see? Imagine answering this question 400 years ago. What did people see then, gazing at the stars? It is remarkable that, in seeing the same thing we see today, they nevertheless saw a different universe with a completely different set of meanings both in itself and for their own personal lives. This marks a highly significant fact: that, at the beginning of the seventeenth century the mind – the mentality, the world-view – of our best-educated and most thoughtful forebears was still fundamentally continuous with that of their own antique and medieval predecessors; but by the end of that century it had become modern. This striking fact means that the seventeenth century is a very special period in human history.

No serious historian would disagree that 'the mind' of European people in 1700 had recently undergone many of the profound transformations that made it essentially modern. Indeed, the important shift to a widespread trust in the scientific method, medical processes and statistics was well underway in the seventeenth century, and I would argue that this marks a fundamental threshold dividing the medieval and the modern – trust in science was replacing faith in God. But Professor Grayling does not give sufficient credit to developments before 1600. It is certainly not the case that the world-view of the Elizabethans was 'still fundamentally continuous with that of their own antique and medieval predecessors'. Let us not forget that the Romans burnt Christians. They encouraged gladiators to fight to the death for the sake of public entertainment. They consulted animal entrails to determine the future. They owned slaves. They were sexually liberated: their public art showed the erect male member and acts of bestiality; their oil lamps and wine cups depicted threesomes and foursomes. None of these things would have gone down well at the court of the Virgin Queen.

One can go further than this. Elizabeth I's world-view was not even 'fundamentally continuous' with that of her own grandparents, who not only were Catholic but also believed that the sun orbited the Earth. Elizabeth, in marked contrast, was Protestant and might well have come across the highly respected astronomer and MP, Thomas Digges, who popularised and extended Copernicus's heliocentric theory during her reign. Elizabeth's and her grandparents' world-views also differed in regard to the interplay between God, saints and people on Earth, and they had hugely varying concepts of the afterlife. Fifteenth-century Catholics believed that if your arm was in pain, it would be healed if you made a model of it, placed it on an altar and paid a priest

to pray for its recovery. Protestants looked on this practice as an attempt
to invoke magic. Indeed, with regard to religion, the world-view of
Queen Elizabeth I had much more in common with that of Elizabeth
II than it did with that of the Roman emperors, who devoutly worshipped an entire pantheon, from passionate Venus to lecherous
Jupiter. These world-views only appear to be 'fundamentally continuous' when you are focused so completely on scientific discovery that
you see everything through science-tinted spectacles.

These three examples illustrate my key point. Even our most
respected public intellectuals believe that society's development largely
depended on technological innovation. My contention is not only that
this view is misleading but also that it results in a cultural denigration
of the Middle Ages as an unsophisticated 'dark ages' in the public
imagination. The medieval period is associated with cruelty, violence,
superstition and ignorance – as summed up by derogatory references
to the Taliban as 'medieval' and the line in the film *Pulp Fiction*, 'I'm
gonna get medieval on your ass'. But this perception is wrong. What
of the Twelfth-Century Renaissance? What of the Italian Renaissance?
What of the great cathedrals? If you think 'medieval' is synonymous
with backwardness, then you are exposing your own ignorance – for
this was the age that gave us universities, Parliament and some of the
finest architecture to be found in Europe.

Just consider the great painters of the Italian Renaissance. Some
people would argue that the achievements of Leonardo and Michelangelo have never been surpassed – that the pinnacle of the painter's skill
was reached around 1500. The original version of the *Madonna of the
Rocks* (now in the Louvre) was created by Leonardo in the early 1490s,
as was his famous *Vitruvian Man* drawing. His *Mona Lisa* was painted in
1503. Michelangelo worked on the ceiling of the Sistine Chapel
between 1508 and 1512. Nothing produced in the year 1000 can compare. There are many points of similarity between an oil painting of
Elizabeth I and one of Elizabeth II – but you will not find any image
from 1000 that compares with a fine Renaissance portrait.

Much the same applies to language. Have a look at the beginning
of the Gospel of St Mark as it appears in the translation published by
William Tyndale in 1526:

1. The beginnynge of the Gospell of Iesu Christ the sonne of God

2. As yt is wrytten in the Prophetes: beholde I sende my
     messenger before thy face which shall prepareð thy waye
     before ye.
3. The voyce of a cryer in the wildernes: prepare ye the waye of
     the Lorde make his pathes streyght.
4. Iohn dyd baptise in the wyldernes and preche the baptyme of
     repentaunce for the remission of synnes.

Apart from the spelling – especially the appearance of an archaic ð
(pronounced 'th') at the end of 'prepareð' – the language is understandable. Little has changed over the last five hundred years. However,
we cannot say the same for the version translated by Aelfric of Eynsham about the year 1000:

1. Her ys Godspellys angyn Haelendes Cristes, Godes Suna;
2. Swa áwriten ys on þæs witegan béc Isaíam, Nu ic asénde minne
     engel beforan þine ansyne, se gegearwað þinne weg beforan
     ðe.
3. Clypiende stefn on þam westene, Gegearwiað Dryhtnes weg,
     doð rihte his siðas.
4. Iohannes waes on westene, fulligende, and bodiende daed-bote
     fulwiht, on synna forgyfenesse.

Having no training in Old English, I cannot even pronounce Aelfric's
words. This is largely because of the way the language developed
before 1250. The rate of change slowed after that, as more people
learned to read and write; it became almost static in the sixteenth century, when the printing of the Bible established standards. But it is
striking that we can understand the English of five hundred years
before our time and yet people living then would not have been able to
understand the language of *three* hundred years before theirs, let alone
five hundred. In this case technology – as in the invention of the printing press – acted as a brake on change, not an accelerator.

When we watch or read Shakespeare's plays we immediately understand 95 per cent of them, and the remaining 5 per cent can be
understood with a little effort.[4] If Shakespeare had listened to a recita-
tion of an eleventh-century English poem he would not have
understood more than a fraction. Nor would he have been moved
emotionally, even if he had been able to understand the words. As I

mentioned in the introduction, we often say that Shakespeare 'speaks for us', even though he knew nothing of our complicated modern lives. The technological innovations of the last four hundred years have not significantly changed the ways in which we think and feel. In marked contrast, no eleventh-century writer expressed such an array of human emotions. No Anglo-Saxon poet could possibly have addressed an audience four hundred years after his own time and have been acknowledged as 'speaking for them'. In literature as with language, the story of the last four hundred years is predominantly one of continuity compared to the huge shifts and leaps of the Middle Ages. The culture of the sixteenth century is as far removed from that of 1000 as a clock is from a sundial.

Despite all this, we still talk about the Middle Ages as being a long period of stasis dominated by violence, ignorance and superstition, until technology came along to make the world a better place in the seventeenth century. Indeed, there is a hidden dimension to our obsession with science and technology. It underpins our belief in progress. Technology tends to reassure us that things are getting better and are always going to get better – that no matter what disasters might befall us, technology will save us. In Technology we Trust. Hence the violent, ignorant, superstitious character of the medieval period has become almost an article of faith.

This presents medieval historians with something of a problem. The fact is that by calibrating social change according to technological development, we have introduced a means for misunderstanding the period entirely. We completely miss other shifts that are just as important as the technological ones. People's everyday lives and their 'world-views' changed immensely between the eleventh century and the sixteenth. They underwent so many revolutions it is difficult to count them all. But that is what we need to understand if we are to have a clear picture of how our modern lives in the West evolved.

That's easier said than done. But if we think about cultural change in terms of expanding and (occasionally) contracting horizons rather than technological innovation, the task becomes much more straightforward. *The Oxford English Dictionary* defines the word 'horizon' both literally, as 'the line at which the Earth's surface and the sky appear to meet', and metaphorically, as 'the limit of a person's knowledge, experience, or interest'. With new building methods and urban expansion, the literal horizon changed dramatically in the Middle Ages – but so did people's knowledge, experience and interests. In this chapter we will consider ten examples of how 'horizons' can be used as indicators of social or cultural change. All of them are so fundamental to our world-view that we don't even think of them as significant historical developments: we simply can't imagine the world without them. But that in itself shows how important they are.

The Physical Horizon

How did the skyline change over the period 1000–1600? At the outset, the tallest building in Christendom was Hagia Sophia in Constantinople, which measures 182ft from the ground to the apex of its great dome. It was built by the emperor Justinian in the 530s. The next largest building was probably one of the great tenth-century abbey churches in Burgundy, which may have stood about half this height. Most church towers in northern Europe at the time were no more than 80ft high. But very soon after 1000 taller buildings started to appear. Within a century many church towers were in excess of 100ft and some more than 150ft – the most famous surviving example being Pomposa Abbey in Italy. By 1106, the threshold of 200ft had been breached by the spires of the Imperial Cathedral at Speyer, in Germany. The south spire of Chartres Cathedral, finished in 1220, is 344ft tall. In fact, at 430ft long, Chartres dwarfs any structure built in Europe before 1000, including Hagia Sophia. The spire of Old St Paul's Cathedral in London reached the height of about 489ft around the year 1300. That of Lincoln Cathedral topped out at about 525ft by 1311 – almost as high as Philadelphia City Hall, the largest free-standing stone building in the world today, which at 548ft is not far short of the maximum one can physically build in stone. Laying aside Hagia Sophia as an anomaly, a survival from the Eastern Roman Empire, we can see that building capability increased fivefold in just three hundred years. It is a salutary thought that between 1000 and 1300, the tallest point on the London skyline quintupled in height whereas between 1300 and the completion of the Shard in 2010, it merely doubled.[5]

This general trend of building higher and larger occurred everywhere in Europe over the medieval period. Huge numbers of churches were built, so that by 1600 every parish had a substantial stone structure at its heart. By 1348 probably every kingdom in Christendom had seen a threefold increase in the height of its tallest buildings. The number of abbeys multiplied several times over – there were more than 12,000 across Europe in 1500 – and many of them had great churches attached. Secular buildings grew more substantial too. What would Harari's peasant have made of the walls and towers of a great medieval castle? Hardly any defensive residential structures existed in 1000, so a 121ft-high castle keep like that built at Loches in France in the early eleventh century would have stunned him. The growth of urban settlements would have been no less astonishing. What would he have thought in 1492 of the sprawl of cities like Ghent, Florence, Granada, Paris and Lisbon, all of which had populations of more than 100,000? What would he have made of Albi Cathedral, a massive structure built entirely of *brick*? What would he have made of the expanses of glass in the windows of medieval churches and halls? He would have seen nothing like them in his own time. Stained glass had only recently been invented in 1000. In fact, if he walked into Chartres Cathedral, with all that fantastic architecture and deep blue and red light, and an iPhone ringtone happened to go off while he was listening to the choir, I don't think it would have been the iPhone that would have caught his attention.

The visible horizon changed just as much for an Anglo-Saxon peasant as it did for Harari's Spanish one. In 1000 he would not have seen anything other than single-storey wooden dwellings, except for a few church towers and manorial bell towers and the occasional royal palace. In marked contrast, in 1492 he would have woken up to see thousands of churches, castles and massive cathedrals. Then there was the growth of the towns, especially London, whose population had quintupled from 10,000 to 50,000. The countryside too would have changed dramatically. He would have seen all the available farmland taken in hand, the waste land entirely used up or turned to commons, and the enclosure of open fields well underway.[6] If we then extend his period of sleep to the year 1600, our peasant would have opened his eyes to see that London had swollen to a population of 200,000 – twenty times its size in 1000. He would have looked up at houses that were five or six storeys in height. He would have noticed the air was acrid with the smell of burning coal. Although many modern skyscrapers are more than twice the height of the tallest medieval spire, and many European cities are more than twenty times the size they were in 1600, it was the medieval period that introduced us to massive engineering feats and urban sprawl, with all its hustle and bustle, noise and stench.

The Personal Horizon

It goes without saying that people have always travelled. You only need to think of Norse ships crossing the Atlantic Ocean to Vinland, in North America, to realise that they did so in 1000. Nor was it just the marauders who were well travelled. Gudrid Thorbjarnardóttir, who was born in Iceland in the late tenth century, sailed to Vinland, Greenland and Norway. She even went on a pilgrimage to Rome, eventually returning to live as a nun back in Iceland. However, a Viking world-view cannot be considered representative of eleventh-century Christendom as a whole. Indeed, Gudrid was not born a Christian, and her people slowly gave up long-distance raiding and trading after they were converted to Christianity. While some adventurous Christian individuals – pilgrims, merchants and royal emissaries – did undertake long journeys in 1000, the majority of ordinary people did not. Men were required to stay at home to farm the land. Women helped with the farm work and provided brewing and dairying services. Most lords did not permit their slaves and peasants to leave the estate where they lived. In addition, travel was dangerous. People were simply safer at home. In short, there were many more reasons *not* to travel in 1000 than there were to do so.

Over the course of the Middle Ages, travel became normal. Markets and fairs proliferated like never before. By 1500, everyone would at some stage of their lives have travelled to a market, many on a regular basis. Pilgrimages were part of this expansion of travel. People journeyed in great numbers to Rome, Jerusalem and Santiago de Compostela. Many of the thousands of abbeys founded in the twelfth and thirteenth centuries made their relic collections available for pilgrims to venerate. Pilgrimages to Canterbury alone would have significantly increased the number of people on the roads in south-east England from the late twelfth century. The changing administration of the law also increased the amount of travel. The circuit judges started to tour the country regularly to administer the king's justice. On a more local scale, constables who arrested suspected felons were responsible for taking them to the county town for trial. In Devon, a journey from a remote spot like Hartland to the county town at Exeter was at least 52 miles, requiring a constable and his prisoner to spend five or six days travelling there and back in winter.

Those summoned to attend a church court might have to travel even further. By the fifteenth century, the system was established whereby, if someone died with an estate that fell entirely within one archdeaconry, their will would have to be proved in the local arch-deaconry court. However, if the estate in question was split between two archdeaconries, then their will needed to be proved in the consis-tory court of the diocese. Thus the executor of a deceased West Cornishman's will with lands in both Devon and Cornwall would have had to make a 100-mile journey to Exeter to perform his or her duty. If that Cornishman had died with chattels in another county, then his executor would have had to travel 300 miles to London to prove the will. Anyone attending the royal courts in Westminster for the purposes of private justice would also have had to undertake a long journey. Those accused of moral crimes would have had to attend their local arch-deaconry court – and that not only entailed *them* making the journey but six or more compurgators as well, to attest to the innocence of the accused.

From the thirteenth century, universities created another need to travel long distances. So did Parliament: those eligible had to make their way to the county town to vote; elected members were sum-moned to Westminster or wherever else in the country Parliament was sitting. Consider too the huge amount of travel undertaken on behalf of the Church: monks travelling between their monasteries and their estates; friars going from town to town; abbots and priors attending convocations of their orders; bishops and abbots attending Parliament; and clergymen travelling abroad to attend the ecumenical councils of the Catholic Church.

Then there was the necessity to travel for war. Although you might argue that men have always journeyed to do battle, in 1000 they did not do so in the numbers they did in later centuries. About 7,000 men accompanied King Harold on his heroic marches to Stamford Bridge and then to Hastings in defence of the kingdom in 1066. More than 30,000 Englishmen appear on the payroll for the siege of Calais in 1346–7; over 15,000 sailed with Henry V on the Agincourt campaign. Large numbers were stationed in France throughout the Anglo-French wars of the fourteenth and fifteenth centuries. No fewer than 48,000 men accompanied Henry VIII to Boulogne in 1544. Further afield too, armies grew rapidly in size. By 1600, the Spanish army numbered 200,000 men, many of whom were stationed in the Netherlands, hundreds of miles from home.

All this means the scale of personal travel changed dramatically over the medieval period. Relatively few men would have ever had to ride or walk more than twenty miles from home in the eleventh century but by 1600 probably the majority had to do so at various times in their lives, and a significant proportion would have had to do so on a regular basis. Over the course of the Middle Ages, travelling away from home became normal. We cannot put a measure on how far the ordinary individual moved. However, it is likely that the increase in the person-miles travelled per year in Europe for commercial, official, legal, ecclesiastical, educational and military purposes was of the magnitude of several hundredfold. The number of inns grew massively to cater for the wealthy among them. Whereas the word 'inn' is not found in English before 1000 and probably only the largest towns had an inn in the twelfth century, by 1577 there were more than 3,000 such establishments in England.[7] This improved infrastructure made it much easier to stay away from home, so that people might even travel for recreation. Certainly, by 1600 most ordinary people moved far beyond the geographic horizon that had surrounded them at birth.

The Collective Horizon

The expansion of personal horizons mentioned above has implications for the whole of society. People's geographical knowledge increases exponentially the further they ride or walk. If you travel up to 20 miles from home, you can potentially see four times as many places than if you only ever travel 10 miles. It is a matter of mathematical radius: the 20-mile traveller can theoretically cover 1,257 square miles as opposed to the 314 square miles of a 10-mile traveller. Moreover, if everyone regularly travels 20 miles from home rather than just 10, they will meet many more people from further away with similarly extensive geographical knowledge. In theory, a man who travels 20 miles from home could meet someone who lives 20 miles beyond that. If that second person has previously travelled 20 miles from *his* home in the opposite direction, the first person might hear a first-hand report of a place 60 miles away from his home town. That theoretically covers an area of more than 11,000 square miles. Obviously the difficulty of negotiating rivers, mountains, moors and coastlines means things aren't quite that simple, but the point is clear: when people travel further, their collective knowledge increases exponentially. With hundreds of thousands of people moving further and further from home as the Middle Ages progressed – in some cases, hundreds of miles – knowledge about England and other countries increased massively. This expansion of the collective horizon helped to spread geographical confidence, as people had a higher level of prior knowledge of what they might encounter when away from home. This confidence in turn allowed them to venture even further.

Laying aside the earlier Viking expeditions as a special case, people started to travel extensively in the twelfth century. The crusades, for example, which began in 1096, saw a massive broadening of geographical horizons. I don't imagine that a great many ordinary northern Europeans in the year 1000 even knew that Jerusalem was in Muslim hands. They certainly came to hear about its capture as a result of the First Crusade in 1099. The Second Crusade saw the Holy Roman Emperor (the elected overlord of the German states) set out in person for the Holy Land, while an English expedition that went to join that crusade took control of Lisbon. The Third Crusade saw the king of England take the Cross and attempt to come back across Europe by a land route. During the Fourth Crusade Christian knights ran riot through the streets of Constantinople. Moreover, after the fighting died down, connections with the Holy Land were maintained. These were not just periodical waves of armed pilgrimage but a movement that led to a constant flow of news to and from the Middle East. By the time of the Sixth Crusade in 1228, the bishop of Exeter saw fit to spend five years away from his diocese with the local knights from the southwest of England, supporting another Holy Roman Emperor in his quest to regain access for pilgrims to Jerusalem. Some of them were the second generation of their families to go to the Holy Land, their fathers having accompanied Richard I on the Third Crusade. English people were increasingly concerned with what was happening more than 3,000 miles away, in the Middle East.

The world beyond Jerusalem was a mystery to eleventh-century Europeans. The world map made in southern England between 1025 and 1050 shows a roughly square shape including Europe and parts of Africa and Asia, with many scattered islands in the Mediterranean and around Scotland. The Red Sea and the great rivers of north Africa are coloured red. Britain appears in the north-western quarter; Babylon (in modern Iraq) is the easternmost city and India is accorded a small honorary position at the eastern edge of the world, depicted as being roughly equivalent in size to the British Isles. This map appears in the same book as a text called *The Marvels of the East*. This includes descriptions of men eight feet tall and eight feet wide with heads in their chests; it refers to cannibals with legs twelve feet long, and other creatures twenty feet tall with mouths like fans and lions' manes.[8] Evidently, knowledge of the distant parts of the world was largely based on fantasy and rumour. The Hereford World Map, which was drawn up at the end of the thirteenth century, is much more detailed than the Anglo-Saxon world map but it too marks no specific places to the east of Jerusalem except the Red Sea and the rivers Tigris, Euphrates and Ganges. Its principal conceptual differences from the earlier map are that it is round rather than square and centred on Jerusalem, not the Mediterranean.

It was in the thirteenth century that some intrepid travellers breached the eastern frontier of knowledge. In 1246, Giovanni da Pian del Carpine, a Franciscan friar, visited the Mongol camp near Karakorum, 5,000 miles east of Paris, returning by way of Kyiv. Ascelin of Cremona, a Dominican friar, met Baiju Khan, the Mongol commander, the following year. When the papal emissary William of Rubruck entered Karakorum in 1254, he met the Hungarian-born son of an Englishman and the Hungarian-born daughter of a Frenchman, as well as the nephew of a Norman bishop, showing that papal missions were not the only reason why people travelled to Asia. In 1271 Marco Polo set out to accompany his father and uncle on their trading journey to the east, which was to last twenty-four years. In 1289 Giovanni de Montecorvino walked across Asia to meet the Chinese emperor Kublai Khan. He reached Peking (Beijing) five years later and was appointed the city's nominal archbishop in 1307.

Long before the maritime expeditions of Portugal and Spain in the fifteenth century, therefore, the horizon of Christendom had already expanded considerably. At the start of the fourteenth century it stretched westwards to Greenland and eastwards to China. The extension of its southern frontier took place later, following the Portuguese conquest of Ceuta on the north African coast in 1415. As a result of a programme of annual voyages championed by Prince Henry of

Portugal, known to history as Henry the Navigator, Africa's western seaboard was gradually charted. These voyages continued after Prince Henry's death, gradually proceeding further and further south. The greatest geographers of the ancient world, Strabo and Ptolemy, had not mentioned the southern tip of Africa. Nor had the earlier maps of the world accurately depicted it. Nevertheless, in 1488 Bartolomeu Dias captained a ship around the Cape of Good Hope – or 'the Cape of Storms', as he called it – and word of his discovery quickly spread.

This is the important point. Viking marauders might have sailed for thousands of miles but their knowledge was not passed on. Portuguese and Spanish explorers, on the other hand, shared their discoveries, and that led to greater confidence in sailing further. If Harari's Spanish peasant had spoken to any of the mariners preparing to set sail with Columbus in 1492, he would soon have learnt that Europeans had already navigated around the southern tip of Africa. Had our peasant seen the earliest extant terrestrial globe – produced at Nuremberg in 1492, just before Columbus's return from Hispaniola – he would have noted that it depicts Europe, Africa and most of Asia. It demonstrates geographical knowledge extending 7,000 miles east, all the way to present-day Indonesia, and 8,000 miles south, to the Cape of Good Hope. From 1570 you could buy a printed atlas, namely Abraham Ortelius's, *Theatrum Orbis Terrarum*, containing the recognisable outlines of continents and individual countries. By 1600, world maps by the best cartographers differed from their modern successors only in respect of the shape of South America, the imaginary form of *Terra Australis* (literally, 'southern land'), the absence of some far-flung regions, such as the Pacific Islands and Antarctica, and their overall precision.

Our discovery of the shape of the world's landmasses was thus predominantly a medieval accomplishment. At least three expeditions circumnavigated the globe in the sixteenth century: Ferdinand Magellan's in 1519–22, Francis Drake's in 1577–80 and Thomas Cavendish's in 1585–8. Ancient writers had established that the world was round – even if they did not always depict it that way – but, as far as we know, no Greek or Roman expedition had ever completed a circumnavigation. Nor had any Viking. Even if they had, their knowledge died with them. Thus the medieval contribution stands supreme. The European collective horizon embraced five of the world's six inhabited continents by 1600.

At the same time, people came to know more about those living in far-flung parts of the world. London was home to Russian merchants. There were men and women from Africa serving in fashionable gentlemen's houses. Going the other way, an English navigator, Will Adams, landed in Japan in 1600, having sailed on a Dutch merchant ship. Two Algonquian Native Americans, Manteo and Wanchese, who had been brought to England in 1584, taught elements of their language to the mathematician Thomas Hariot, so he could speak to their people when he visited North America the following year. No one can reasonably claim that the 'world-view' of European mariners in 1600 was fundamentally the same as that of their predecessors in 1000, let alone in the ancient world.

All this is pretty impressive, especially when you consider the dangers that those pioneering mariners faced on their travels. However, the true importance of all these voyages – in particular, Columbus's discovery of Hispaniola and the eastern coasts of South and central America – is that they proved to well-educated people that the great writers of the ancient world were fallible. For centuries, people had believed that the wisdom of the Greeks and Romans was unsurpassable. The discovery in the twelfth century of hundreds of translated texts in the Muslim libraries of Spain and Sicily had only emphasised the wisdom of Greek and Latin writers. Aristotle above all others had come to symbolise the depth of ancient learning. Then, suddenly, it turned out he was incorrect on some important points. Obviously, if there were some things that Aristotle did not know about the world's geography, there were other things he could be wrong about too. This amounted to a cognitive revolution – a truly pivotal moment in intellectual history. Aristotle had completely missed the continents of North and South America. Everything was now open to question.

The curiosity of Christendom blossomed, like a flower opening. People tried to collect items from around the world, stretching out their arms to touch the glories of Creation. Anyone visiting London in 1599 could go to Sir Walter Cope's house and admire an African charm made of human teeth, the horn and tail of a rhinoceros, porcelain from China, a magnifying mirror and a Native American canoe.[9] At banquets the well-to-do tasted the new-found produce of the New World – potatoes, tomatoes, turkeys and tobacco. Through the expansion of their collective horizon, people had challenged the thinking of the ancient world and found it lacking. A beautiful spirit of investigation had been born.

The Commercial Horizon

No eleventh-century peasant waking up in the sixteenth century could have failed to notice the increased level of commercial activity. In 1000 in many parts of northern Europe, you could easily have travelled thirty miles or more without passing through a market town. Even a hundred years later there were just 169 markets in England. But by 1516, the government had granted rights for a further 2,274 markets to be held.[10] This turned out to be an over-provision: only about 676 of them were going strong in 1600. But that still means you would have come to a market town every ten miles.

This increase in the number of market towns over the course of the Middle Ages does not reveal the whole picture, however. Money too is an important feature of medieval change. Although large numbers of silver pennies were minted in the eleventh century, a great deal of trade still depended on barter. In some places, such as the south-west of England, it was the default form of exchange.[11] In others, money was an aspect of everyday life. Throughout England, there is a strong correlation between eleventh-century coin finds and the population except in those regions which had very few markets. The implication has to be that, where there were no markets, there was little need for money. In remote areas, the economy still depended on subsistence farming and barter. But by the early fourteenth century, the shift to a market economy was complete. A subsistence farmer from 1000 would have been utterly perplexed to wake up in 1492 and find that money was king.

The importance of this goes far beyond our poor peasant being charged cash for everything in every town through which he might pass. If he had wanted something in the eleventh century he had to make it himself, grow it or obtain it by barter. It is likely that everything that he used had been made within twenty miles of his home. Harvest failure automatically meant deprivation and possibly starvation. But after markets and fairs were established in large numbers, anyone with sufficient money could buy essentials such as food and cloth, and luxuries including dyes from the Mediterranean, silk from

China, carpets from north Africa and spices from Indonesia. The six great international trading fairs held in Burgundy in north-eastern France – known as the Champagne Fairs, after the province – supplied the markets of northern Europe with exotica. In return, the merchants of northern Europe provided Mediterranean traders with wool and silver. Banking developed over the course of the thirteenth century, facilitating the long-distance transfer of money and the ability to finance speculative trading enterprises through debt. In 1600 joint stock companies were doing business internationally; the East India Company was set up that very year. A northern European peasant from 1000, wandering through a fair and seeing silks, spices, carpets and dyes on sale, would have regarded an iPhone ringtone as just one of so many previously undreamt-of marvels.

The Horizon of Memory

In 1000 there were several sorts of document in England to preserve knowledge of the past. Charters were written to record leases, boundaries and rights. A few wills were drawn up, by nobles and leading clergymen. Kings issued writs, some of which survive. Clerks were compiling the *Anglo-Saxon Chronicle*. Asser's *Life of Alfred* also dates from about this time, as do Aethelweard's chronicle and a number of saints' and kings' lives. There were some older texts too – such as the works of Gildas, Nennius and Bede – and of course there were historical poems composed for entertainment. But that accounts for almost all the writing about the past that existed. Aethelweard's chronicle drew on just three sources: the *Anglo-Saxon Chronicle*, Bede's *Ecclesiastical History* and a now-lost set of annals for the years 893–946. Moreover, apart from Bede's work, these sources were rare. The *Anglo-Saxon Chronicle* today survives in just five manuscripts, Asser's *Life of Alfred* in two. As for charters pre-dating 1066, we know of about 2,000 such texts but many of them are later forgeries made by monks to claim lands and rights. We have to conclude that in 1000, there was relatively little writing about the past in England. The horizon of memory was largely a matter of personal recollection, the reminiscences of community elders, and a very thin scattering of documents.

Document creation massively increased over the next six centuries. Just think about Domesday Book: a survey of all the property in

England completed in just eight months in the year 1086. Clerks went out to examine every manor and compare it to records of what it had been worth under the old Saxon taxation system twenty years earlier. This required them to employ four languages: Latin, various forms of Old English, Norman French and Old Cornish. All these notes were then compiled into drafts for each region and finally all the drafts were systematically copied into the two volumes that today form Domesday Book. It is an astonishing achievement.. Despite the advent of computers and ease of transport, you cannot imagine all the substantial property in England being documented in just eight months today. But Domesday Book was just the first instance of what turned out to be an explosion in record-keeping.

The twelfth-century Exchequer saw many bureaucratic innovations, from the compilation of more surveys of knights' lands in the *Red Book of the Exchequer* and the *Black Book of the Exchequer* to the royal accounts known as 'pipe rolls', produced annually from the reign of Henry I. In the years around 1190 the royal chanceries of both England and France were reorganised and started to keep copies of all outgoing official correspondence. Thus in England we have thousands of rolls of medieval royal letters. We have large numbers of royal account rolls too. Every bishop started to keep a register of his official deeds and correspondence, and had his lands surveyed. Every lord in the country soon started to follow suit. Monastic houses and landowning families started to keep cartularies in which they recorded all their charters. In the late thirteenth century a second major escalation in record keeping took place, when lords started to keep manorial records: court rolls, rentals, accounts and surveys. By 1300 the government was keeping taxation records which named every taxpayer in the country. Private letters started to circulate, and private accounts were drawn up. Probably every major household was creating an annual account book of its income and expenditure by 1400. By then churchwardens were also compiling annual accounts for their parishes. Hundreds of chronicles were kept, either by monks or private citizens. And this revolution in record keeping took place before the third major expansion of the horizon of memory – namely, printing.

So significant is the advent of printing that we do not tend to regard it as medieval. In the same way that people associate the medieval period with negativity, ignorance and violence, and everything that appears civilised in this period with a Renaissance mentality, printing is just too powerful a development to be regarded as 'medieval'. Yet by 1500, about 250 printing presses across Europe had produced 27,000 editions of books. If each one of those editions had an average print run of 500 copies, 13 million books would have been in circulation among 84 million people.[12] Printing was unquestionably a medieval phenomenon.

The changing horizon of memory marks a profound break in continuity between the old world and the new. Literacy in England increased from a tiny fraction of the male population (probably less than 0.25 per cent) at the start of the eleventh century to over 10 per cent by 1500, and 25 per cent by 1600. Among women it was still less than 1 per cent in 1500 but 10 per cent by 1600.[13] The country saw a commensurate surge in the number of documents created – parish registers, court records, state papers, letters and thousands of books. The number of publications in England rose from about 40 per year in the first decade of the sixteenth century to 400 in the last – about 20,000 editions in all. If each one of those was of 500 copies, then that put about 10 million books into circulation in England over the course of the sixteenth century. They passed among some 400,000 readers – an average of twenty-five books per person. But their owners also lent them out. Each and every *reading* – not just each and every book – contributed to a growing literary culture and the gradual extension of the horizon of memory.

The implications of this multi-dimensional expansion of our collective memory were significant. The law, for example, was hugely strengthened. People could expect judgments on property and rights to be based on written evidence rather than personal recollection. Natural philosophers could make and circulate astronomical observations and calculations more easily. Music in particular was completely transformed. Musical notation as we know it was developed by Guido of Arezzo in the early eleventh century. Prior to this, there was no way of preserving a tune except to indicate above the lyrics whether it went higher or lower in pitch. As a result, singers had to remember the music and teach it to the next generation of minstrels. However, reliance on memory prohibits the passage of complicated, multi-part works. (Imagine trying to memorise a symphony and then teach it to a series of musicians who have never heard it.) Writing music down therefore allowed it not only to last for generations – centuries, even – but for it to become more and more sophisticated. Today we tend to label all music written before 1600 as 'early music' but in reality, it was the musicians of the Middle Ages who created the system that allowed music to become more complex than it ever had been before. By the end of the sixteenth century, Italian composers were working on operas. Without the medieval innovation of multi-part scoring, the great composers of the eighteenth and nineteenth centuries would not have been able to perform at anything like the level they did, let alone pass down to us their musical legacy.

Over the course of the Middle Ages private individuals began to record matters of fact with great enthusiasm, whether in the form of histories, accounts of travels, medical and culinary recipes, or astronomical or mathematical treatises. Medieval people started to print scientific works – and the printing was crucial, for it allowed difficult texts and diagrams to be produced accurately and in large numbers for rapid circulation. New theories and findings could be communicated directly to distant recipients without fear of miscopying. Between 1000 and 1600, we passed from a world in which the total number of words written down or printed every year in England, for all purposes, escalated from about a million to roughly a hundred billion.[14] This amounts to a fundamental change which is all too easily taken for granted – and which marks a complete break from the illiterate world of Harari's and Morris's peasants. And none of the achievements of the age of genius that Grayling so rightly applauds would have been possible without it.

The Religious Horizon

We all think of the medieval period as being characterised by religion. Whether the foremost images in our minds are cathedrals, abbeys, pilgrimages or crusades, the cross stands for the Middle Ages in much the same way as the phone does for the last 150 years. However, just as the phone means different things to the various generations that have used it, so the cross changed its meaning over time.

At the start of our period, several kingdoms had only recently converted to Christianity. Large parts of the Iberian peninsula were still Muslim. Parts of eastern Europe were still pagan. It follows that Christendom was much smaller in 1000 than it was in 1500. In addition, within its boundaries, papal authority was weak. Many dioceses had very few church buildings or even priests. Popes had little power over kingdoms' religious leadership, let alone their kings. As late as the Council of Sutri in 1046, popes were little more than archpriests appointed by the Holy Roman Emperor. But from that point on, things began to change. For the next 470 years, papal authority grew stronger and reached ever further outwards.

The crucial pontificate was that of Gregory VII (1073–85). Even before he took office, Gregory had helped reform the process by which popes were elected, putting their position beyond imperial control. After he had become pope himself, he embarked on a great struggle with the emperor, Henry IV. He famously ordered Henry to cross the Alps to come to him to do penance at Canossa in 1077, thereby establishing the principle of ecclesiastical rule over secular Christian kings. Gregory also pioneered sweeping reforms that brought the clergy under the central authority of the Church, forbidding simony, usury and clerical marriage. Popes now sought to exercise authority over all priests in whichever kingdom they lived. By the time of the Fourth Lateran Council in 1215, the papacy was at the height of its authority, having successfully reformed the clergy and regimented not only their behaviour but also that of the whole of Christendom – seeking to regulate the moral life of every man, woman and child in Europe.

A more united Church was a more purposeful and powerful organisation. It also grew phenomenally wealthy, expressing its prosperity in the building of tens of thousands of abbeys and parish churches and the foundation of monastic orders. Its wealth was partly a result of the Medieval Warm Period – a period of favourable climate change, discussed in chapter three – but an even more important factor was the scale of the donations it received. The idea of Purgatory, where your soul lingered before being projected Heavenwards through the power of prayer, was a new concept in the twelfth century. It meant that many thousands of priests were employed to sing Masses for the benefit of the departed. In return, huge sums of money and amounts of land were given to the Church. The idea of the plenary indulgence, whereby all your sins were forgiven in return for an act of devotion (such as a crusade) had not existed in 1000; now such indulgences were accepted as ways of easing your path to Heaven. Pilgrimages too were phenomenally popular, as ordinary people invoked the healing power of saints and their relics. Whereas once few people had left home for religious purposes, now millions were on the move across Europe, enriching all the churches they visited with their donations. Christendom's religious horizons had widened and the Church's penetration into society had deepened, flooding like rainwater after a storm into every private crack and corner of daily life.

Although the Catholic Church continued to expand geographically throughout the Middle Ages, it did not remain united. From the twelfth century, significant fractures appeared. Many Christians were appalled by the growing wealth of bishops and archdeacons and urged a return to the poverty of Christ. Fervent believers were concerned above all else with the salvation of their souls – to the extent that they prioritised their own consciences over religious obedience. Scepticism crept in, resulting in many expressions of belief that the Church deemed unacceptable. Popes responded in a number of ways. One was to increase their ability to supervise and intervene directly in ordinary people's lives. Pope Innocent III and his successor, Honorius III, officially recognised the first two orders of friars, the Franciscans and Dominicans, in the early thirteenth century. Unlike monks, who were required to remain in their cloisters, friars were required to go out into the world, to preach the word of God in the streets and marketplaces. They were answerable directly to the pope, not to their local bishops, and so remained above national interests. Inevitably they became agents of papal authority. Their ability to enter universities and take advantage of educational opportunities also made them exceedingly useful as religious diplomats – not only in seeking out and eradicating threats but by enlisting the allegiance of Christian kings in pursuit of papal aims. By way of these orders and by enhancing the powers of local ecclesiastical courts, the Church tightened its grip on the behaviour of everyone who dwelt within Christendom.

The other principal form of papal direct action was to stamp down hard on heretics. In 1179 the Third Lateran Council imposed upon kings and lords the duty of extirpating heresy in their respective kingdoms. Burning alive became the standard punishment. A number of followers of Peter Waldo (known as Waldensians), who supported ecclesiastical poverty and rejected the authority of the Church, were burnt at the stake in 1211. The bloodbaths of the papal war against the Cathars – the Albigensian Crusade – began in 1208 and continued periodically for another twenty years. Although the later thirteenth century saw fewer persecutions, the rise in literacy sowed the seeds for more people to question the authority of the Church in the early fourteenth century, especially with regard to subjects not mentioned in the Bible. As Marsilius of Padua put it in the early fourteenth century, Jesus did not claim to have any temporal power, so why should the leaders of the Church claim to wield any in his name?

Despite the horrific punishment of burning, the numbers of heretics grew again after the Black Death of 1347–51. People began to ask why God had cursed Christians with such a terrible disease. Was this a second Flood? Some believed that it was indeed a punishment for Man's decadence. There were renewed calls for the Church to return to its original poverty. Obviously, these views were no more popular with the wealthy Church hierarchy than they had been in previous centuries. The early fifteenth century thus saw the regular lighting of pyres to consume outspoken Christians. The Catholic Church had become a victim of its own success. For more than two hundred years it had promoted the foundation of schools and the reading of God's word: the result was ever-increasing levels of literacy and, ironically, ever-increasing diversity of opinion on what the word of God actually meant.

The Church also started to splinter along nationalistic lines. Philip IV of France took decisive action to limit the power of Pope Boniface VIII in the 1290s after the pope tried to limit Philip's power to tax the clergy in his domain. Under French pressure, Clement V moved the papal see from Rome to Avignon in 1309. A whole succession of French popes followed. It amounted to a successful takeover of the papacy by the French. That only heightened the tension between France and its neighbouring states, especially England and the principalities of the Holy Roman Empire. Thanks to tensions between French and Italian rulers, an antipope was briefly appointed in Rome in 1328. In 1378, the papacy split in two, with a French pope continuing to rule at Avignon and an Italian one presiding in Rome. Rival European rulers accordingly chose which pope they supported. An attempt to reconcile the divisions in 1409 was unsuccessful; in fact, it resulted in the election of a third pope, based at Pisa. Only in 1417, with the final resolutions of the Council of Constance, was the integrity of the papacy restored. By then, the damage was done. Popes were seen as being not only corrupted by wealth and power but also as being manipulated by powerful kings in the interests of their respective nations. You did not need to be preoccupied with your own salvation to realise that that was not the way the Church was originally intended to be.

All these religious tensions finally exploded in the Reformation of the early sixteenth century. In 1517 Martin Luther nailed his ninety-five theses to the church door in Wittenberg in Germany, thereby starting the Reformation. Within a few years, the whole of Christendom was torn between those who supported the pope as the ultimate authority on Earth and those whose secular rulers successfully established their own national churches. Within those churches too there were multiple splits, most significantly between different forms of Protestantism. Such developments only amplified the divisive nature of the Christian faith. As people began to read the Bible for themselves, so the different beliefs multiplied and amplified. A decisive shift had taken place from communal religion towards conscience-led individual belief. By 1600, the people of Europe were divided by their faith, not united by it. Whereas the Roman Catholic Church had been a reason for Christian kings *not* to fight each other in 1000, now it had become a factor exacerbating their political differences.

The Scientific Horizon

It is science that underpins Professor Grayling's belief that the world-view of the Middle Ages was simply a continuation of that of antiquity and that it did not fundamentally change until the seventeenth century. In support of that belief we might observe that divine forces were still seen to exercise a dominant influence on the planet. Astrology too still had an official role: the date of Queen Elizabeth's coronation was subject to a forecast for a propitious moment by Dr John Dee. And superstition was still legally recognised in the Witchcraft Acts of 1563 and 1603. However, a few continuities with the past do not imply that people's world-view had not changed significantly. Just because physicians today swear the Hippocratic oath does not mean they are exponents of Hippocrates' methods.

The starting point has to be education, which underwent a revolution over the course of the Middle Ages. Schools were almost unknown in 1000 but waves of educational reform completely changed that situation. The Third Lateran Council of 1179 decreed that every cathedral should operate a school. The Fourth Lateran Council of 1215 added that every church with sufficient wherewithal should do likewise. Many schools were established over the course of the thirteenth century but even more were set up over the next two centuries, so that every town had one by 1600. In addition, universities came into being. Oxford was established in the twelfth century; Cambridge in 1209. There were seventeen other universities across Europe by 1300 and dozens more by 1500. They taught grammar, logic and rhetoric (the *trivium*), and geometry, arithmetic, music and astronomy (the *quadrivium*). Some additionally taught natural philosophy – a forerunner of scientific thinking – giving new life to Aristotle's ideas on physics and biology, among other things. Most of all, the universities taught students to think and to argue, thereby giving them the tools to make original contributions of their own.

It is true that a medieval university education was largely a series of received readings from the ancient world. But plenty of original elements emerged that became significant in finally battering down the walls of Aristotelianism, allowing thinkers to explore the world and the heavens anew. Nowhere is this more apparent than in cosmology. Aristotle believed that the Earth was at the centre of the universe and surrounded by a series of rotating nested spheres that contained the stars and planets. Nicholas of Cusa questioned that notion in the mid-fifteenth century and Nicolaus Copernicus put forward his heliocentric theory in a manuscript for his friends in 1514. This eventually resulted in his ground-breaking book, *De Revolutionibus Orbium Coelestium*, which was published in 1543, the year of his death. It could be argued that Aristarchus of Samos had had the same idea in the third century BC but that would be missing the point about continuity. Just as no one in the year 1000 remembered the mathematics of Euclid or the logic of Aristotle, no one in 1000 remembered Aristarchus or his theory: the scientific knowledge of the ancient world had been lost.

In the later sixteenth century, Italian thinkers such as Galileo Galilei and Giordano Bruno, and Englishmen like Thomas Digges and William Gilbert, became convinced that Copernicus was right to state that the Earth revolves around the sun. Digges, like the Danish astronomer Tycho Brahe and others, witnessed the appearance of a 'new star' in November 1572 and realised that it was physical proof that Aristotle's theory of fixed celestial spheres was wrong. In 1576 he extended Copernicus's theory by suggesting the universe was of infinite size. In 1584 Bruno proposed that the stars are other suns with their own planets. In 1600 William Gilbert correctly postulated in *De Magnete* that the

Earth is a giant magnet revolving in the vacuum of space. He also referred to a force between objects that he called *electricitas*. It is perhaps fitting that our period ends with the first mention of electricity.

The simplest symbol illustrating the advance in European scientific thinking between the eleventh and sixteenth centuries is a small circle: zero. The ancient Romans had no understanding of it; their numerical system had no zero. Imagine how difficult it is to do multiplication and division sums – or any scientific calculation – using just Roman numerals. Zero came to Europe by way of Muslim mathematicians whose works were translated in the twelfth century. By the early thirteenth, Leonardo of Pisa was familiar with the concept, as he experimented with Arabic or Indo-Arabic numbers. Natural philosophers and astronomers frequently used Arabic numbers in the fourteenth century. Roman numerals remained the most common form of accounting for merchants until the early sixteenth century but gradually the greater mathematical power of Arabic numbers took over. By the late sixteenth century, Arabic numerals were common enough that datestones on buildings usually employed them. And where you had Arabic numbers, you had zero. Modern science would simply not have been possible without it. There could be no better refutation of the idea that 'the mentality . . . of our best-educated and most thoughtful forebears' did not change between Roman times and 1600.

The proof that medieval people advanced the scientific horizon lies in such aspects of life as this: innovations so fundamental that they go unnoticed. Time is another one. After all, how long is an hour? It is easy enough for us to say 'sixty minutes', but if you don't have a clock by which to measure minutes, only a sundial or an hourglass, that is a meaningless answer. In the year 1000 an hour was a twelfth of the daylight and a twelfth of the darkness. This means an hour was twice as long at the height of summer as it was in the depths of winter, as there is approximately twice as much daylight in summer. But when exactly does the daylight start? How do you measure it?

In order to create a clock that mechanically tells the time, you have to be able to measure a standard length of the day. For this you need to employ an hourglass or a similar timepiece. Then you need to find a way of creating a circle of metal that rotates through exactly 360 degrees over the course of a day measured by your hourglass. Once you have created a clock, you have to get everyone else to adopt your new concept of regulated time, not the God-given natural one. Otherwise all you have created is a meaningless machine that does nothing but tick. Nevertheless, medieval thinkers solved the technical problems and rulers confronted the social ones. Over the course of the fourteenth century mechanical clocks were developed, refined and adopted. By 1400, many royal palaces, cathedrals, abbeys and noblemen's houses worked to the sound of bells. In the fifteenth century more and more places adopted the 'hour of the bell' or the 'hour of the clock' as their means of communal time keeping. Wealthy people had portable clocks in their chambers. By 1500 clock time was ubiquitous. Just as Harari's peasant would have experienced some confusion upon hearing a ringtone, he would also have been confused by the sound of a chamber clock chiming the hour by itself.

The standardisation of time was fundamental to scientific research. As medieval achievements go, it is no less significant than the building of the cathedrals, the circumnavigation of the Earth, and the development of printing. Many seventeenth-century scientific experiments would have been impossible if there had been no standard unit of time measurement. But the Middle Ages did more than just standardise the hour. Beginning with Roger Bacon in the thirteenth century, astronomers repeatedly pointed out to a succession of popes that the Julian Calendar – the calendar of the ancient world named after Julius Caesar – was wrong by a factor of $1/130$th of a day, or eleven minutes and four seconds per year, and that this was throwing out the calendar. The lack of precision was gradually disrupting the seasons. After more than three hundred years of nagging, Gregory XIII finally took notice, and established the Gregorian Calendar in 1582. Not just the theory but the actual implementation of the standard year we adhere to today was a medieval achievement. How much more difficult would the work of all the mathematical astronomers of the seventeenth century have been if they had still used a length of year that was incorrectly calibrated? To praise the work of the scientific geniuses who put these medieval tools to good use in the seventeenth century and to ignore those who conceived of them is like lauding the goal scorer and ignoring the rest of the team. It is missing a fundamental point about science. Without accurate units of measurement, it is pointless to try and measure anything.

The Technological Horizon

As the case of the clock shows, it is a grave error to assume that medieval people were incapable of technological innovations. Imagine how different the modern world would be if you could not plot your geographical position on Earth. What would the twentieth century have been like without explosives? What if the Second World War had been fought with bows, arrows, spears, crossbows and catapults? Think how different your life would be today if everything had to be written down by hand and never typed or printed. It is simply impossible to think of the modern world without the compass, guns and printing.

It was the natural philosopher Francis Bacon who pointed to this trinity. Seeing a significant discontinuity between the world-view of his own era and that of antiquity, he wrote in 1620:

> It is well to observe the force and virtue and consequence of discoveries, and these are to be seen nowhere more conspicuously than in those three which were unknown to the ancients, and of which the origins, although recent, are obscure and inglorious; namely, printing, gunpowder, and the magnet. For these three have changed the whole face and state of things throughout the world; the first in literature, the second in warfare, the third in navigation; whence have followed innumerable changes, insomuch that no empire, no sect, no star seems to have exerted greater power and influence in human affairs than these mechanical discoveries.[15]

All three 'mechanical discoveries' were originally made in China – printing in ancient times and gunpowder and the compass around the year 1000. But all three were known in Europe long before 1600. The compass was first recorded in the West in the twelfth century, gunpowder started to be used in the thirteenth, and printing with moveable type took off in the fifteenth. If Harari's peasant from 1000 wondered whether he was in Heaven or Hell when he heard a mobile ringtone, he would have had little doubt he was in Hell the first time he heard a cannon fired. A gun of the scale of Mons Meg, the 6.6-ton bombard cast in 1449 with a calibre of twenty inches, would have scared him to death. To hear the report of the 17-ton Dardanelles Gun, cast in 1464, which has a calibre of twenty-five inches, would have been far more frightening than any electronic device. Much had changed by 1492 to shake our peasant's world-view. Even more had changed by 1600: in Elizabeth's time cannon were made of cast iron and were of various sizes, depending on range and purpose, and fired standard-calibre cannonballs. Battles were now won by superior firepower and states had to tax their citizens more heavily to pay for men, training and guns in ever greater numbers.

In terms of world-views, it is important to note that late-sixteenth-century thinkers were fully aware that their technology surpassed anything known by less technologically sophisticated people. In 1585–6 Thomas Harriot visited the North Carolina region of America and demonstrated the devices he had brought with him from England to the local Algonquian-speaking people. He reported that:

> Most things they saw with us, [such] as mathematical instruments, sea compasses, the virtue of the lodestone [magnet] in drawing iron, a perspective glass whereby was shewed many strange sights, burning glasses, wild fireworks, guns, books, writing and reading, spring clocks that seem to go of themselves, and many other things that we had, were so strange unto them, and so far exceeded their capacities to comprehend the reason and means how they should be made and done, that they thought they were rather the works of gods than of men, or at the leastwise they had been given and taught us of the gods. Which made many of them to have such opinions of us, as that if they knew not the truth of God and religion already, it was rather to be had from us . . .[16]

Perhaps Harari's Spanish peasant would have reacted similarly. He too would have been unfamiliar with everything on that list, unless he had seen a priest reading aloud. Nor would he have seen windmills, overshot waterwheels, chimneys, ships' rudders, spinning wheels, spectacles or mirrors, all of which had come into regular use by 1492. For him to imagine living with all these changes is as impossible as it is for us to imagine them never having been invented.

One last technological innovation should be mentioned here, because it is so fundamental to our culture. Paper. Without it, the printing revolution mentioned above would have been impossible, the horizon of memory would have been dependent on handwritten parchment scrolls, and the spread of knowledge would have been

erratic and restricted. Yet it is often overlooked by historians of medieval technology – just as Francis Bacon overlooked it – perhaps because
it seems to be just another form of lowly writing material. In reality it
was much more than that. Invented by the Chinese about two thousand years ago, it came to Europe by way of Arab traders dealing with
Italian merchants in the twelfth century. It was fragile by comparison
with parchment or vellum: it was easily torn. For this reason, in 1145
Roger II of Sicily ordered that every charter written on paper in the
time of his predecessors should be copied out on vellum and then
destroyed.[17] But paper had some subtle qualities that Roger did not
appreciate. Whereas you could scratch out a number on a vellum
document and write something else over the top, with paper – if you
used an appropriate ink that soaked into the surface – the writing
became indelible. It could not be erased. Thus it was more secure.
When the Italian banking houses started to make large loans over long
distances in the thirteenth century, paper became important for guaranteeing the security of the sums paid out and received. In 1275,
Edward I urged the mayor and aldermen of London to create a new
administrative system using paper.[18] He had probably learnt about the
value of paper from his clerks in Gascony, where its use was already
well established.

By 1450, paper was common. It was still predominantly made in
France and Italy but it was regularly exported across Christendom.
In England, most lordly households drew up their accounts on paper
books imported specially for the purpose. Many clerks used paper
for drafts of documents. Letters that might need to be quickly
destroyed for security reasons were written on paper. Therefore it
was already widely available when printing was developed in Europe
in the 1450s. While it was possible to print on vellum, paper was
much cheaper. Each vellum Bible printed by Gutenberg required the
skins of about 300 sheep: hence he produced only 30 vellum copies
compared with 180 paper ones. Paper was lighter too and easier to
transport, and if bound properly, it would last as long as vellum. By
1500, printing and paper production were steadily advancing hand in
hand. Whereas there had been no paper in Europe at the start of our
period, thousands of tons of it had been produced by the end, facilitating the spread of knowledge across the world on an unprecedented
scale.

The Horizon of Law and Order

Every part of Europe was more dangerous in the early eleventh century than it was in the late sixteenth. Personal violence was a fact of life. Of the seventy-seven laws issued by King Alfred, thirty-four were purely concerned with the specific amounts of compensation to be paid for severing limbs and injuring people.[19] Many of his other laws were similarly concerned with violent acts, including murder, violence in inappropriate places, killing a pregnant woman and the rape of nuns, young women and children. From the late thirteenth century onwards, we can calculate homicide rates. In England, the rate of violent deaths declined from about 23 per 100,000 people per year in 1300 to about 7 per 100,000 in the late sixteenth century.[20] Going on these figures, extreme violence declined by more than two-thirds in the late Middle Ages, so that by 1600 it was about as safe as modern-day America – to which most people travel without great concerns for their safety.

The Middle Ages saw a dramatic shift in the law and how it was applied. Of course, the tenth century had not been devoid of law. Alfred's is just one of several Anglo-Saxon law codes that have survived, and we know of others that have not. However, there was no systematic application of justice. The legal system was based on the 'tithing', a group of ten householders who were collectively responsible for their good behaviour. If one member of the tithing transgressed, all ten could be called upon to answer for his wrongdoing. When a crime took place, the discoverer was required to raise the 'hue and cry', calling for all able-bodied men in the vicinity to help him pursue the culprit. He was also expected to report the offence to the officer in charge of the hundred (a subdivision of the shire). Justice was thus subject to local people's understanding of the law and it was accordingly simple. In many places the lord of the manor had the right to hang anyone he deemed guilty of breaking the law, and to drown a woman if she was caught red-handed committing a felony. Not until the twelfth century did the common law as we know it develop, in which a strong centralised legal system took the place of local justice. Trained royal judges were appointed to sit in the county courts, normally visiting every region on a seven-year cycle to judge the most serious crimes. In the late thirteenth century these seven-year circuits were replaced by assize court judges performing a similar function on a six-monthly rota.

In the fourteenth century, local justice was also made more efficient with the introduction of justices of the peace – otherwise known as magistrates – who presided over county courts in prosecuting a great number of crimes. By the sixteenth century, a whole overlaying series of courts dealt with every conceivable form of misdemeanour. At the lowest level were the manorial courts, which addressed such things as blockages of drains and obstructions of the highway, breaking fences and damage to roads. At a higher level were the petty sessions, over-seen by magistrates, which dealt with minor crimes such as playing unlawful games, vagabondage and paying servants and workers exces-sive wages. (You might not think of paying workers high wages as being a crime but it was.) Next up were the quarter sessions, again presided over by magistrates, dealing with a very wide range of matters – from road repairs and the licensing of inns and alehouses to libel, slander, forgery, trespass, housebreaking, burglary (theft from a house by night), larceny (theft from someone in his or her absence), robbery (theft involving violence), common assault and poaching. The most serious offences were referred to the assizes, overseen by the royal judges who dealt with treason, sedition, murder, arson, rape, ser-ious assault, witchcraft, riot and infanticide. The expansion of the court system over the Middle Ages can be seen as a widening of the entire legal horizon, in which more and more crimes and disputes came within the longer and more professional arm of the law.

On top of all this, by 1600 there was a whole hierarchy of ecclesias-tical courts that did not exist in 1000. The involvement of the Church in administering justice began in the eleventh century with the reforms of Pope Gregory VII. Archdeacons were appointed to oversee the moral rectitude not only of priests but all the parishioners in the dio-cese. Today we seem to have forgotten about these courts and the consistory court of the bishop but they dealt with hundreds of thou-sands of cases every year. Millions of wills were proved in ecclesiastical courts. In 1000 only a very few nobles and prelates would have drawn up a will, but by 1600 anyone might. The church courts also dealt with a truly staggering number of moral offences that included bridal preg-nancy, sexual incontinence, prostitution, bastardy, incest, defamation, drunkenness, usury, absence from church, and heresy. The scale of litigation was colossal. One historian has calculated that in the reign of Elizabeth I there were about 27,000 reported sexual offences in the county of Essex for a total adult population of about 35,000.[21] A peasant in 1000 might have involved himself in a blood feud if he had seduced another man's daughter, and even been summarily executed if she was from an important family. Either way, the matter was a local one. Things had entirely changed by the late Middle Ages, when an archdeaconry court would probably have forced the seducer to do penance for his sin by standing at the door of his local church in a white gown and bearing a white wand.

It was also in the Middle Ages that the central courts were established. In England, there were three – the courts of the King's Bench, the Exchequer and the Common Pleas – and all three sat at Westminster. These brought financial matters within the law. They also opened up the law to private cases and international plaintiffs. If you were a French merchant in 1000 and you had a grievance against an Englishman, there was little you could do about it. You might appeal to the king but, since he was preoccupied with fighting the Norsemen, you would have had difficulty getting his attention for so trivial a matter. Besides, he would naturally be inclined to take his subject's side of any argument. From the thirteenth century onwards, however, there were royal law courts to which you could take your case, and a recognised system for doing so. In this way, slowly, the law courts replaced the blood feud. Whereas there had been next to no jurisprudence in 1000, by 1500 many lawyers were making a living from it. In Elizabeth's reign, some of the richest men in the country were lawyers.

Whichever type of law we are talking about, whether secular or ecclesiastical, royal or private, it was far more systematically applied in the sixteenth century than in the eleventh. In this way we can see how the legal horizons of a kingdom such as England expanded to embrace everyone – from traitorous nobles to embarrassed debtors and adulterous peasants. And when all these various legal horizons are taken together, one can appreciate how 'order' itself became established. Few matters can be more important in any age. Just think: what would concern you most when planning a visit to another country? What would put you off going there? Poor phone signal? Probably not. The quality of the food? Perhaps. Total breakdown of law and order? Definitely. Unless you are a journalist or a mercenary soldier, you would almost certainly prefer to go somewhere else or stay at home. You simply would not want to visit a country in which there were no safe-guards to prevent you being robbed, raped, beaten, enslaved, tortured or killed.

The Medical Horizon

In certain respects, there was a continuity of medical understanding from antiquity to 1600. The works of Galen, the second-century phys-ician and philosopher, were still the basis of medical education; his theory of the humours continued to be widely accepted at an even later date. But Galen's ideas were circulated and applied very differ-ently in the eleventh and sixteenth centuries. For a start, there were almost no professional physicians or surgeons in 1000, nor was there yet a distinction between the two sides of medical practice, physic and surgery. A few short Galenic texts were preserved in the West but the majority were unknown, quietly biding their time in Arabic transla-tions from the Greek originals in Muslim libraries. There were a few herbals and leech books, which combined smatterings of ancient med-ical works with spells and recipes made from plants and animals. However, very few people used them – for the simple reason that hardly anyone could read. What's more, priests made up the majority of the literate population and the Church had an ambivalent attitude towards medicine. Some took the view that a disease was a divine pun-ishment and that it was wrong to stand in the way of the judgment that God chose to inflict on the patient. This view persisted well into the twelfth century. St Bernard, the great abbot of Clairvaux, declared that 'to consult physicians and take medicines befits not religion and is contrary to purity'.[22]

It was the Twelfth-Century Renaissance – the rediscovery of all those Greek and Latin works that had been translated into Arabic, together with the inspiration they provided – which gave rise to the systematic arrangement of medical knowledge. Among the works that made their way to the West were hundreds attributed to Galen and Hippocrates. There were also treatises of the most prominent Arab physicians – Avicenna, Rhazes and Albucasis – and Johannitius's syn-thesis of Galen's works, entitled the *Isagoge*. The idea that there was a continuity between the ancient world and the Middle Ages is thus clearly exposed as a delusion: most of the medical, geographic and scientific knowledge of Greek and Roman writers had been lost for more than half a millennium. And of all these aspects of ancient learning, medicine had fallen furthest into decline. Accordingly, its rediscovery had a profound impact on society. In the early thirteenth century, a model medical syllabus developed at Salerno: the *Articella*, based around the nucleus of the *Isagoge*. By the end of the century the royal physicians of Europe were formally educated and often held medical degrees. The fact that much of their knowledge was based on ancient medical understandings is less important than the fact there was now an accepted corpus of medical information that the learned physician or surgeon had to master. That provided a foundation on which later centuries could build.

The Church continued to restrict the expansion of the medical horizon for a long time. From the 1160s, monks and canons were strictly forbidden from leaving their cloisters in order to study medicine. The Fourth Lateran Council of 1215 forbade priests from practising surgery. Four years later, Pope Honorius III issued a bull, *Super speculam*, which prohibited those in holy orders from studying medicine of *any* sort.[23] Technically, this did not mean they could not practise medicine – and some men who turned from medicine to the Church did continue to exercise their former art – but effectively it barred almost all educated clergymen from advancing the medical frontier. Pope Boniface VIII prohibited the dismemberment of corpses in 1300 'for any reason'.[24] His purpose was not to stop dissection *per se* but the practice of the wealthy having their bones buried in one place and their heart and entrails in another. Nevertheless, the result was a general poor view of the practice of dissection. It became ever more difficult to persuade families to give up their dead relatives' bodies when to cut them up might damage their souls' chances of entering Heaven.

Despite the ecclesiastical restrictions, the medical horizon continued to expand. Even the Church at the height of its authority could not prohibit the appearance of new diseases and the growing or declining virulence of some old ones. Leprosy, the most feared disease of the early Middle Ages, had practically vanished from Europe by the sixteenth century. Its demise was sadly more than compensated for by the arrival of a range of new afflictions – including plague, syphilis, the sweating sickness and influenza – and the spread of tuberculosis, smallpox and typhus. If a peasant from 1000 had awoken in 1492 and found himself infected with plague, or seen his loved ones suffering from it, I don't think he would have 'felt at home' any more than you or I would.

The world-view of the educated elite did not remain unaffected by these diseases. After the Black Death wealthy people commissioned *memento mori* – sculpted skeletal cadavers that show worms crawling out of skulls' eye sockets and bowels – to be their own memorials. Some wore jewellery that also showed dead bodies. The idea seems to have been a belief that the plague had indeed been sent like a second Flood to destroy mankind for their sins; thus these constant reminders of mortality were intended to safeguard against being punished by divine affliction. The wills of Lollards (followers of the Church reformer, John Wyclif) similarly show the deepest self-abasement, as if to indicate they bore no shred of pride that might incur the wrath of God. Even the wills of some kings and archbishops show this sense of extreme humility in the wake of the plague. At the same time, ideas about contagion as outlined in the pages of Galen's translated works started to spread. The sale of poor-quality meat became a particularly sensitive issue as corrupt flesh was thought to lead to plague. For this reason, many regulations were passed to uphold the cleanliness and freshness of food markets.

These developments and ideas – resulting from causes as varied as the mutation of a virus and the translation of an ancient medical text – prompted responses from those in the know. Accordingly, medical knowledge inched forwards. The Holy Roman Emperor, Frederick II, whose free-thinking approach to learning was centuries ahead of that of his thirteenth-century contemporaries, urged that a corpse be dissected at least every five years for the benefit of medical students. The universities of Perugia, Padua and Florence made it compulsory for candidates for the doctorate in medicine to attend at least one dissection. When new diseases arrived, people questioned what had actually caused them. In the early sixteenth century, syphilis changed people's attitudes to morality and sex. It also changed their attitudes to immersing the body in water. Before 1500, those who could afford to do so would regularly have baths. But when the prostitutes who ran bathhouses started spreading syphilis, their clients were scared off. Moreover, they came to realise that, just as good things could be conveyed into the body through immersion in water, so could corruption and disease. The more doubts, questions and problems people faced, the more answers they wanted. Dozens of medical faculties were established in universities across Europe by 1600. Thinking people no longer accepted that diseases were simply a sign of God's will, as St Bernard had done four centuries earlier.

In the sixteenth century the Church effectively lost its power to stand in the way of medical progress. Although attitudes towards dissection had meant that anatomy students in 1500 were still using an early fourteenth-century work by Mondino de Luzzi as their basic textbook, enough dissections had taken place for surgeons to realise that it was far from an accurate account of the human body. It was simply blown away in 1543 when Andreas Vesalius published his *De Humani Corporis Fabrica*, which included accurate engravings of the muscles and bones of the human body. Just as significant were new ideas concerning medicines. Many people came to believe God had created the antidotes to all the diseases of mankind in the flora and fauna of the world and it was mankind's duty to seek out these antidotes and to derive their essences to cure diseases. Theophrastus von Hohenheim, the great sixteenth-century German medical philosopher and practitioner also known as Paracelsus, taught people how to think of inorganic substances as remedies that would counteract a physical ailment. Already by 1600, the volume of medical ingredients being imported into London had significantly increased.[25]

By the end of our period, people were actively seeking out new substances, believing that medical intervention was a divine act and to refuse it was to scorn God's bountifulness. In 1608 Maria Thynne wrote to her husband, who was then ill, saying,

> Remember we are bound in conscience to maintain life as long as is possible, and though God's power can work miracles, yet we cannot build upon it that because He can, He will, for then He would not say He made herb[s] for the use of man.[26]

This marks a complete revolution from Bernard of Clairvaux's anti-medical stance 480 years earlier. The acquisition and application of medicine, once regarded as being against God's will, had become a godly act. At the same time, medical practices had become codified, systematised and professionalised. Whereas in 1000 there were no trained medical practitioners in England and very few amateur ones, by 1600 in some parts of the country (such as the south-east) the ratio of active physicians, surgeons and apothecaries to patients was 1:400.[27]

That is over half the level of the provision today, when we have the NHS. The importance of this change cannot be overestimated. One of the most important developments of the last thousand years – if not *the* most important – is the shift from trusting God to safeguard our interests to trusting our fellow human beings when they have gained a professional competence in their field. In terms of our health, that shift began in the Middle Ages.

The above ten points demonstrate how our cultural horizons expanded dramatically between 1000 and 1600. The philosophical lesson we might take away from arranging them like this is that some aspects of the past are best seen when viewed from a different point of view than the one with which we are familiar. An understanding of social change based on technology focuses our attention on the most sophisticated achievements, which disproportionately emphasises the final stage of centuries of innovation. Such an approach leaves the earlier phases of our cultural and intellectual development looking primitive and unimpressive by comparison. It leads us to believe that the development of the latest Ferrari is of far greater importance than the invention of the wheel. This is obviously wrong-headed: few of us will ever own a Ferrari whereas billions of lives depend on the wheel.

An emphasis on technology also casts into shadow our ancestors' non-technological achievements, as if they did not matter. It obscures the fractures of the past – such as the Black Death, the shock of projectile warfare and the loss of medical writing from the ancient world – and makes everything regarded as 'medieval' seem merely primitive. The benefit of looking at the past through a series of expanding horizons is that it allows us to see change in the context of the starting point in time, without labouring under the baggage of modern value judgements. The rising skyline and the expansion of travel and trade; growing literacy and the advent of printing; the standardisation of time; the transition of the Christian religion from collective ritual to individual faith; the arrival of guns and the widening of the medical horizon; the extension of the arm of the law – all these we take for granted. Ultimately, the greatest achievement of our medieval forebears was unlocking humanity's potential. And this too we take for granted.

Let me finish this chapter with a famous analogy. In 1676 Isaac Newton wrote to Robert Hooke saying that, if he had been able to see a little further than Hooke and their colleague Descartes in his work on optics, it was because he was 'standing on the shoulders of giants'. That phrase was actually first coined in the twelfth century by John of Salisbury, who claimed he had heard it from the philosopher Bernard of Chartres. Even in his choice of analogy, therefore, Newton was drawing from medieval thinkers. How many other aspects of medieval culture and innovations underpinned his work? Trade, law and order, printing, lenses, medicine, education – the list is a long one. Newton and his contemporaries did not stand solely on the shoulders of a few 'giants' of science but on the far greater human pyramid of the past, formed by everyone who had ever lived.

And so do we.

2

War

The Development of Attitudes to Violence[1]

It is surely the greatest irony of civilisation that the more we develop as a society, the more we advance our ability to destroy ourselves. Whereas medieval kings had few ways of killing large numbers of people, today the complete annihilation of life on Earth is within the power of our political leaders. It seems, therefore, that the nature and character of war have changed entirely, so that modern conflict bears little resemblance to its medieval equivalent. But although this is undoubtedly true in respect of the technology employed, is it correct in all other respects? Did people's attitudes to war change in the course of the Middle Ages? Or are our modern attitudes to conflict a wholly post-medieval phenomenon?

There is one easy way to demonstrate that our modern attitudes to war owe much to medieval thinkers. If we look at how the morality of modern warfare is discussed, we can see it normally reflects one of two positions that were outlined in the early sixteenth century. The first is that war is a calamity in every respect, and to be avoided at all costs, without exception. This was the view of the early-sixteenth-century Dutch scholar, Desiderius Erasmus, who wrote that 'the most disadvantageous peace is better than the most just war' in his treatise *Against War* (c. 1515). The second moral position, espoused by Erasmus's near-contemporary, the Englishman Thomas More, is that war is a necessary evil. As More wrote in his *Utopia* (1516), the people of his imaginary New World island

> detest war as a very brutal thing and which, to the reproach of human nature, is more practised by men than by any sort of beasts. They, in opposition to the sentiments of almost all other nations, think that there is nothing more inglorious than that glory that is gained by war. And therefore, though they accustom themselves daily to military

exercises and the discipline of war . . . yet they do not rashly engage in war unless it be either to defend themselves or their friends from any unjust aggressors . . . or [to] assist an oppressed nation in shaking off the yoke of tyranny.

Between them, Erasmus and More speak for the majority of people in the Western world over the last five hundred years. However, they do not have much in common with earlier writers on the subject. Both of them imply that war is *always* regrettable. Even More regarded it as an 'inglorious' last resort. Such negativity is totally at odds with the hundreds of medieval texts that glorify war, applaud its strategies and hero-worship its leaders. Both writers ignore the theological justifications for fighting that were devised before the start of our period. Their views similarly clash with those of the ancient world, which produced many texts in favour of war – including some that lasted long enough to be pored over by medieval commanders. The fact is that most medieval people thought of war very differently from Erasmus and More and, indeed, from us. In other words, our most common moral positions on warfare today were not devised in recent times as a reaction to modern war but are the results of medieval thinking and experiences. They have simply been reinforced, over and over again, by the occurrence of ever more horrific calamities and atrocities.

The medieval origins of the modern rejection of war on moral grounds are not obvious and are rarely discussed. As a result, it is very easy for us to misunderstand medieval warfare. We are likely to presume our modern attitudes have always prevailed, with the result that we fail to see how people could ever have taken a favourable view of it. We also fail to notice how changes in the nature and character of conflict during the Middle Ages created the very doubts that now prevent us seeing it in a positive light. As the quotations from Erasmus and More indicate, criticisms of war were being articulated in educated circles long before 1600. We might also take the great playwrights' views into consideration. 'Accurst be he who first invented war', wrote Christopher Marlowe in his *Tamburlaine the Great* (1590). Shakespeare similarly referred to 'the hideous god of war' in his *Henry IV Part Two* (1600). It did not require the advent of modern tanks, bombs and missiles for people to back away from armed struggles on principle.

This chapter is an attempt to look beyond the views of Erasmus and More and show how attitudes changed between the eleventh century

and the sixteenth. It requires us temporarily to hold back on our modern opinions and open ourselves to the idea that people *can* see war as
positive, glorious, heroic, enriching, ennobling, spiritually rewarding
and exciting. If we start off with the predisposition that all war is a failure of humanity, we will never understand the reasons why people
went to war in the first place. And there were many. After considering
the culture of violence that predominated in the eleventh century, we
will look at changes in medieval tactics and technology, the chivalric
imperative encouraging the knightly class to fight, the spiritual benefits
of holy wars, the political opportunities afforded by military aggression, and the increasing regulation of war. In both concept and practice
we will see a waning of personal enthusiasm for fighting as individual
vulnerability grew greater and the opportunities for personal glory
diminished. And that personal element is the key. It is the difference
between a genuine willingness to fight and Thomas More's extreme
reluctance to endorse violence and Erasmus's complete refusal to do so.

Eleventh-century War

Human beings are violent by nature. Long before the development of
the written record, social groups carried out acts of hostility against
other social groups, ranging from raids and skirmishes to full-scale
conquests. As Thomas Hobbes stated in *Leviathan* (1651), and as
numerous modern archaeological studies have confirmed, war was the
norm among prehistoric tribes. The only exceptions seem to have been
remotely situated settlements, such as Skara Brae in the Orkney Islands.
This pattern of everyday warfare continued into historical times. The
Roman Empire was rarely at peace. Its collapse led to an escalation in
fighting as small kingdoms vied for supremacy and waves of people
moved across the Continent. The Viking incursions saw further violence. War was so common it required no formal declaration of
hostilities. If a large number of grim-looking men rushed into your
village wielding axes, you knew you were at war. You therefore had to
be prepared for it at all times. This is why it is no exaggeration to say
that in the year 1000, war was normal. Peace was merely a lull in the
hostilities – during which people prepared for the next attack.

The familiarity of war in the eleventh century does not imply it was
without its horrors. However, they were very different from those of

modern mechanised warfare. There were no 'fronts' of soldiers facing each other for hundreds of miles. There was far less indiscriminate killing – and nothing on the scale seen today in the use of missiles, machine guns, tanks and chemical weapons, let alone nuclear warheads. It was not possible to kill tens of thousands of people in a medieval campaign unless a commander ordered his troops to employ a scorched-earth policy and thereby brought about a famine. War was horrific in other ways. People were cut down in hand-to-hand fighting. Assailants could see whom they struck with an axe, slashed with a sword or stabbed with a knife. Contemporary chroniclers do not normally go into graphic detail about who did what to whom but if we need a reminder of just how appalling wartime atrocities can be – even when they have to be committed by hand – we can refer to plenty of examples from recent times. Just think of the ethnic cleansing, rapes and massacres in the Bosnian war in 1992–5, or the Rwandan genocide of 1994, in which more than 600,000 people were systematically butchered by militias with machetes, many of the women and children being raped and sexually mutilated beforehand. At the time of writing, Ukraine is yet to reveal the full scale of the butchery and savagery being committed there but already a number of horrific incidents have been reported. At Nanking in 1937–8, it is said that two Japanese officers had a race as to which of them could most quickly slaughter one hundred Chinese people with their swords. It is not difficult to imagine eleventh-century European warriors similarly taking pleasure in killing vulnerable peasants for sport.

Some eleventh-century chronicles do describe the horrific acts that were committed. Accounts of the First Crusade are among the most vivid. One knight who was present at the fall of Jerusalem in 1099 reported how

> Some of the pagans were mercifully beheaded; others . . . tortured for a long time, were burned to death in searing flames. Piles of heads, hands and feet lay in the houses and the streets, and men and knights were running to and fro over corpses.[2]

According to another source,

> After a great and cruel slaughter of Saracens, of whom ten thousand fell in that same place, [the crusaders] put to the sword great numbers

of gentiles who were running about the quarters of the city, fleeing in all directions on account of their fear of death. They were stabbing women who had fled into palaces and houses; seizing infants by the soles of their feet from their mothers' laps or their cradles and dashing them against the walls and breaking their necks.[3]

Whether or not these actions took place at the time is not the point: these are *Christian* accounts of what Christians did in the course of conquering the city. They illustrate what people believed happened in the course of such an attack. These are the sorts of atrocities we need to imagine when we read in the *Anglo-Saxon Chronicle* of Viking 'raids', and men 'doing evil' or carrying out 'a great slaughter'. They may have been small in scale compared to twentieth-century massacres but they were both horrific and tragic nonetheless.

Such acts of brutality were predominantly carried out by the most privileged members of society. Although we traditionally use the word 'gentlemen' to describe Englishmen of an elevated social position, in the eleventh century the most powerful members of society – the feudal lords, who controlled the land – were anything but 'gentle'. Contemporaries had no qualms about describing them in terms of violence, because violence was what the nobility did. In the tenth century, Aelfric of Eynsham wrote:

In this world there are three kinds of men: those who work, those who pray and those who fight. The workers are those who by their labour provide us with the means to live; praying men plead for us with God; and warriors protect our cities and defend our land against invading armies.[4]

The same conception of the three orders existed across Europe. The bishop of Laon stated in the eleventh century that the three orders 'are joined together and may not be torn asunder, so that the function of each rests on the work of the others, each in turn assisting all'.[5] The warrior was thus an integral part of the divine structure of society and as essential to its functioning as workers and churchmen.

To become one of 'those who fight', a man needed to be recognised by his lord as a companion in arms and given his war gear. He would then swear an oath of loyalty: to do whatever he was told and to protect his lord with his life. It is important to remember that these ties of loyalty and duty were maintained only among members of the upper classes. No obligations were owed to the mass of the peasantry, whom the military order deemed infinitely beneath them. A high-status warrior might ride through his peasants' crops with his men one day, take advantage of their womenfolk when he came to their village, demand the best food – and then the next day give orders for the villagers to repair his barns or help with the construction of his castle. In carrying out his military duties in their defence, acts of wanton destruction against an enemy justified his position. By hurting his enemy's peasantry and slaves, he was harming the enemy himself. And vice versa. The peasantry were merely the collateral damage in this repetitive cycle of violence and misery.

As a result, many people lived with the fear of war every day of their lives. Those who lived on the coast or beside a major river were especially vulnerable, as they could easily be surprised by a water-borne attack. Villages near the border between rival lords' lands were equally dangerous places to live. And when a country was invaded by a foreign king, nowhere was safe.

Everyday life was full of violence too. Even when not killing each other, destroying crops and stealing cattle, people were cruel. In a society where the arm of the law was short, it was a case of every man for himself. Disagreements were frequently resolved by violence and killing. Feudal lords fought each other on a regular basis. The blood feud was still in operation, requiring an eye for an eye in domestic squabbles. Even judicial proceedings were bloody. The Normans introduced the custom of trial by battle into England. This required a legal matter to be decided by armed combat, although weaker claimants could be represented by a third party. Even monasteries sometimes employed this method of settling land disputes, each one choosing its champion. Such undercurrents of violence carried through to the treatment of women and children. In short, peacetime was not that much more peaceful than war.

The English saw almost constant conflict in the eleventh century – among themselves and with the Danes, the Scots and the Welsh. The Norman invasion was followed by a number of rebellions by dispossessed Anglo-Saxons and ambitious Norman lords, and further campaigns against the Welsh and Scots. Just over half the eleventh-century entries in the *Anglo-Saxon Chronicle* include a passage concerned with war. Those that do not refer directly to a military campaign are hardly any more peaceful. Apart from the countless annals concerned with the deaths of bishops, there are references to payments of tribute, famines, pirate raids, pools bubbling with blood, murders and men having their eyes put out. The Irish chronicles are just as bloody. One lord kills another, only for that lord to be killed by his victim's kin in revenge. You would have thought that, with famine and miserable living conditions, life was tough enough and people would have endeavoured to live in peace. But 'those who fought' made sure violence was constantly on the agenda.

The Church had an ambivalent attitude to war in the eleventh century. On the one hand, it was obliged to teach that 'thou shalt not kill'. On the other, from the time of St Augustine in the early fifth century, the idea of a 'just war' had developed. This held that war was justifiable if the cause was a moral one and the desired outcome was peace. The Church sought to maintain this balance by providing a theological framework justifying war alongside a series of moral initiatives limiting the suffering. The Peace of God movement was an attempt to protect unarmed people in areas where conflict took place. Repeated Church councils from 975 urged political leaders to distinguish between soldiers and non-combatants and ordered warriors not to commit rape or kill women, children, merchants and churchmen. The later Truce of God was an attempt to limit violence to certain days of the week. No fighting was to take place between sunset on Wednesdays and dawn on Mondays, nor during Lent and Advent. Such a compromise allowed Church leaders a degree of influence in military matters, while at the same time it showed them attempting to limit the destruction.

It is doubtful that either the Peace of God or the Truce of God led to a significant reduction in the levels of violence. But what is interesting about the latter movement is that the restriction on fighting resembles the forms of abstinence imposed by the Church on people indulging themselves. For example, eating meat was forbidden on Fridays and Saturdays, and in Lent and Advent. Sexual intercourse was not permitted on Sundays, saints' feast days and during Advent and Lent. This gives the impression that eleventh-century fighting was seen as an aristocratic self-indulgence, like feasting and sex. The doctrine of a just war was not an exhortation to commit violence but a theological justification of what warriors were wont to do anyway.

Viking culture had certainly celebrated violence, to the extent that the Norse religion promised daily warfare in the afterlife as a form of reward. This positive view of killing did not noticeably diminish with the conversion of the Scandinavian kings to Christianity, as the conquest of England by Sweyn and his son Cnut demonstrates. In the first year of his reign Cnut ordered the murder of all the powerful Englishmen whom he suspected might conspire against him. His caution was understandable. As a later king of Norway, Magnus Barefoot, succinctly put it, 'kings are for honour, not for a long life'.

At the outset of our period, therefore, war was normal and constant preparation for it was essential. War defined lordship and the ruling elite derived satisfaction from it. And many of their men enjoyed the fighting, committing acts that caused enormous suffering but which they regarded as their right – either by virtue of their privileged position or as the spoils of war.

Tactics and Technology before 1500

The medieval castle is one of the icons of the Middle Ages. And rightly so, for its development in France around the year 1000 was one of the most important innovations in the history of the Western world. Previously, an invading army could easily enter a country and seize control; there were no borders and few defences to stop them. This meant that early medieval kings were essentially lords of *people*, not of territory: they only governed their kingdoms by ruling over their subjects. This began to change with the growth of fortified towns, which were capable of resisting attacks. But it was the advent of castles that completely revolutionised political rule. A series of fortified lordly residences amid a landscape of walled towns meant that an invading army had to attack and seize control of every single defensive structure. Each siege would delay them and leave them open to attack themselves. Kings, by being rulers of the lords who held all these castles, were in a far stronger position to defend their kingdoms as a result. Kingship was now defined as rule over people *and* territory. One of the reasons frequently cited for the rapid conquest of England by the Normans in 1066–9 was the lack of castles. William the Conqueror and his companions in arms soon remedied that. By the end of the eleventh century, approximately five hundred castles had been constructed across the country, firmly linking lordly authority with the land.

The castle quickly evolved, its design being adapted to the tactics of siege warfare. Early wooden castles were rebuilt in stone in the twelfth and thirteenth centuries. Encircling walls were defended with projecting towers. Round towers with walls of great thickness were constructed to protect the inhabitants against stone-throwing siege engines. Machicolations were included to stop attackers scaling the walls. Drawbridges and portcullises were developed to trap assailants who breached the defences of a gatehouse. Angled entrances were employed to plunge assailants into darkness if they broke through the outer defences. Murder holes were devised as a way of killing trapped men from above. A prominently situated castle thus became an aggressive way of controlling the land, not merely a defensive one. By the thirteenth century, such fortifications had become the prime strategic tool of government. As soon as Edward I took control of North Wales in 1272, he sought to consolidate his power over the principality with the construction of a series of powerful castles. Robert Bruce, in trying to wrest control of Scotland from the English in the early fourteenth century, systematically attacked all the castles with English garrisons north of the border. Prior to the Black Death, castles and power were synonymous.

By the late fourteenth century, things had begun to change. Cannon had started to prove their worth in sieges. By 1400, a large cannon could take out a castle tower or a large stretch of curtain wall with a single shot. At Warkworth Castle in 1405, Henry IV needed only seven blasts from one of his large cannon to wreck the defences and force the garrison to capitulate. Castles were no longer the bastions of power they had once been. They were still important for regional control but they were less frequently the deciding factor in determining the security of the realm. More important was the unity of the political classes. All that was required to keep cannon and soldiers in the field – and thus dominate the land, including its castles – was money and political support. Castles were simply less versatile.

Medieval conflict also developed with regard to tactics and weaponry on the open field. At the opening of the eleventh century, battles in England were mostly fought on foot. The Normans introduced the mounted charge, which soon proved a battle-winning tactic. It featured a number of knights in armour on horseback charging together in close formation, with a seemingly unstoppable momentum. The knights trained for such charges by jousting. In the early days, jousts took the form of group fights or *mêlées*, which were hardly any more peaceful than the battles for which they were preparing. Later, knights rode head-to-head against each other in the lists. Their protective clothing developed from chainmail into a complex adornment of plate armour. Thirteenth-century foot soldiers in leather jerkins and mail coats, armed with axes, spears and swords, would have quailed at the sight of a large number of knights on *destriers* (specially bred heavy warhorses), charging towards them with an array of sharpened steel lances projecting in front.

The power of the charge of aristocratic knights began to be met and matched in the early fourteenth century. At Bannockburn in 1314, Robert Bruce employed sharp metal caltrops across ground where he expected the English knights to charge. He organised his men in circular *schiltroms* or shield-walls with long protruding pikes, their bases firmly embedded in the ground. Any knight driving his valuable horse onto a 15ft-long pike risked having it killed underneath him. From the 1330s, an even more effective way of combating the chivalric charge was developed as longbowmen were deployed among the pikemen. Just as a mass of mounted knights was more terrifying and effective than a handful of individual riders, so it was discovered that longbow archery was more effective when large numbers of arrows were loosed at once. Longbowmen could shoot very rapidly and with sufficient force to penetrate plate armour at a short distance. Although a squadron of knights charging at full speed left each longbowman only enough time for one or two shots within armour-penetrating range, large numbers of archers could shoot sufficient arrows to stop the front ranks of a charge, slowing down the following knights who stumbled on their wounded and dying colleagues and their horses. The victories won in this manner by Edward III over the Scots at Halidon Hill in 1333 and over the French at Crécy in 1346 heralded the demise of the power of the knightly charge.

The massed cavalry attack did not disappear overnight, however. Only the English could amass enough longbows on a large scale to nullify its impact. This was because Edward III insisted on the compulsory training of archers at the butts on a weekly basis and the large-scale production of longbows and arrows for this purpose. Other countries continued to value men-at-arms more than lowly archers. And there was sense in them doing so, for the longbow advantage was not as significant as English nationalist histories would have you imagine. When the French arrived at Agincourt in 1415 with thousands of knights and only a few bowmen, they fully expected to be able to sweep the English army, including the archers, from the battlefield by the use of cavalry alone. They might well have done so, had it not rained so heavily the night before the battle. As it was, the ground was too soft for the French knights to charge at speed, so the English archers had time to shoot several arrows into each *destrier* at close range – and thereby destroyed the impetus of the French charge.

By the end of the fifteenth century, however, the massed charge was practically redundant. Armies had grown larger and were now employing specialist pikemen to resist a cavalry charge. Knights' high social status meant that they were coming to cherish their independence and refused to see themselves as members of a pack. They no longer trained as groups to charge *en masse*. What's more, to sustain a knightly charge, you needed a large expanse of open ground, but the land was increasingly being broken up into small fields surrounded by hedgerows and walls, making it impossible for a large body of knights to charge at an enemy at full speed without breaking ranks. At the same time, guns increasingly played an important role in battle, especially when it came to attacking castles and walled towns. Thus by 1500, armies were composed of large numbers of infantry employing pikes, swords, bows and powerful cannon. The cadre of well-trained knights charging together was a thing of the past.

The Enthusiasm for War

It is not difficult to see the attractions of being a medieval warrior. Just *being* one conferred a considerable degree of respect and authority. In addition, your armour and weapons gave you power to take what you wanted from the defenceless peasants that formed the vast bulk of the population. If a similarly well-equipped group of warriors tried to stop you and your companions, then there was the excitement of combat. The very culture of fighting was a powerful incentive to initiate and participate in wars. Equally there was a sense of pride in being one of the defenders of your own community, which in turn gave men rights and power over their own people.

The delight the upper classes took in displaying their martial prowess can be seen in the popularity of jousting. According to one twelfth-century chronicler, a man was not ready for battle – and thus not fully a man – if he 'had never seen his own blood flow nor heard his teeth crunch under the blow of an opponent nor felt the full weight of his adversary upon him'.[6] Young men were sometimes so keen to take part in tournaments that they would defy the king's express orders *not* to do so – as twenty-two English knights showed in 1306. Although the *mêlée* was exceptionally dangerous – in 1241 eighty knights were reported to have died in a single tournament at Neuss in Germany – men rushed to take part.[7] A hundred years later, in December 1341, in the context of the Anglo-Scots war, Sir William Douglas and twelve men twice challenged the earl of Derby and twelve of his companions to jousts of war – with sharpened steel lances, not blunted ones – at Roxburgh and Berwick. They agreed to fight on the astonishing condition that no one wore any armour. We do not know how many were injured but, at the second of these events, three men were killed on the tournament field. At the St Inglevert tournament in 1390, three French knights took on all comers for forty days, including the future king of England, Henry IV. Every participant opted to fight with sharpened lances, even though there was no requirement for them to do so. Men clearly enjoyed this form of deadly combat.

The same bellicose spirit can be glimpsed on the actual battlefield. At the battle of Bannockburn in 1314, Sir Giles d'Argentein is reported to have announced, 'I am not accustomed to fleeing a battle; I choose to bide here and die rather than shamefully flee!' And die he did. At the battle of Crécy in 1346, John of Luxembourg, the blind king of Bohemia, asked to be led into the fray by his household knights, so he could die in the thick of the fighting. To these you can add the thousands of examples of soldiers displaying reckless courage on the battlefield in order to win the respect of their fellow men, regardless of whether they died or not. Such men were bred to fight, trained to fight, and, by God, they were going to fight.

The culture of war was enhanced by chivalric storytelling. The most famous examples are the Arthurian tales of courage, adventure and morality, harking back to the utopian reign of King Arthur. From the twelfth century, English kings and lords regularly re-enacted them and had them read aloud to create a sense of brotherhood among their leading knights. Such stories were hugely popular but they also served a more serious purpose: to instil in knights the values of honour, fairness, commitment and self-sacrifice that Arthur's companions showed. We can see this bravado culture played out repeatedly in the fourteenth century. One example that leaps to mind is the night-time attack on the camp of young Edward III by the Scots patriot, Sir James Douglas, who was so bold he rode through the English army up to the king's tent and slashed through the guy ropes. Another is the fortitude of Sir Thomas Dagworth and his force of eighty men-at-arms and a hundred archers in holding off an army perhaps twenty times the size in 1346. Many more examples could be mentioned in connection with the English in France. Recounted in Jean Froissart's chronicle and the *Brut*, such deeds were inspirational to a wide readership.

This chivalric culture lasted into the fifteenth century. Although some pious knights began to turn against war on religious grounds in the 1390s, most continued to believe that chivalric leadership was the best way to command an army. That was certainly still the case in 1415, when Henry V was able to command strong support for the campaign that resulted in the battle of Agincourt: more than half of the Knights of the Garter took part in person. Even though the battle was won by longbowmen massacring the chivalric champions of France, the English chivalric champions clearly believed they still had an important role to play. However, by the time Sir Thomas Malory composed *The Death of Arthur* in about 1450, tales of chivalry were already tinged with nostalgia. Although Arthur's post-Roman Britain could be modernised to include castles, jousts and plate armour, it could not go so far as to include guns. Chivalry was *personal*: a machine that killed brave warriors indiscriminately was the very opposite of chivalric. A shocking moment that foreshadowed the death of chivalry came at the siege of Meaux in December 1421, when Sir John Cornwaille witnessed his beloved only son's death. The young man, then aged seventeen, was standing beside his father when a cannonball decapitated him. Sir John was so deeply affected by the tragedy that he swore never again to take up arms against fellow Christians.[8] But knights did not need to witness such events themselves to understand their supremacy was coming to an end. As the fifteenth century drew to a close, guns increasingly did at long range what longbows had started to do at short range: they made warfare more dangerous – more indiscriminate, less personal and less chivalric.

Holy War

One of the most important elements inspiring medieval men to take
up arms was the hope of winning God's favour. Given the degree to
which war was a part of everyday life in the eleventh century, you can
understand the immediate popularity of the crusade when Pope Urban
II preached his famous sermon at the council of Clermont in November 1095 exhorting the men of Western Christendom to fight in the
Holy Land. If you were a warrior who found satisfaction in vanquish-
ing your enemies, you could now satisfy your desire to fight while
gaining glory *and* obtaining forgiveness for all your sins, guaranteeing
your passage to Heaven. That was an extremely attractive proposition.
On the First Crusade in 1099, Tancred de Hauteville, having made his
way to the Holy Land, stood on the Mount of Olives and looked down
on the walls of Jerusalem. The chronicler tells us that

> He turned his gaze towards the city, from which he was separated only
> by the Valley of Josaphat, [and saw] the Lord's Sepulchre . . . Drawing a
> great sigh, he sat down on the ground and would willingly have given
> his life there and then just for the chance to press his lips to that most
> holy church.[9]

Whether or not Tancred actually felt this is not the point; it was what
the chronicler and his readers believed people felt. The possibility of
conquest, riches and lordship in those parts only added to the spiritual
incentives. The message was clear. War against non-Christians met
with divine approval, as well as being a means to prove oneself and
enjoy the spoils of war.

Over time, the crusading ideal became corrupted. The knights who
gathered for the Fourth Crusade of 1204–5 found themselves heavily in
debt to the Venetians before they set out. They had unwisely con-
tracted with the Italian city state to supply three times as many ships as
they needed to transport them to the Holy Land. Attempts to repay
the debt resulted in them acting as a Venetian mercenary force against
Christian targets, namely the port of Zadar on the Adriatic coast and
the city of Constantinople. The Sixth Crusade of 1228–9 saw the Holy
Roman Emperor negotiate and *pay* for Christians to have access to
Jerusalem; it was thus a business transaction, in which no atrocities

were committed, no sins were forgiven and no souls guaranteed entry to Heaven. Nevertheless, the crusading spirit endured. Towards the end of the fourteenth century, Chaucer described his knight as a man who 'loved chivalry, truth and honour, freedom and courtesy' and who was renowned for fighting crusades in Alexandria, Prussia, Lithuania, Granada, Algiers, Turkey and several other places. Until the battle of Grunwald in 1410, knights from Western Europe regularly took ship for Lithuania to participate in the annual campaigns or *reysen* against the pagan Lithuanians in support of the Teutonic knights. Such wars of aggression in God's name were neither 'a necessary evil' nor can they be simply dismissed as imperialism. They were military as well as spiritual indulgences. When the season's fighting was over, the knights returned home.

The nature of holy war changed in the late Middle Ages. Several European kings had joined the crusades in person in the twelfth and thirteenth centuries; their successors promised to do so but never sailed. The turning point was the fall of Acre and the loss of the last Christian outpost in the Holy Land in 1291. With no hope of recovering Jerusalem, kings were reluctant to commit significant resources to a campaign so far from home, especially when their presence was required to manage domestic threats. In 1312 the Knights Templar – one of the two main military orders established to protect pilgrims travelling to Jerusalem – was abolished. Thereafter, holy warriors became more individualistic. The knights taking part in *reysen* and other late-fourteenth-century campaigns only travelled in small bands. They did not employ large bodies of archers or massed guns. They were more akin to jousting champions who fought for personal glory. By 1391, when Henry of Lancaster (the future Henry IV) went on a *reyse* in Lithuania, crusading had become a personal test of faith. But with the annihilation of crusader armies at Tunis in 1390, Nicopolis in 1395 and Grunwald in 1410, the idea of crusading withered. Thus the enthusiasm for holy war decreased at roughly the same time as cannon diminished the chivalric impetus to engage in secular conflict.

Raiding

In order to train 'those who fought' so their potential force was maximised, armies needed to practise by raiding. Viking raids into England,

Christian raids into Muslim Spain, Angevin raids into the county of Blois or the duchy of Brittany, English raids into Wales – all of these were undertaken in the spirit of testing the mettle of those taking part. Thus, the Scots' incursions into England throughout the Middle Ages were not just jabs at the English lion's rump or patriotic declarations of Scottish independence, they were also means by which warriors demonstrated the military strength and prowess of their kingdom.

Some kings escalated these training exercises to full-scale wars of aggression. When Edward III came to the throne in 1327, his highest priority was to stop the fighting among his magnates. The previous reign had been characterised by just such a series of conflicts, resulting in deep discontent with the king's administration and, ultimately, the collapse of the government and the enforced abdication of the king. Edward had no intention of making the same mistakes. He pursued a policy of international raiding on a massive scale. Military leaders and their men were given real wartime experience in both Scotland and France, on both land and sea. But his policy was always to keep the fighting on foreign soil. As Edward himself put it in 1339,

> According to the theory of war, which teaches that the best way to avoid the inconvenience of war is to pursue it away from your own country, it is more sensible for us to fight our notorious enemy in his own realm, with the joint power of our allies, than it is to wait for him at our own doors.[10]

Thus his wars had a multiplicity of purposes. They provided his troops with outlets for their chivalric aspirations. They gave them military experience. They secured the support of his allies by keeping alive a common cause. They kept his enemies – the French and the Scots – under pressure. And they successfully put an end to conflict among his nobles for the duration of his reign.

War, therefore, was not 'a necessary evil' but a political expediency. It might have served Henry IV in the same manner, as he acknowledged when he publicly declared in 1400 that he would take an army further into France than even his grandfather, Edward III, and his uncle, the Black Prince. Henry never set out – ill-health prevented him – but he did permit English soldiers to take part in the French civil war that erupted in 1407. This English intervention was also not 'a necessary evil' but an opportunistic move to gain a political advantage.

Henry V even more deliberately continued Edward III's policy. Not only did all the advantages of war apply equally in his day, he had the additional incentive of needing to prove his dynastic right. As a claimant to the throne of France, Henry could show God's approval of his claim to both kingdoms by defeating the French in battle. But the days of invading a foreign land for domestic purposes were coming to an end. National sovereignty and the importance of trade were threatened by the very idea of kings and magnates taking up arms against neighbouring states. So too were the legal systems of each nation involved. These were too valuable to be jeopardised simply for the sake of training warriors or demonstrating divine approval of a claim to the throne. Over the course of the fifteenth century, fewer military raids were sanctioned by European monarchs. It became increasingly necessary to justify war – for there to be some specific reason or objective that made conflict a necessity. The normality of war as it existed in the eleventh century, in which a king or a lord might attack his neighbour at will, had given way to the normality of peace.

The Regulation of War

As shown above, it was predominantly in the fifteenth century that positive attitudes to war – as displayed through crusading, jousting and international raiding – declined. However, even before this, a series of regulations had started to change the nature of warfare and take it further away from the privileged indulgence it had been at the outset of our period. The earliest of these came from the Church in the early eleventh century, in the form of the Peace of God and Truce of God movements. In addition, the rise of the papacy meant that kings increasingly needed to justify their wars to the pope. They could not simply invade other Christian kingdoms and expect there to be no diplomatic fallout.

What ultimately restrained kings' power to go to war, however, was that armies were costly. As markets multiplied and money became ever more important in the thirteenth century, the ability to go to war was limited by financial constraints. In England, this meant that kings had to secure a grant of extraordinary taxation by Parliament to carry on a protracted military campaign. In 1297 Edward I accordingly acknowledged that a decision to go to war lay in the hands of Parliament. In 1339, Edward III told papal envoys that any truce he made with France would also have to be ratified by Parliament as Parliament had the final say on all matters of war and peace.[11] This was perhaps a little disingenuous – real decision-making still lay with the king – but discussions about war could no longer ignore Parliament's opinion and its ability to withhold the necessary taxation. As a result, in England at least, foreign wars had to have the support of Parliament and thus acquired an official, legal basis. War was no longer the everyday activity it had been in the early Middle Ages. It needed consent, special agreements and legal provisions.

The conditions under which kings might go to war were not the only regulatory limitations imposed over the course of the Middle Ages. There were also the rules of engagement. We often assume that war was always prosecuted to the full, and that belligerent nations would do whatever it took to win, regardless of conventions, regulations, rules and codes of conduct. This was not always the case. Conflict tended to be conducted within the moral environment of chivalric codes. In particular, 'those who fought' had to acknowledge the high status of their opponents, treating them with dignity and respect if they captured them. They would normally choose to ransom men of high rank, not kill them. Such was the importance of chivalric principles in this matter that it resulted in patterns of behaviour that seem extraordinary to us. It was not uncommon to let a captured knight go back to his own country to raise his ransom. Even more extraordinarily, he might well return to submit himself again to captivity if he failed to find the money. On a wider scale, James IV of Scotland was so chivalrous that in 1513 he gave a month's advance notice of his intention to invade the north of England. In this case, unfortunately, James's avoidance of unleashing a surprise attack probably contributed to his defeat and death on the battlefield.

We can see the taming effects of chivalry also in the ordinances issued from the fourteenth century for the conduct of armies on foreign soil. In 1346, Edward III stipulated that 'no town or manor was to be burnt, no church or holy place sacked, and no old people, children or women in his kingdom of France were to be harmed or molested'.[12] The set of ordinances issued by Henry V in 1415 included clauses instructing his soldiers to protect churches and religious buildings and not steal from them; not to capture or harm any clergymen or women, or to take prisoner any clergymen unless they were armed and hostile; and not to rape any women, on pain of death. Similar ordinances were repeatedly renewed and reissued over the next two hundred years and they defined people's understanding of war. When Shakespeare talks about 'mercy', 'sparing' and 'honour', he is drawing on the common culture of war. Of course, such laws and codes were hugely idealistic and the reality usually looked very different. Edward III's instructions in 1346 were broken in every respect as towns and manors were burnt and many women raped. Nevertheless, they were at least aspired to. There is evidence that on the Agincourt campaign, a high moral standard was not merely expected of the army, it was imposed: a man who stole from a church was hanged. The bottom line is that a regulatory code that prohibits looting, the murder of prisoners, the raping of women, the despoliation of churches and the killing of children and peaceful civilians, is a more humane approach to war than that of obtaining victory at all costs. It certainly provides a framework for troops to be far more considerate towards peasants, children, women and priests than they were in the eleventh century.

The Sixteenth Century

Despite the association of war with the Middle Ages in the public imagination, the medieval period saw the steady decline of warfare. The unfettered, primitive aggression displayed by the Vikings and Normans and their contemporaries was no longer a feature of daily life by 1500. Wars between kingdoms became less common as their borders became more firmly established in the twelfth and thirteenth centuries. Violence, which had been part and parcel of war in 1000, had become limited by rules and regulations by 1400. The loss of key outposts in the Holy Land, shifts in lords' priorities, and fractures in the unity of the Church had reduced holy war to a shadow of its former status by 1420. Cannon and longbows had largely eliminated the element of individual prowess by 1450. Lords and knights were more frequently to be found living in manor houses than castles. In 1504, in the wake of the Wars of the Roses, Henry VII passed an Act that prevented lords from maintaining their supporters in livery, thereby effectively banning private armies in England. By then war had become nationalised and institutionalised, subject to Parliamentary approval. It had become a political strategy of last resort, a 'necessary evil' requiring special justification, as Thomas More said it should.

Significantly, all this decline had happened before handguns had become the dominant force on the battlefield. Large cannon had proved capable of bringing sieges to more speedy conclusions before 1500, but pitched battles were still won or lost with steel blades, whether the blades in question were swords, pikes or arrowheads. More than a century before Francis Bacon's observation that guns (along with printing and the compass) had changed the world, warfare had already altered beyond all recognition. Castles, the rise of the papacy, chivalry, longbows, the decline of crusading, moral regulation and the economic advantages of peace had all had an effect.

Despite this, Francis Bacon was not wrong. The advances in handguns that took place in the sixteenth century fully justified his statement. And as he implied, the effects were much more profound than a simple influence on the outcomes of battles. The historian Michael Roberts argued in the 1950s that the rise of hand-held guns led to a military revolution in Europe between 1560 and 1650. Changes in tactics, strategy, the scale of conflicts and the impact on citizens meant that war was completely transformed, with far-reaching political and economic consequences for society. There have been several criticisms of Professor Roberts's theory, and I would suggest that most of the changes to which he drew attention were already evident in England in the fourteenth century. Long before guns and large armies changed the face of European warfare, longbows had had the same effect in England, with a similar requirement for taxation and Parliamentary approval. Still, it can hardly be denied that guns affected the battlefields of Europe on a much larger scale.

The key to understanding the aforementioned military revolution is that, when fighting with long-range projectile weapons, you are more likely to win if you have more of them than your enemy. It follows that the more guns you have, the stronger your army. And, in turn, large and well-equipped armies have to be financed by taxation, resulting in new relationships between those who pay taxes, the government, arms manufacturers and military commanders.

Let us begin with the matter of scale. In the early Middle Ages, battles were often small-scale affairs, fought by a few thousand men at most. The battle of Hastings was fought by armies of 7,000–8,000 men on each side. Most battles before 1300 were even smaller than this:

skirmishes between a few dozen men were the most common form of action. When chroniclers claimed that 60,000, 80,000 or even 100,000 men faced each other, these fantastical figures were inspired by the reputed sizes of biblical armies. More reliable financial accounts reveal that it was rare for a campaign to involve more than 10,000 fighting men on each side. About 12,000 Englishmen and Welshmen were with Edward III at Crécy in 1346. At Agincourt, 8,000–9,000 Englishmen faced 12,000–15,000 Frenchmen (stories of 30,000 or more are contemporary exaggerations).[13] By the time of the Wars of the Roses, armies had swelled: perhaps a total of 50,000 men were present at Towton in 1461. In Italy, at the battle of Pavia – the decisive event in the struggle between France and Italy in 1525 – approximately 26,000 Frenchmen were defeated by a slightly smaller number of Habsburg troops.

In the sixteenth century, armies grew much larger. By the 1590s, the Spanish government had 200,000 men under orders – ten times the number it had had in the 1470s. The French army doubled over that time to 80,000 men. Even the English had increased their troops, from 25,000 to 30,000.[14] The reason for these increments was that all these armies now had guns. War had become a game of numbers. Sixteenth-century commentators therefore had two good reasons to urge political leaders not to fight. First, there was the horror of war, which was more extreme when massive armies rampaged across your land, looting, raping and killing. And second, there were the financial costs and the necessity of higher taxation.

The shift from chivalric war – typified by the massed charge of knights and hand-to-hand fighting – to projectile war also changed the social composition of 'those who fought'. In the eleventh century this position had been exclusively occupied by high-status men. In the late fourteenth century, 'those who fought' were generally men-at-arms, pikemen and archers, who in peacetime were yeomen and husbandmen. Thus the identity of the warrior had shifted from the top end of the social pyramid to a much lower position. As the sixteenth century demanded more and more men who could shoot a weapon, this trend continued down the social ranks. Why should a nobleman or a prosperous yeoman or merchant risk his life in the line of fire? It was much better to pay men who had no other prospects. Anyone could be trained to shoot a musket or hold a pike alongside a musketeer. In this way, guns not only blew away chivalric principles but also reduced the need for men of high status to take part in war. Whereas in the early

Middle Ages, the entire male nobility had been expected to fight, by 1600, the only aristocrats involved were those who took on positions of command. As a result, the percentage of English noblemen suffering violent deaths steadily declined from 25 per cent in 1400 to 2.5 per cent in 1750.[15]

Kings similarly began to withdraw from the battlefield. Early medieval monarchs had no choice but to be warriors. Everyone expected it of them, including 'those who prayed' and 'those who worked'. The defence of the realm in war was one of the two prime responsibilities of medieval kingship (the other being the delivery of justice to his subjects). But when guns came on the scene, the embodiment of political power and military command in one person began to disintegrate. Increasingly, kings did not risk their lives on the battlefield but rather delegated command to senior noblemen. James IV of Scotland was killed while commanding at Flodden in 1513; Francis I of France was captured at the battle of Pavia in 1525; and Louis II of Hungary was killed in 1526 fighting the Ottomans. After those events, royal appearances on the battlefield were rare. King Sebastian of Portugal perished at El-Ksar El-Kebir in Morocco in 1578. Very few battles after 1600 were attended by a monarch. In 1632, Gustavus Adolphus of Sweden became the last European king to die leading his troops in battle, but his personal commitment to generalship marks him out as exceptional. Heads of state no longer risked putting themselves in positions of danger. They and their subjects had too much to lose.[16]

At the opening of his book, *War and the Liberal Conscience*, the military historian Sir Michael Howard stated that 'it is likely that ever since the origins of human society, men – or at least some men and most women – have intermittently lamented the existence of war'.[17] It would be hard to disagree. Men lost their lives and saw their friends and kinsmen killed; women and girls were raped; peasants saw their homes and fields destroyed and non-Christian people were massacred on account of their beliefs. But we can be equally sure that war was so much a part of everyday life in the eleventh and twelfth centuries that men and women lived with its horror and did not lament it more than they lamented enslavement, plague, pestilence and extreme weather conditions. In fact, throughout the Middle Ages, plague and harvest failure were far deadlier than war. Obviously, the loss of a loved one in battle was a tragedy but so too was the loss of a family member from disease or starvation. To the ever-practical medieval mind, lamenting the existence of war was rather like complaining about the existence of winter. Just as winter came around every year and was best used in whatever ways were possible, so the key to limiting the damage inflicted by war was to use it to your advantage.

At the same time, there were many positive reasons why eleventh- and twelfth-century men wanted to go to war. These included proving themselves in battle, adventure, prestige, honour, loyalty, financial gain, the opportunity for sexual indulgence and, in the case of crusaders, the chance to obtain the forgiveness of their sins and a place in Heaven. To these we can add military responsibility. A king could not allow himself to become the victim of war: his neighbours would grow strong at his expense and the borders of his kingdom would become vulnerable. If, on the other hand, he kept the pressure up on his neighbours by raiding, so that his troops' practical training was always at his enemy's cost, then he did not have to worry so much about defending his own kingdom. An aggressive policy was thus often a popular one with the whole community. The best way of securing the necessary force was for society to be organised around a military nobility that was bred and trained to fight. Security, prosperity and honour were the rewards for the people whose king could lead his lords and men successfully into battle. Vulnerability, atrocities, hard- ship, humiliation and death were the alternative fates that awaited the people whose king was hesitant or unsuccessful in war.

As we have seen, the late Middle Ages saw all the personal incentives for going to war diminish. The means by which military victory could be obtained were increasingly impersonal and unchivalric. The heroic element was removed from war. So too was the divine element, in the sense that crusading fell out of favour. War was increasingly a financial and logistical problem, orchestrated by politicians and sanctioned by parliaments. At the same time, the potential losses increased. It is a tell- ing fact that exactly a century separates the glorious but unnecessary battle of Agincourt from the remarks of Erasmus and More, quoted at the start of this chapter. It is highly likely that the Latin chronicle entitled *The Deeds of Henry V* was specially commissioned by the king soon after the battle to give an account of his victorious kingship for a European readership. Yet one hundred years later, Erasmus would declare that war was 'stupid' and all war leaders 'military idiots, thick- headed lords . . . not even human except in appearance'.[18] The source of Henry V's pride had come to be seen not only as unwise but also inhuman. The divine order of 'those who fight', 'those who pray' and 'those who work' had fallen apart. When the cataclysmic wars of the seventeenth century broke out – the Civil Wars in England; the Thirty Years War on the Continent – there were no such distinctions. Everyone fought, everyone prayed and almost everyone worked. There was no chivalric glory. No sins were forgiven. No souls went to Heaven. Men and women suffered in their thousands as 'a necessary evil' was allowed to slash nations in two and rip through society. By the time these wars were over, their political leaders and their causes were exhausted. War had become a deterrent in its own right.

This is a situation we all recognise today, even as the president of Russia instigates wars of conquest against the neighbouring countries of Georgia and Ukraine. Our abhorrence of war and our understanding that it can only be justified through extreme necessity is the result of developments that happened in the Middle Ages. In war as in all those other aspects of life mentioned in chapter one, the differences between us and our medieval ancestors are not due to our actions or our ways of thinking but to theirs. And since this chapter began with one irony – that the more we develop as a society, the more we increase our ability to destroy ourselves – it seems fitting to end it with another. The period we associate with knights, castles, battles and long wars was actually the one that delivered us the expectation – if not the reality – of long periods of peace.

3

Inequality

Disparities of Wealth and Status in England

Medieval society was riven with inequality – that will not come as a surprise to anyone. Few people, however, realise quite how unequal it was. We don't publicly discuss slavery in England in the eleventh century, even though in some regions the proportion of slaves was as high as it was in eighteenth-century America. Similarly, we do not appreciate the extent of racial and sexual prejudices. Instead, we just presume that society was extraordinarily unequal and that rich and powerful men lorded it over everyone else. If we are forced to be more particular, we tend to approach the subject in one of two ways, depending on whether we are trying to entertain people or to inform them. Hence a few words need to be said about popular perceptions of medieval inequality before we can start to investigate the subject itself.

To begin with the entertainment side of things. If you were to make a film about violent, sexist, racist warlords whose wives and daughters wholeheartedly endorsed their abusive behaviour, you would have a hard time making your audiences sympathise with any of your characters. For similar reasons, historical novelists are reluctant to show everyone in their novels as exploiters of the poor. Any storyteller even partially reflecting the wanton acts of cruelty to be seen every day in a medieval city would instantly render that society repulsive to his or her readers. This is why historical authenticity is even harder to achieve than historical accuracy: the truth is likely to offend.[1] What's more, audiences don't like to think that medieval people would simply have accepted these things. They do not want to see slaves and peasants happily accepting their lowly status, nor women allowing themselves to be downtrodden and abused. We find it hard to believe that the vast majority of disadvantaged people meekly accepted their oppression. Thus, we impose our own prejudices on the past and reinvent it as 'how it must have been' to conform with our outlook. To appeal to a modern audience, therefore, a medieval heroine in a book or film must be shown as having control over her own life. Alternatively, she must appear constantly fighting her oppressors. Male peasants must similarly include at least one plucky, Robin Hood-like character who leads the others in defying authority. The result is a reproduction of modern society draped in medieval clothing. Indeed, 'Robin Hood Syndrome' is an appropriate term for the obligation on writers and artists to bring the Middle Ages into alignment with the expectations of our own age.[2]

Things aren't much easier when it comes to works intended to inform the public. We tend to judge medieval people by our own standards because what is good and right appears to be a timeless moral code, applicable to everyone in every age. We know that we would not want to experience the hardships that a medieval peasant did, so we accordingly presume that oppressed and persecuted people suffered just as much in the Middle Ages as we would if we were treated as they were. That may or may not be the case. The trouble is that when we condemn an eleventh-century slave owner, for example, in the same way that we would a nineteenth- or twentieth-century one, we obliterate the medieval perspective. More generally, in judging medieval people for failing to live up to our standards of behaviour, we shut our eyes to their own moral values. We see no morality in slavery, so we think a medieval peasant who sold his child into slavery cannot have done so for anything other than immoral reasons. But if the alternative was the child's starvation, it *was* a moral decision, and might even have proceeded on account of the parents' love for the child. Similarly, we would naturally criticise a medieval lord who forbade one of his peasants from marrying the man of her dreams; such action seems heartless. But in condemning him, we would be ignoring the medieval point of view. This is disastrous in terms of understanding the Middle Ages. We can't apply our twenty-first-century standards to eleventh-century people and imagine they will live up to our expectations any more than we ourselves should be judged by the values of the thirty-first century.

Eleventh-century people were different from us. They generally believed that the powerful figures who ruled them had been chosen by God. The rights of a divinely appointed king or lord therefore took priority over the suffering of the oppressed. Peasants were simply there to support the powerful and the religious members of the community. A woman's well-being depended entirely on her husband and, if she did not have a husband, then on her father and her lord. Opportunities for self-betterment simply did not exist. Had Shakespeare been born in 1064 rather than 1564, he would have been forced to work on his lord's manor as an illiterate labourer. He might never have had the opportunity to recognise his genius, let alone exercise it. But as we will see in this chapter, many changes took place between the eleventh century and the sixteenth. Those at the bottom of the social scale came to enjoy greater freedom. The sons of the most prosperous farmers were educated and became clerks, lawyers, merchants and bishops. They acquired manors of their own. They achieved a degree of political power through Parliament. They began to resist the rule of warlords. Women too saw their status and freedoms improve. The horizons of liberty and equality that first began to expand in the Middle Ages continue to affect our lives to this day.

Liberty

As we saw earlier, it was generally understood in the eleventh century that society was composed of three sorts of people: 'those who fought', 'those who prayed' and 'those who worked'. Domesday Book provides a more detailed breakdown of these groups. At the top of society was the king. Then came about 190 magnates and several thousand monks, nuns and priests of various ranks, with the archbishops, bishops and abbots ranking as high as the secular lords. These were 'those who fought' and 'those who prayed'. Together with their families, they made up less than 2 per cent of the population. 'Those who worked' included freemen, villeins, bordars, cottars and slaves. Freemen accounted for about 13 per cent of the population. The remaining 85 per cent were unfree. The villeins, bordars and cottars were serfs, bound to the land. They made up the majority. The remainder were slaves, bound to their owner.

Serfs could not leave the manor in which they lived without their lord's permission. They worked their lord's land as well as their own and were bought and sold along with it. This affected every aspect of their lives. Imagine not being able to marry the man or woman of your choice because he or she was from another manor and bound to another lord. Imagine not being able to send your son to school because the lord demanded that your son work on his land. A serf's status varied according to how much land he held, courtesy of his lord. Those of the highest standing, the villeins, had the use of 30 acres or more. The poorest, known as cottars or bordars, held just 5 acres or less. Life was tough. In the hardest years, families faced starvation. But even those with enough land to raise their children had few opportunities to better themselves. They had no choice in what they did in life. Their fate was to work for the benefit of their lord, in hope of their own survival.

Slaves accounted for about 10 per cent of the population nationally in 1086, although in the south-west, that figure was much higher, about 20 per cent. They were bought and sold as chattels, in slave markets. If you were a slave, any money you made legally belonged to your owner, as did any possessions you owned. Your lord owned your children too. If he wanted to sell your child, he could do so. If he wanted to rape a female slave, no one had the right to stop him. One of the Kentish laws specifies that slaves were not at liberty to eat when they wanted but only when they were fed.[3] According to Athelstan's law code, if you were a slave and your owner suspected you were a thief, he had the legal right to have you killed by his other slaves – by being stoned to death if you were a man or by being drowned or thrown off a cliff if you were a woman. Likewise, he could require you to kill one of your fellow slaves. If you failed to do so, you yourself would be whipped as a punishment.[4]

Female slaves were often bought and sold for the purpose of sexual gratification. Around the year 1000 Bishop Wulfstan of Worcester denounced those men who clubbed together to buy a girl so they could all have sex with her. When they grew tired of her, they would simply sell her to a slave dealer and buy a new girl.[5] Obviously, not all slaves were subjected to such torment and abuse, but many were. For most, slavery meant a life of hard labour. Sometimes favourite slaves were freed by their dying owners in the hope that the good deed would make it easier for the owners' souls to enter Heaven. For the majority, however, there was no respite except by their own death.

You might have thought that the Church would have promoted the abolition of slavery, but it was awkwardly positioned. When wealthy men and women left their estates to endow monasteries, they included in the gift the slaves who worked the land. If the Church had freed those slaves, it would have diminished the value of the gift. The Church therefore made a distinction between morality on the one hand and business on God's behalf on the other. While it taught that slavery was regrettable and that it was good to free slaves, it also held that slaves given to God should be retained for God's benefit. You might consider this hypocritical but the early medieval Church did not see things that way. Slavery, like war, was a fact of life and the Church had to accommodate such realities, even if it disapproved in principle.

The first discernible shifts in the horizon of liberty can be detected in Continental Europe. The causes are hotly debated by historians due to the large number of factors that had an impact on the economics, politics and social acceptability of slavery. But one deserves special notice. There was a period of slight global warming in the early Middle Ages, known as the Medieval Warm Period. This amounted to a rise in the average annual temperature of between 0.5 and 1 degree Celsius. This doesn't sound dramatic, but just half a degree difference means that the last frost of spring occurred about ten days earlier and the first frost of autumn about ten days later than before.[6] This resulted in improved harvests and a greater food supply. The mortality rate of the most disadvantaged members of society dropped. The upper ranks had always had enough to eat but the surplus crops now meant more of the poor survived into adulthood. This gave the lords more serfs under their control, and their wealth increased. More land could be cleared of woods, rocks and undergrowth and brought under the plough. More agricultural surpluses could be sold. This in turn led to the increase in commercial activity described in chapter one, with more markets and fairs being established and more people making use of money rather than barter.

These changes prompted lords to wonder why they should maintain their slaves when they could require them to fend for themselves, like their serfs. Moreover, if they freed their slaves by making them serfs, those ex-slaves had an incentive to clear more of the land and enrich the lords still further. The lords could still take advantage of their labour and exercise their rights over them, so they stood to lose nothing. In fact, they could gain spiritual benefits for themselves, as churchmen on the Continent increasingly extolled the virtues of manumission. For the lords, it seemed to be a win-win. Or, rather, a win-win-win: at one stroke they could reduce their financial liabilities, improve the agricultural value of their manors and smooth their souls' passage to Heaven.

In the British Isles, however, lords did not rush to give up their slaves.

It seems that they *liked* owning other people. Besides, many traders did good business selling English children as slaves in Ireland. That slavery in England was abolished about a century earlier than in the other countries in the British Isles was the result of the Norman Conquest.[7] The Normans not only introduced the Continental view that slavery was morally wrong, they imposed it by displacing almost the entire Anglo-Saxon landowning and slave-owning class. William the Conqueror himself was instrumental in bringing about this revolution, declaring his opposition to the slave trade in the 1070s. The English Church finally forbade the buying and selling of slaves in slave markets in 1102. After that, slavery rapidly declined. Children of slaves continued to be born into slavery, so the condition lingered on in some places: Peterborough Abbey still counted the slaves on its estates in the 1120s.[8] But by 1200, slavery in England was rare, if not extinct.

Serfdom lasted much longer. Peasants were still predominantly unfree in the thirteenth and early fourteenth centuries, working the land for their lord. However, after the Black Death of 1348–9, serfdom also declined. Lords were given a sharp reminder how dependent they were on their peasants. When their workers died, their estates were left unproductive. Crops were allowed to rot in the fields. Animals were abandoned to stray. All a lord could do was offer good wages in the hope of persuading peasants from neighbouring manors to run away from their places of birth and come and work for him. Where this happened, the runaway tenants left their feudal obligations to their previous lord behind. The king passed legislation to try to stop this from happening but the economic forces were too strong. Higher wages and social freedom were just too great an allure. In some places, so many people left their manor that only a small number of peasants were left. Then the manorial court ceased to be held and any remaining serfs became *de facto* freemen, obtaining leases and paying rent. Over the next two centuries, more and more manorial tenants gained their freedom so that by 1600, less than 1 per cent of the English peasantry remained bound to the land.[9] This means that, between the eleventh century and the sixteenth, the horizon of liberty expanded from including less than 15 per cent of the population to embracing almost everyone.

As a result of these changes, the lowest classes in 1600 were no longer serfs and slaves but servants, labourers and paupers. Ordinary men and women could not be prevented by a landowner from marrying their partner of choice. Nor could they be stopped from leaving the manor. A labourer's child might be forced through poverty to become an apprentice in the house of a wealthier neighbour but, upon reaching adulthood, he or she was free to choose whom to marry and where to work. Status was no longer defined in terms of legal restrictions but financial ones. If a sixteenth-century pauper was denied the hand in marriage of the daughter of a prosperous yeoman, it was not the lord of the manor who prevented the match but her mother and father.

Individual freedom is thus a major development of the Middle Ages. Indeed, given the emphasis we place on our liberty in the modern world, many would regard it as the most important element of the entire medieval legacy. Although in later centuries, certain English families became owners of slaves overseas, slavery as an institution was never again legally recognised in Britain (except for two years in the sixteenth century, 1547–9, when enslavement was made the legal punishment for vagabonds). Serfdom too was formally abolished in 1660. These changes make the juxtaposition of Harari's peasant listening to the ringtone of a mobile phone seem much less impressive. No electronic device could possibly be so desirable that it would be an adequate compensation for enslavement.

Land Ownership

When economic historians discuss changing levels of wealth inequality, they tend to employ the statistical tools used by modern economists. However, economists' models are inappropriate for societies that were so different from our own. For example, you will often come across references to the proportion of the country's total wealth that was in the hands of the richest 1 per cent or 10 per cent of the population. Thomas Piketty's *Capitalism in the Twenty-First Century* (2013) is a case in point: it contains many historical graphs showing the share of the wealth owned by the top 1 per cent and top 10 per cent of a nation since 1800. This method concentrates on the very wealthy; it places the distressed poor and destitute in the same bracket as everyone else who is not in the top 10 per cent – including the second-richest 10 per cent. It hardly needs saying that the problems of that group are dwarfed by those facing the poorest in society. The 'top 10 per cent' method is a good way of assessing the comparative wealth of the rich but it obscures poverty rather than revealing it.

Another method employed by economic historians is to calculate the Gini coefficient at various points in time. This is a technical measurement of how far a society deviates from perfect equality. It is expressed either as a percentage or as a figure between 0 and 1, with the lower figure being the more equal: zero thus reflects perfect equality. For context, the Gini coefficient for the UK today is 0.37 – more unequal than Germany (0.29) but slightly more equal than the USA (0.39). The problem is that it reduces all forms of inequality to a single statistic. This is like asking 'What is the meaning of life, the universe and everything?' and coming up with the answer '42', as Douglas Adams did in his *Hitchhiker's Guide to the Galaxy*. The simplicity of the solution does not reflect the complexity of the question. The Gini coefficient also fails to acknowledge that, in medieval society, some people's wealth and possessions were not their own but their lord's. It is not designed to measure inequality in a society in which some people owned wealth and other people *were* that wealth. It not surprising, therefore, that attempts by economic historians to calculate Gini coefficients for late-thirteenth-century England have produced wildly varying results.[10]

How then should we proceed? The answer is that we must be clear what we mean by 'wealth' and employ a means to be both specific and consistent in our measurements. In the modern world, we normally measure wealth in two ways: capital and income. Concentrating first on capital, the obvious benchmark for us to use is the ownership of land. Almost all rich individuals in the Middle Ages held a manor. Although prosperous merchants were a significant exception, even they often consolidated their success by buying a country estate. Thus the extent of land ownership is one way to gain an appreciation of how wealth inequality changed over the Middle Ages.

As we have seen, in 1086 England was entirely owned by the king and held from him by a relatively small number of lords, prelates, freemen and religious institutions. The total number of manorial lords in 1086 was about 2,650. Some of these 'lords' appear anonymously as 'four thanes' or 'two free Englishmen' but even so, there cannot have been more than 3,000 men and women holding land outside the boroughs. Including their families, the whole country was in the hands of less than 2 per cent of the population. Land ownership was therefore extraordinarily unequal.

This situation changed over subsequent centuries. In 1873, there were 959,552 landowning individuals and 14,459 landowning institutions in England and Wales.[11] In other words, when the population had grown thirteen times, there were more than 300 times as many landowners. Today, although the distribution of land is still unfair, about 36 per cent of UK dwellings are owned outright by their occupiers and another 28 per cent are owned by way of a mortgage. Almost two-thirds of the 24.7 million householders in the UK own their own home in one form or another.[12] Obviously the vast majority of them own *only* their own home and little or no land outside their back door: collectively their plots and gardens cover just 5 per cent of England. A minority of families and organisations own vast swathes of the countryside and valuable urban estates. Nevertheless, the horizon of land ownership has expanded hugely over the last nine centuries. The question is, how much of this expansion took place in the Middle Ages?

The following table compares the percentages of land owned by the various classes in Domesday Book with land ownership in England as estimated by the statistician Gregory King in 1695. The figures from the 1873 *Return of Owners of Land* are given for comparison. The three datasets show that land ownership changed significantly before 1695 – and less so in the two centuries afterwards.

Percentage of England owned by each class[13]			
	1086	**1695**	**1873**
The Crown	>17%[14]	6%	1%
The Church	26%	2%	3%
Leading barons (1086)/lords and baronets (1695)	25%	16%	17%
Lesser tenants-in-chief (1086)/gentry (1695)	29%	31%	37%
Freeholders/yeomen	<3%	45%	38%

Although Gregory King's figures are only approximations, they leave no room for doubt that land was redistributed on a massive scale between 1086 and 1695. The royal family's holdings diminished by two-thirds, principally as a result of royal grants to noblemen and knights before Edward I sought to put a stop to such losses in 1279. The Church lost 90 per cent of its estates, largely during Henry VIII's reign. Between them, Crown and Church gave up ownership of more

than a third of the country. The obvious beneficiaries were the yeomen. Whereas in 1086 the country had been in the hands of about
3,000 families and institutions, in 1695 it was shared between 204,000
families and 4,000 institutions. In other words, the redistribution of
more than a third of England had resulted in an expansion of land
ownership from less than 2 per cent of the population to more than 15
per cent. Obviously some families owned much more than others: the
140,000 smaller freeholders in Gregory King's list owned an average of
just 47 acres. Nevertheless, it is clear that the Victorian pattern of land
ownership in England was principally the result of changes that took
place between 1086 and 1695 – most of which pre-dated 1600.[15]

What about the rest of society? Clearly, 84 per cent of the population in 1695 still did not own any land at all. Some of these people were
able to acquire the use of farms by way of copyhold from the landowner, which gave them short-term rights. Others were able to lease
farms. According to King, 150,000 families were in one of these classes
in the late seventeenth century: another 11 per cent of the population.
These groups of farmers might be considered alongside the freeholders on account of their economic independence. Despite a significant
difference in status between landowners and lease-holding husbandmen, both groups derived an income from land they themselves
managed, which marked them out from the labouring class. Combin-
ing the two, control of the land in 1695 was shared by about a quarter
of the population. This marks a considerable expansion from the less
than 2 per cent of the eleventh century.

Incomes

Was society in 1600 more equal than it had been in 1000? It is tempting
to say it was, because slavery no longer existed, serfdom had almost
been eradicated and many more people owned and controlled the
land. Still, how 'equal' people really were is a matter for debate. It was
not just a question of wealth. Was it better to be a free but starving
pauper in the sixteenth century, whipped half-naked from town to
town and branded in the ear for vagrancy, than an eleventh-century
slave whose food, shelter and clothing were provided by an owner? As
we have seen, one of the reasons why freemen sold their children into
slavery in the eleventh century was the moral one of giving them a

better life – in the hope that both the child and its birth family might thereby escape starvation. We risk imposing modern values on the past if we set a higher priority on personal liberty than on the need to eat, however principled that prioritisation might appear.

Given this problem, the assiduous historian will reach for some statistics to see whether income equality also improved over the Middle Ages. But what figures should we choose? In theory, we could just take the average income of the poorest in society and compare it to that of the richest. But this would not be satisfactory. For a start, such figures do not exist for the eleventh and twelfth centuries. Many people did not have an income as such. Money was not universal. If you grew your own crops in a remote area of the country where there was no market, you might not handle silver coins at all. This makes it very difficult to compare incomes.

This brings us to another problem that historians often gloss over with regard to income inequality. Which matters more: the number of people who are disadvantaged? Or the scale of their disadvantage?

If we want to find out whether society in 1600 was more equal than it had been in 1000, we need to examine inequality in more subtle ways than by simply comparing income. To this end, it is worth starting with a basic model of differences. Consider which of the following two societies is the more equal: Society A, in which 1 per cent of the population receive £100 per year and the remaining 99 per cent all earn £1; or Society B, in which the richest 1 per cent receive £100 per year, the next richest 1 per cent £99, the next richest £98, and so on, all the way down to those in the poorest centile, who earn £1 per year.

Most people would argue that the second society, Society B, is the more equal, because it doesn't seem quite as unfair as Society A. In Society A, everyone is poor in comparison to the richest 1 per cent. In contrast, there is a good chance someone will be worse off than you are in Society B. However, there are other ways of looking at this. In Society A, 99 per cent of the population are equal in only having a modest income. They all earn about half the average. Aside from the top 1 per cent, no one is more disadvantaged than his neighbours. So, although it seems both unfair and unequal, there is no stratification of income and no underclass. There are no obvious financial barriers to people mixing – either for work, society or marriage. In Society B, the poorest 10 per cent of the population have an average income of roughly a *tenth* of the overall average. Even though it is comparatively more prosperous – more than twenty-five times as rich as Society A – many people earn much less than half the average income. The poorest are unlikely to be able to make ends meet or offer anything by way of hospitality to the richer sort. The richest groups will probably not want to consort with the poorest or allow their sons and daughters to marry the offspring of such unfortunate individuals. The greater divergence of incomes thus leads to an underclass. Although the Gini coefficient of Society B is 0.33 – significantly nearer equality than the 0.49 of Society A – more people are severely disadvantaged in the statistically more equal society. In short, the more stratified a society is, the more likely it is that the poorest members will suffer.

This is why income inequality was far more important than wealth inequality in the Middle Ages. Not owning land didn't kill people; not having enough to eat did. When prices rose, the least well-off starved. Women were unable to produce milk to feed their babies and infants (who were breastfed for much longer than they are today). Weakness from lack of food stunted children's growth, leaving them small and deformed. Hungry people were weak and more likely to die from illness or injury.

As noted above, a top-down approach to wealth inequality is misleading because it focuses on those who did *not* suffer from it. It follows that we should look at it instead from the point of view of those who *did* suffer, namely the poor. Just as beauty lies in the eye of the beholder, so inequality lies in the hunger of the beggar.

This sets us quite a challenge. Traditionally historians have reached for wage and price indices to see whether workers' ability to buy a basket of goods was increasing or decreasing over the course of time. One such dataset is known as the Phelps Brown-Hopkins index, which measures fluctuations in builders' real wages from the 1260s to the 1950s.[16] It shows that real wages declined in the late thirteenth century, then rose significantly after the Black Death and continued to rise in the fifteenth century before plummeting to their lowest-ever levels in the 1590s. However, its figures are all just *averages*; they say nothing about inequality. They tell us the ordinary fifteenth-century builder's family had a better diet than his great-grandparents in the fourteenth century or his great-grandchildren in the sixteenth. But the incomes of the poorest members of society fell well below these averages.

The key to understanding income inequality as it was experienced by the poorest people in medieval England is, once again, land. This time, however, it is not the *ownership* of land that is the significant factor but the use of it. If you did not farm any land, you had to buy all your food. In order to do so, you had to have an income. For someone to employ you, he or she had to have a surplus of cash. But in times of dearth, when prices went up, such surpluses dried up and so did the jobs market. Therefore it was essential to have the use of enough land to grow enough food to feed yourself and your family. As a rule of thumb, if a medieval peasant had 30 acres, he could grow sufficient grain to see his family through the worst weather that England might throw at him. If he had between 15 and 30 acres, his family was more precariously positioned. And if he had less than that, he and his family were at constant risk of starvation.

Population was a critical factor. It grew from about 1.71 million in 1086 to 3.1 million by 1190 and 4.43 million in 1279.[17] The more people there were, the less land there was to go around, especially after the clearing of almost all the remaining usable moors and wasteland for agriculture by about 1220. The percentage of unfree peasants with the use of 30 acres or more dropped from 40 per cent in 1086 to less than 26 per cent by 1279 (when the next major land survey was drawn up).[18] The proportion on the cusp of survival, with between 15 and 30 acres, declined from 40 per cent to 36 per cent over that period. The poorest sector of the community, who never had enough to be self-sufficient, grew from 20 per cent to at least 38 per cent. Although the land was more productive in 1279 than in 1086, due to the effects of the Medieval Warm Period, the proportion of peasants who could be confident of feeding their families diminished.

As the above figures show, nearly three-quarters of the population teetered on the edge of disaster in 1279. Famines were deadly. And good years did not solve the problems of poverty. If a smallholder had a number of sons who survived the hardships of youth, and if there was no other available land in the manor, either the smallholding had to be subdivided – with the result that the separate parts were each insufficient to feed a family – or the eldest son was given the whole smallholding and the younger sons were left landless. Those younger sons then had a choice of searching for labouring work, learning a craft or turning to crime. And in the period 1279–90 they did survive: the population grew by more than 7 per cent in those eleven years alone, reaching 4.75 million.[19] Inequality grew even more extreme. Rents rose as more people competed for land. And in many places, there was simply no more land available. At Martham in Norfolk, 60 per cent of the peasants were reduced to having just 2 acres each.[20]

'It never rains but it pours', we often say. And that is exactly what happened around 1290. The Medieval Warm Period started to come to an end. In the early fourteenth century, deluges devastated the crops for several successive years. Temperatures plummeted and pandemic cattle diseases broke out. Criminal gangs began to roam the land. The breakdown of law and order of the 1290s and early 1300s – which left its mark on England in the form of hundreds of moated manor houses constructed by owners wanting to defend their property – was a consequence of chronic social inequality.

No statistic can do justice to the plight of the landless poor at the turn of the fourteenth century. Between 1290 and 1325 the population shrank to 4.12 million – a drop of more than 13 per cent in one generation. And those 600,000 deaths do not represent the full extent of the suffering. Many of those who survived experienced extreme hunger, stunted growth and nutrition-related diseases and grief. Many more were the victims of crime.

While the poor saw their lives become more and more difficult, those at the top of society saw their incomes rise. That of the bishops of Worcester more than trebled, from £345 in 1212 to £1,307 in 1313.[21] The annual profits of the bishops of Ely increased two and a half times, from £920 to £2,550, between 1170 and 1299. Canterbury Cathedral Priory's revenue rose from £1,406 in 1200 to £2,540 in 1331. Some of these increments were due to grants and gifts. But others were the result of charging higher rents to ever more desperate people. As in the Industrial Revolution half a millennium later, when the incomes of the workers diminished, the profits enjoyed by their employers and landlords increased.[22]

The Black Death changed this pattern. Between 1348 and 1351, it destroyed about two million lives in England alone. It used to be said that a third of Christendom died in those few years. Now we know that was an underestimate. The actual figure for England is more likely to have been in excess of 45 per cent, and some scholars even put it at over 60 per cent.[23] It was the most catastrophic event in Europe of the last thousand years.[24] For those who survived, however, it had a silver lining. It freed up land and capital on a scale never seen before. The reduction in size of the agricultural workforce gave peasants unprecedented bargaining power. As we have seen, the result was the rapid decline of serfdom. Men and women who had previously been bound to the land departed in search of a better life. Lords who had once commanded a large, unfree workforce now became prospective employers offering good wages. They were forced to reduce rents. Many sold up, parcelled out farms as freeholds or leased their estates to risk-taking merchants and those working their way up from the ranks of the peasantry. The accounts of wealthy abbeys all show a decline in income from their estates over the period 1350–1450.[25] Overall, real wages among the peasantry doubled while aristocratic incomes fell by 10–20 per cent. Given the discrepancy between a lord receiving £400 or more per year and a hard-working peasant with 30 acres bringing in perhaps £4 or a skilled worker earning £5, this hardly amounts to a revolution. However, it did result in less income inequality than in the thirteenth century.

This situation lasted until the mid-fifteenth century when the population hit a low point of just under two million. As it started to grow again, so too did aristocratic and ecclesiastical incomes. The better-off peasants who had invested their surpluses in freehold estates or had acquired farms on long leases with low rents, also saw their incomes rise significantly. Those who had not been so lucky found their younger sons stranded without land. The lower classes thus became more and more stratified and those at the bottom of the scale more vulnerable. At the same time, lords began to enclose the manors of central England, removing the common fields and pastures from community control and turning them into private fields. Poorer tenants were left with even fewer assets than before. No longer could they use the community oxen to draw a plough. No more could they graze their animals on the common. Often they had no choice but to let go of their four or five acres and move to a town to look for work. This led to further inequality, especially when prices began to rise. Over the period 1450–1600, meat prices increased four times and grain prices five times. Workers' wages merely doubled.[26]

By 1600, the population had recovered to four million. Freedom from feudal bonds and new opportunities to rent, lease or buy more land had broken up the classes that had once been termed 'those who work'. Some were so wealthy they could no longer be called workers: they had become local gentry. Those who had nothing to sell but their labour found themselves forced to work for these newly wealthy families. And the more the population grew, the more labourers there were, and the lower their wages sank. The lowest real-wage levels on the Phelps Brown-Hopkins index almost certainly indicate periods when the poorest people suffered the most extreme hardship. Many sixteenth-century labourers were unable to eat meat as regularly as their fifteenth-century forebears, living with malnutrition and even facing the prospect of starvation. The numbers of those who were forced to travel the country in gangs – either looting or in search of work – reached critical levels in the 1590s. Every county complained of vagrants. Stratford-upon-Avon had 700 homeless people sleeping in barns. London was reputed to have 30,000. In towns such as Norwich, a quarter of the population was destitute and in need of charitable relief to survive.

All this makes it difficult to argue that society was more equal at the end of the sixteenth century than it had been in the eleventh. Just because almost everyone had been given their freedom does not mean they all enjoyed a better standard of living. Many did, that is not in doubt. There was certainly more equality of opportunity than before, and there was greater social mobility among those who had some capital. However, those who had no capital were just as vulnerable as they had always been, if not more so. Society was more stratified than ever and, as we have seen, the more stratified a society is, the more likely it is that the poorest members will suffer. They bore the brunt of every harvest failure and every price rise. Had you been one of them, you would not have regarded income inequality as diminishing, rather the opposite. When prices rose, you'd have seen and felt its pernicious effects with your own eyes. And it would have been of small consolation to you that some of your neighbours had been able to acquire 80 or 90 acres and become employers.

Having said that, on the basis that 'inequality lies in the hunger of the beggar', there was one important area in which late-sixteenth-century England differed enormously from its pre-Black Death counterpart. Systems of relief were introduced in some towns in the sixteenth century to give sustenance to those who were starving. In 1597, following the food shortages of the previous three years, the Old Poor Law was introduced. As will be shown in greater detail in chapter six, this made provision for people to be taxed locally to feed the poor of their parish. In conjunction with the maturity of a market system that circulated food in times of dearth, it saved thousands of lives. You could say that, through the enforcement of charity on the well-off,

English society found the means to alleviate the worst suffering created by its greater stratification. But charity does not lessen inequality. It is a painkiller to help people cope, not a cure.

Political Power

The number of educational and professional opportunities open to the developing middle classes in sixteenth-century society vastly outnumbered those in the feudal eleventh century. Much the same can be said for political power. As the horizon of wealth expanded further to take in more and more families, so the political horizon widened to embrace them.

In the eleventh century, the king's will was the law. King Ethelred II banished or confiscated the lands of lords he did not trust and ordered a cold-blooded massacre of all Danes in England on St Brice's Day in 1002. Cnut executed four important lords without trial at Christmas 1017. Those who were bold enough to defy William the Conqueror did not normally live to regret it. The only check on royal power was that of a small number of lords and bishops who advised the king. The king could not be compelled to accept their advice but wise kings at least took it seriously. From this handful of influential men, the political horizon started to expand outwards, to include more and more individuals. The agreement by King John to accept Magna Carta in 1215 and the subsequent confirmation of its provisions by later kings made the monarchy accountable to the most powerful men in the realm. The development of Parliament in the late thirteenth century amplified this accountability. Occasionally from 1265, and regularly from 1295, seventy-four elected county MPs and the representatives of about 160 towns joined with the lords and higher clergy in advising the king and creating or revising statute law. The role of each MP may have been small but political power was no longer vested in the monarch alone.

Parliament acquired even greater authority in the fourteenth century. Most notably, in 1327, English MPs agreed to depose Edward II, forcing him to abdicate in favour of his son. Then, in 1399, Parliament deposed Richard II and appointed his successor. The difference between the two events is significant. No one quite knew whether Parliament had the legal right to depose a king in 1327. Seventy years later, there was no doubt: Parliament was the arbiter of whether Richard's reign was finally over, not the king himself, by his abdication. Thus the development of an electorate composed of burgesses and yeomen with an income of as little as £2 per year from freehold land did a great deal to expand political power, even if it still only extended to a minority of the populace. Whereas the king's will had once been law, now their will could dethrone a king.

Female Independence

In English law, from at least the twelfth century, a married couple was a single legal entity, one flesh and blood, represented in law solely by the husband. A woman was required to obey her husband in all things, and he was permitted to beat her to make sure she complied. Women were not allowed to hold office (with very few exceptions). Daughters only inherited land and titles in the absence of a male heir. If a manorial tenant died, his widow normally continued to enjoy his estate as long as she did not remarry; no such bar against remarrying was placed on a man if his wife died. And so forth. It would be wrong to say, however, that all men were privileged over all women. The inequalities of sex were overlaid by those of status. When a householder was away from home, his wife was in charge, and no male servant in the household was in a position to disobey her commands. Similarly, many a lord's wife would have been able to influence the steward who held the manorial courts in her husband's name, even if she was not the lord of the manor herself.

Carrying on from this pattern of tacit influence, wealthy women might enjoy a degree of unofficial power. Isabella de Fortibus, widowed in 1260 at the age of twenty-three, and countess of Devon in her own right two years later, was twice able to resist the king's command that she marry a man of his choosing. Such defiance could even extend to military matters. The redoubtable Agnes, countess of Dunbar, successfully defended Dunbar Castle for six months in 1338 against a substantial English army led by the earl of Salisbury. Unofficial power also applied to politics. Although women could not vote or sit in Parliament, powerful ladies who controlled boroughs that sent men to Parliament in the fifteenth and sixteenth centuries could guarantee that their interests were represented by making sure their friends or yes-men were elected by their tenants. When aristocratic women could defy the king's directions, and many women of less exalted birth could control their husbands through sheer force of character – as Chaucer's Wife of Bath reminds us – it would be misleading to describe the inequality of the sexes in purely legalistic terms. To do so would be to study the law, not the people.

Given all these things, can we discern any change in women's rights and power over the course of the Middle Ages? Can we identify a shifting horizon of female independence – and if so, in which direction did it move?

Although there were many instances of women appearing in prominent positions in Anglo-Saxon society, it would be difficult to argue that there was less sexual discrimination before 1066. Striking examples of female leaders like Aethelflaed of Mercia may be attributed to their royal or noble birth, their wealth, their husband's status or – as in Aethelflaed's case – all of these things. Such women were exceptional. The same applies to female landholding. About 350 manorial lords were female in 1066 but approximately half of all the land they held was in the hands of just three women: Gytha, the widow of Godwin, earl of Wessex; Queen Edith, her daughter; and Edith, the mistress of her son King Harold II.[27] This says more about Earl Godwin's family than about the position of women generally. Thus any examination of women's freedom and achievements in the eleventh century needs to take into account the status of the women in question.

Many of the inequalities women faced were due to marriage. Therefore it is easy to overlook this as an area in which women's status changed significantly for the better. In the early eleventh century, aristocratic marriage declined to being a civil contract that a powerful husband could set aside at will. According to the *Anglo-Saxon Chronicle*, in 1051 Edward the Confessor 'forsook the lady who had been consecrated his queen and had her deprived of all that she owned in land, and in gold and silver, and of everything, and committed her to his sister at Wherwell [Priory]'.[28] Although she was later restored to favour, this is indicative of how a man could treat his noble wife. Even men who took official wives might have concubines whose children were treated as legitimate offspring. King Harold took Edith Swanneck as his mistress and had five children by her, marrying another woman after most of Edith's children had been born and while Edith herself was still alive. Cnut similarly had a concubine. William the Conqueror was the product of his father's affair with Herleva before she married Herluin de Conteville, a minor Norman lord.

The acceptability of such unions was hugely threatening to women. They had no guarantee they would remain in favour, nor that their children would enjoy their paternal birthright if their 'husband' took another woman as his wife or concubine. Thus it was very much to women's advantage in the eleventh and twelfth centuries that the Church enforced the recognition of the sanctity of marriage across Christendom. Following the reforms of Gregory VII, marriage increasingly became a holy bond that no one, not even a king, could set aside. Banns and marriage settlements were introduced. Illegitimate children were barred from inheriting: in the early twelfth century there was no question of any of Henry I's illegitimate sons becoming king. A wife was henceforth for life. Repudiation was impossible (with a few rare exceptions, mostly relating to consanguinity and non-consummation) and the inheritance of any legitimate children was underpinned by law. If we think of the bigger picture, it marks the start of a long process. Marriage ceased to be an institution that the husband alone could dissolve at will. From the late eleventh century, only the Church could do so. In later centuries, Parliament took on that role. And finally, in the nineteenth century, it became possible for women to seek a divorce. Pope Gregory VII might seem an unlikely champion of women's rights but, indirectly, he was.

Further subtle shifts in the expansion of female independence can be detected in the rights of widows. Initially, a rich widow could be forced to marry against her will. Henry I declared that he would not tolerate this but his Angevin successors were of an opposite mind. Richard I and John both gave permission for men to marry widows without their consent. Magna Carta, however, stamped on the practice:

> At her husband's death, a widow may have her marriage portion and inheritance at once and without trouble. She shall pay nothing for her dower, marriage portion, or any inheritance that she and her husband held jointly on the day of his death. She may remain in her husband's house for forty days after his death, and within this period her dower shall be assigned to her.
>
> No widow shall be compelled to marry, so long as she wishes to remain without a husband. But she must give security that she will not

marry without royal consent, if she holds her lands of the Crown, or without the consent of whatever other lord she holds them from.

Despite the readiness of later kings occasionally to overlook these clauses, they became accepted as law by the end of the thirteenth century.

Official recognition of marriage implied the recognition of the state of widowhood too, which held other advantages for noblewomen. A married woman could not be given an official appointment on behalf of the king, as she was bound to obey her husband in all things. A widow, however, could be expected to be loyal. The early thirteenth century saw the appointment of at least two female sheriffs. Nicolaa de la Haye, hereditary castellan of Lincoln Castle, was made sheriff of Lincolnshire by King John. And Ela de Longespée became sheriff of Wiltshire in the reign of Henry III. These were important positions with a range of significant powers; they were not merely symbolic.

The downside of the official recognition of marriage by the Church was that it confirmed the marital pre-eminence of the husband. Sexual discrimination is blatant in Magna Carta, which stipulates: 'No one shall be arrested or imprisoned on the appeal of a woman for the death of any person except her husband.' A woman's testimony was therefore practically worthless as evidence in a murder trial. It was just part of a whole gamut of prejudices against women. Women could not attend grammar schools or universities. They could not be priests or teachers. There were no more female sheriffs after Ela de Longespée. In every aspect of life, a married woman had to have her husband's permission – from making a will to allowing someone into the marital home.

The most interesting point of tension is where royal status and sexism clashed. Although Henry I saw no reason why his daughter Matilda should not rule as queen after his death, he was in a minority. When he died in 1135, his nobles decided that her sex barred her from the succession, even though they had collectively sworn oaths on at least three occasions during her father's lifetime to support her right to the throne. Edward I similarly considered his daughters' sex no impediment to their becoming queens regnant and drew up a settlement of the throne to that effect in 1290. It is open to question whether his wishes would have been respected if he had not left sons. Edward III was more sexist than his ancestors on the matter, specifically ignoring his daughters and granddaughters when he drew up an order of the succession in 1376. Henry IV also tried to restrict the inheritance of the throne to his sons' male progeny by Act of Parliament in 1406. But his eldest son, Prince Henry, objected to the idea. The king was forced to pass a second Act, allowing for Prince Henry's daughter to inherit in her own right rather than the prince's next brother, Thomas.

The royal glass ceiling did eventually shatter, as we can see from the fact that two women succeeded to the throne in the sixteenth century. We might therefore see 1406 as a turning point, with the revolution being complete by the time of Mary I's accession in 1553.

What had changed? One of the most important factors affecting the possibility of the succession of a woman was the calamitous reign of Stephen. It was not difficult for people to make the link between his controversial succession and the anarchy that followed. This led to the principle, adopted from 1154, that the inheritance of the throne by a child or grandchild of the deceased king was of paramount importance, even if the late king's only living descendant was a woman. A second, not unconnected factor was that other kingdoms had supported female succession. Two queens of Naples were early examples: Joanna I in the fourteenth century and her kinswoman Joanna II in the early fifteenth. An even more important queen in English eyes, however, was Margaret of Denmark, who had not only united the kingdoms of Denmark and Norway with that of Sweden but had arranged the marriage of her heir, Erik, to Philippa of England, daughter of Henry IV, in 1406. More significant still in Tudor eyes was Isabella of Castile, the Spanish queen who completed the *Reconquista* in 1492 and united Spain by marrying her second cousin, Ferdinand of Aragon. Her daughter was Catherine of Aragon, Henry VIII's first wife. Given that these foreign queens had not only ruled successfully but had been endorsed by the English royal family, it would have been difficult for anyone to deny that Isabella's own granddaughter could become queen of England in her own right.

Another important factor affecting the potential succession of women was that the nature of kingship had fundamentally changed. Whereas in the eleventh century a king was required to lead his men in battle and to administer justice, a sixteenth-century monarch was expected to be more circumspect. Private armies had been banned in 1504, so English kings and queens no longer needed to march against an upstart earl at the head of a large body of men. Besides, as mentioned in the previous chapter, kings who personally led their troops into battle were liable to be killed by a cannonball or stray bullet, so they increasingly left the business of war in the hands of professional military commanders. There were similar developments when it came to the king's other main duty, the administration of justice. When King Stephen resisted the introduction of Roman law in the twelfth century and insisted that his subjects should retain their English customs, it placed a responsibility on his successors to codify and develop the common law. Consequently, by the fifteenth century, the principles of English law were no longer a vague gathering of laws but a legislative corpus that required professional supervision and Parliamentary clarification rather than royal intervention. With bodies of professional men taking charge of military leadership and jurisprudence, the role of the monarch was increasingly confined to politics and policymaking. And as Margaret of Denmark and Isabella of Castile both showed, there was nothing to stop a woman excelling at both.

The promotion of peace and the extension of the rule of law did not only benefit royal women. In the eleventh century it was exceedingly difficult for a woman to be a merchant, even if she inherited the business of her deceased husband. The necessary travelling was dangerous and the law was insufficiently developed to safeguard both her and her goods in transit. Trips abroad were out of the question, unless the woman was accompanied by a large band of men. But as the legal systems in England and Europe developed, so too did the safety of trade. In 1412 Margery Russell of Coventry, the widow of a wealthy merchant whose business she had taken over, petitioned the king to help her recover more than £800-worth of goods in Spain.[29] Chaucer's fictional Wife of Bath was similarly a businesswoman with overseas interests in the cloth trade. Domestically, the legal system provided a mechanism whereby women could enforce their legal rights over men. Such empowerment marks a significant difference in women's ability to act independently in the later Middle Ages compared with the eleventh century.

The increased efficiency of the law and the protection it afforded women – especially those from well-connected families – had a positive effect on women's independence. Emanuel van Meteren, a Flemish diplomat, remarked in 1575:

Although the women [in England] are entirely in the power of their husbands, except for their lives, yet they are not kept as strictly as they are in Spain or elsewhere. Nor are they shut up but have the free management of the house or housekeeping, after the fashion of those of the Netherlands and other neighbouring countries. They go to market to buy what they like best to eat. They are well-dressed, fond of taking it easy, and commonly leave the care of household matters and drudgery to their servants. They sit before their doors decked out in fine clothes in order to see and be seen by the passers-by. In all banquets and feasts they are shown the greatest honour; they are placed at the upper end of the table where they are served first . . . This is why England is called 'The Paradise of Married Women'.[30]

Thomas Platter, a young Swiss physician who came to England in 1599, wrote a similarly vivid description of the freedom Englishwomen enjoyed at the end of our period:

Now the women-folk of England . . . have far more liberty than in other lands, and know just how to make good use of it for they often stroll out or drive by coach in very gorgeous clothes, and the men must put up with such ways, and may not punish them for it, indeed the good wives often beat their men . . . And there is a proverb about England, which runs: England is a paradise for women, a prison for servants and a hell for horses.[31]

Women's individual horizons had clearly broadened since the early Middle Ages, when the dangers of leaving home without protective male company were too great for most women to contemplate it.

Perhaps the most significant advance for middle-class women, however, was literacy, which depended heavily on the printing of books in English. It is impossible to teach yourself to read in a language you do not understand, and Latin was hardly ever taught to women or girls. But a book in your own language offers you the chance to recognise the written word. Moreover, whereas schools required their pupils to be male, books did not. Many sixteenth-century women were able to teach themselves to read. This allowed them to study and reach their own conclusions. They were also able to write letters and books themselves, and thereby exchange information with other women. Some could argue with intellectual men on their own terms. Knowledge ceased to be a male privilege.

Society in 1600 was still fundamentally sexist. A married couple was still a single legal entity represented solely by the husband. Many parish incumbents still recorded children being baptised as the sons and daughters of their fathers alone, as if their mothers played no part in bringing them into the world. But sexual inequality in 1600 was different from that of 1000 – in respect of a woman's legal position, her independence and her ability to share in wider learning and knowledge. Women from the new middle class were able to realise their intellectual potential in ways quite unimaginable in the eleventh century. To return to our image of the slumbering peasant from 1000: if he had woken up in 1600 to hear a woman reading to him from the Bible, he would certainly not have felt 'at home'. 'Is this Heaven?' he might well have asked himself. 'Or, perhaps, Hell?'

Racial Intolerance

All the horizons of inequality we have so far looked at shifted significantly during the Middle Ages. Even that of income saw movement, albeit with a return to greater inequality in the sixteenth century. Sadly, race is the exception: deep-seated racial prejudices were evident in England at both the start and the end of our period. This is perhaps partly a result of geography. Unlike southern Europe, the country is a long way from Africa. Unlike the eastern European states, it is even further from the Orient. The Channel too separates the English – physically and psychologically – from the Continent. And lack of familiarity with people from these other regions resulted in suspicion, prejudice and deep inequality.

It seems that no Jews lived in England before the Norman Conquest, after which small numbers settled in the largest trading towns, including London, Canterbury, Winchester, Southampton and Lincoln. They occupied an awkward position. While they were able to access the highest echelons of society as money-lenders and medical men, they were reviled by the English as a race apart. They were hated on account of their religion. People bitterly envied them their wealth. They were officially forbidden from owning land. And they were often the victims of racial violence. In York in 1190, the city's entire Jewish community was forced by a mob to take shelter in the royal castle. Most committed suicide, with men killing their wives and children before taking their own lives; the remainder were murdered by the mob or died in the burning castle. A century later, Edward I expelled all Jews from

England; the only Jews permitted to live here after 1290 were physicians. Henry IV is known to have employed a Jewish doctor and Elizabeth I did likewise, each monarch giving them and their families special permission to live in the kingdom. Although English people were familiar with Jews and the opprobrium that many Christians felt towards them – as shown by the centrality of the character Shylock in Shakespeare's *Merchant of Venice* – most would never have met a Jew in person. Not until 1657 were Jewish people allowed to settle here freely once more.

Racial intolerance also explains the hostile reaction to nomadic 'Egyptians' or Gypsies in the sixteenth century. Their arrival in Scotland is noted in 1505, which is probably also when they came to England. By 1530 they were perceived to be a problem by the government. The Egyptians Act of that year prohibited more Gypsies from entering the realm and gave those already here sixteen days to leave. A similar Act in 1554 continued their criminalisation; a third in 1563 made it a capital offence simply to be a Gypsy. The last man to be executed under the Act was hanged in 1628; it remained on the statute books until 1783.

Although black people had come to Britain in Roman times, their bloodlines were absorbed long before the eleventh century. Some travellers arrived in England over the next centuries – such as a prince of 'India' who visited in the reign of Edward III – but otherwise the medieval English did not meet many people of colour. They knew about them though. A description of the local people by an anonymous monk at Tynemouth, written about the middle of the fourteenth century, states: 'The men living by the seashore are like Moors, the women are like Ethiopians, the maidens are filthy, the boys are as black as Hebrew boys.'[32] Information about black people – rarely of any accuracy – continued to be circulated in popular travel books, such as *Sir John Mandeville's Travels*. From 1500 we can be more confident that they permanently resided here. By 1507, there was a black trumpeter at court, John Blanke, who may have arrived in the entourage of Catherine of Aragon when she married Prince Arthur in 1501. Some of Catherine's female companions may also have been black. Traders from Portugal and Spain brought north African sailors and servants to Britain in the early sixteenth century. Some may have settled here: at least two skeletons found on the shipwreck of the *Mary Rose*, the Tudor warship that sank in 1545, are believed to have had north African ancestry. Interestingly, the presence of black people in England before 1550 is not accompanied by any evidence of racial tension. They certainly did not come in for the sort of condemnation and legal persecution that Gypsies did, probably on account of their small numbers and royal patronage.

This changed when English slave-trading expeditions in the 1550s and 1560s brought more people from Africa to England. A sense that black men and women had many vices and no virtues started to seep into English texts, driven by slave-trading explorers. Robert Gainsh, writing after an English expedition to Africa in 1554, states that 'The people which . . . were in olde tyme called *Ethiopes* and *Nigrite*, which we now call Moores, Moorens, or Negros [are] a people of beastly lyvyng, without a God, lawe, religion, or commonwealth . . .'[33] He adds that, among them, 'women are common: for they contracte no matrimonie, neyther have [they] respecte to chastity', casting all black women, and by implication all black men, into an immoral shadow. It became easier to justify buying and selling such people if they were seen as flagrantly and regularly breaking Christian moral laws.

Racial tensions continued to grow. In 1578 George Best explained that black people were the descendants of Noah's son 'Cham', who had sex with his wife on the Ark, contrary to his father's instructions.

> For the which wicked and detestable fact, as an example of contempt for Almighty God and disobedience of parents, God would that a son be born whose name was Chus, who not only itself but all his posterity after him should be so black and loathsome that it might remain a spectacle of disobedience to all the world. And of this black and cursed Chus came all these black moors which are in Africa.[34]

Six years later, in his book *A Discoverie of Witchcraft*, Reginald Scot described a devil as having skin like a black man.[35] Black skin was presumed undesirable in Shakespeare's *Much Ado About Nothing* (1598/9), where Claudio declares that he would love Hero even if she were 'an Ethiope'. English playwrights started to describe black men as beasts of burden. Christopher Marlowe refers to two Moors drawing Bajazeth in his cage in part one of his *Tamburlaine the Great* (1590). George Peele's play, *The Famous Chronicle of Edward the First* (1593), contains the stage direction, 'The trumpets sound. Queene Elinor in her litter borne by foure Negro Mores'. Several other almost identical references to great rulers being drawn by black men, sometimes specifically naked, can be found in English works from the late sixteenth century.[36] Although slavery was outside the English common law – law courts sometimes refused employers' claims to ownership of a black individual – black people were regarded as *de facto* unfree and discussed in deeply insulting language.

All this resulted in a declining trajectory of the status of black people. A Privy Council order of 1596 allowed a German merchant to buy them in England and transport them out of the realm for sale abroad. Part of the motive seems to have been a presumption that growing numbers were unwelcome. Either way, it emphasises how low in society the position of black people was. The government clearly considered them eligible for deportation and sale as slaves purely on account of their skin colour.[37] A follow-up petition from the same German merchant dated 1601 indicates that he had been unable to obtain any black people in England on the previous occasion as their masters refused to relinquish their servants. This is an interesting fact in itself: they all had masters. At the end of the sixteenth century, all black people living in England were servants of one sort or another and many powerful men considered them suitable for sale as slaves outside the kingdom.

Over the course of the Middle Ages, the horizons of inequality shifted dramatically in almost every respect. Those shifts even included the horizon of income, which saw an expansion in the proportion of the population able to make ends meet in the fourteenth and fifteenth centuries, prior to a contraction in the sixteenth. The notable exception examined here is race. Legal slavery shrank rapidly and disappeared. Serfdom did too. A third of England's farmland passed from the royal family and the Church into private hands. The proportion of landowners, including leaseholders, increased from less than 2 per cent to 25 per cent. However, there were losers as well as winners. On the one hand, a man could become exceedingly wealthy from reinvesting his agricultural surpluses in land when prices were low. Eventually he might turn the income accruing from his freehold estate into educational advantages for his sons, who might then go on to achieve lucrative positions in the Church, the government or the law. On the other hand, the same man's kinsmen might struggle to produce enough food on their smallholdings to feed all their children, who would have grown comparatively poorer in relation to their newly enriched cousins. This in turn restricted their opportunities for self-improvement. By the Elizabethan period their descendants might have been town labourers or vagrants. The differentiations of wealth and income that we see in society today are not just the consequences of the exploitation of labour in the Industrial Revolution. They owe a great deal to the longevity of medieval estates and the stratification of society over the course of the Middle Ages.

At the same time, the horizon of political power expanded to embrace those who did become landowners. By 1400, yeomen could vote in Parliament to change the law and even dethrone the monarch. You cannot imagine the unfree villeins of eleventh-century England having a hope of getting rid of William the Conqueror, but some of their descendants' representatives did just that to William's eight-greats-grandson, Richard II, three hundred years later. As for women, there were subtle but important benefits, especially for the better-off. The recognition of the sanctity of marriage, the expansion and refinement of the law, and the spread of literacy all helped reduce their inequality in relation to men. Women enjoyed far greater freedom in the sixteenth century than they had done in the eleventh or twelfth. That a woman could not become queen in her own right in 1135 but could in 1553 was merely the recognition of far wider social changes that had taken place. Although society was still prejudiced against women, there were now legal limits to that prejudice. Few women would have wanted to turn the clock back to the days of endemic violence and concubinage. Given all the other changes that had taken place in society, it is unlikely that many men would have wanted to either.

4

Comfort

Standards of Living in England

An English peasant falling asleep in the year 1000 would not have believed his eyes when he woke to see the skyline of 1600. But his amazement would not have stopped at the roofs. At the beginning of our period his own house would have been a smoke-filled hut, with smoke-blackened walls of timber or turf. How could he have even begun to imagine the tapestried interior of a sixteenth-century stately home like Burghley or Hardwick Hall, let alone a royal palace like Richmond or Whitehall? Or what luxuries were to be found within the townhouses of rich merchants? People's living standards changed just as radically over the course of the Middle Ages as the heights of their churches and the sizes of their towns.

When we think of a medieval house we usually imagine a late-medieval building with heavy beams and a broad fireplace. But that's only because these are the examples that have come down to us. No domestic architecture from the early eleventh century survives in Britain and there is very little fabric of that antiquity to be seen anywhere in Europe. Indeed, the very fact that thousands of late-medieval dwellings are still standing is testament to how much houses improved over the course of our period. They reached a level of solidity and comfort that made them last for centuries. In contrast, the standard of housing in the eleventh and twelfth centuries was unacceptable even in the eyes of late-medieval people.

We can say much the same for sixteenth-century furniture: a great deal of it survives because it was well-made and either practical or handsome enough to be valued until modern times. Very little furniture from the previous century survives, and almost none from before 1400. The evolving domestic interior saw the material possessions of the previous centuries replaced with something better. But by the sixteenth century, many household items had reached a state of sophistication that merited permanent retention. Chests, bedframes, tables, benches, chairs, cupboards and dressers all survive in substantial numbers from the sixteenth century whereas not even the best furniture does from the eleventh.

This is not the place to attempt a detailed history of the medieval home; the subject is too vast, even if we just concentrate on England. Instead I will briefly sketch how our ancestors' homes improved over the course of the Middle Ages. The metaphorical horizon is a particularly useful tool in this respect. When applied to domestic comfort, we can see how it expanded to embrace larger houses with loftier ceilings and more rooms. It grew with regard to its utensils and furnishings. It developed in terms of the rituals and functions that took place within its walls. In fact, the period from the eleventh century to the sixteenth saw living standards change beyond all recognition, taking us from the smoke-filled wooden halls of axe-wielding warriors to the oil paintings and lute music of sophisticated courtiers in Shakespeare's time.

The Homes of the Wealthy

Most of us today live in just one house. As we all know, wealthy people often have more than one home, and exceedingly rich individuals might have four or five on different continents. No one today has twenty or thirty in one country. But just such a situation describes the domestic arrangements of powerful figures in the early eleventh century. Many lords had dozens of estates and travelled between them on a regular basis, so as to be able to take advantage of the produce of each place without running out of food. Thus there is a fundamental disjuncture between our idea of a home – a residence with which we have a personal relationship – and an eleventh-century nobleman's house. If you were a Saxon lord constantly travelling between thirty residences, none of them was your home. Instead, your 'home' was what you carried from place to place – your valuables, clothes, tableware, furniture and weapons – and the people in your household, who travelled with you. When you left one house to move on to the next, you left behind little more than a wooden shell.

For this reason, the difference between the comforts of the hall when the lord's household was in residence and when it was not would have been striking. Turn up to an eleventh-century aristocrat's house when he was absent and you would have thought you were visiting a farm. Once you'd entered through the gates in the enclosing palisade, you would have seen an agglomeration of buildings laid out around the largest and most imposing structure, the hall. This was built of timber, with oak posts sunk into the ground rather than foundations. Its walls were formed of tree trunks sawn in half (like a log cabin, except vertically arranged), with two doors: either one at each end or one in each side. The roof was thatched. Given the difficulties of heating such a building, there were only a few small window openings. These were unglazed and covered with a wooden shutter or a semi-translucent sheet of scraped sheepskin. The bowers or bedchambers for the lord and his family were separate wooden buildings elsewhere in the precinct. So too were the kitchen, chapel, slave quarters, women's quarters, stores, stables and all the other farm buildings.

All these structures were made of wood and a single storey in height. Inside they would have been bare when the lord was absent, occupied only by the manorial reeve and a small number of servants and slaves. When the lord was in residence, however, it would have had quite a different appearance. The timber-walled hall with its central hearth would have been hung with tapestries and embroidered hangings. Fresh rushes would have been spread across the earth floor. Tables would have been set up for everyone to dine at, with fine tablecloths covering the lord's own table. The lord's chests would have been unpacked to provide him and his attendants with drinking horns and goblets. His bed would have been set up in the main bower and covered with his brightest embroidered bedclothes. In the chapel, the lord's own priest would have set up the best altar decorations. The place would have been utterly transformed.

Lordly houses continued to be made of timber for centuries, even though this necessitated their rebuilding every thirty years or so, after the earth-fast posts had begun to rot. This also applies to the majority of castles built in the wake of the Norman Conquest. The use of stone in the construction of dwellings was introduced only slowly from the twelfth century, but stone buildings soon became the peripatetic nobles' preferred residences. Now a lord's sleeping chamber was normally adjacent to the hall, which remained the most important space in the residence. But whereas wooden Saxon halls had almost always been single-storey buildings, in twelfth-century stone houses the hall was normally located on the first floor, with a cellar for storage below.

One of the best-preserved twelfth-century stone houses in England is Boothby Manor House at Boothby Pagnell in Lincolnshire. This is the solar block – the lord's private apartments – of a manor house. It consists of two main rooms on the first floor – the hall and a chamber – above a vaulted undercroft. The hall has a fireplace with a chimney stack above. It also has a window seat and cupboards built into the walls. Outside there would have been separate buildings containing the great hall for the servants, kitchen, stables, lodgings for important guests and brewhouse. There would also have been a pantry for bread, dry foodstuffs and linen, and a buttery for ale, wine and moist foodstuffs.

This type of upper-class building provided a far more secure and comfortable arrangement than before. The placing of the hall on the first floor meant that now the floor was made of stone, not earth, which made sweeping up the old rushes and detritus much easier. As anyone who has spent any length of time in a hall heated by a central-hearth fire will tell you, the smoke gets everywhere, so the fireplace in the wall marks a huge step forward in domestic luxury. Given the lack of light in most medieval halls, the windows (covered by wooden shutters at night) were another significant improvement. The window seat allowed more intricate tasks such as needlework to be performed indoors. Nevertheless, it is worth noting that there are just two living spaces for the lord's family. Only the lord had a chamber of his own; the best any other family member could hope for was a space on the floor of the hall on which to lay a straw-filled mattress. Whereas we think of having our own bedroom with our possessions arranged around us, the emphasis in the twelfth century was still very much on communal living.

By 1300 the advances in comfort to be seen at Boothby Manor House were in evidence in all newly built aristocratic houses and castles. Every high-status residence had large fireplaces and chimneys in the solar range. The grandest buildings had glass in the windows of the private chambers. Glass was precious, so lords sometimes took it with them as they moved from one house to the next, transporting it in wagons along with their other furniture. The walls might be painted or hung with tapestries and carpets. In the great hall, doorways now led directly to the pantry and buttery. Often a covered passageway led to the kitchen, which took the form of a double-height stone room, with two or three large fireplaces and ovens in the side walls.

In the fourteenth century, the provision of markets throughout the country meant lords were no longer dependent on travelling between their various manors for food. Instead, they could concentrate on making their principal manor house or castle as secure and as comfortable as possible. Many invested heavily in improved sanitation, such as the truly impressive latrine blocks at Ludlow Castle and Warwick Castle. Everywhere the number of private chambers increased, so it became normal for people of high status to sleep in their own room. Perhaps the most striking development of all, however, was the number and scale of windows. Several factors contributed to this improvement. First, the end of the 'normality of war' meant that windows no longer had to be small and inward-facing for defensive purposes. Then there was the sense that light was healthy and that sunlight purified the infecting miasmas that built up in unventilated spaces. In addition there was the comfort factor. If you could have a large, glazed window by which you could sit and do needlework or read, how much more comfortable was that than sitting beside a guttering candle in a draughty hall? And what did it say about your status? Huge amounts of glass represented wealth, which in turn implied power. The windows of great halls accordingly grew bigger and were permanently glazed. Some were given metal frames so they could be opened to let in fresh air.

Dartington Hall in Devon, built by Richard II's half-brother, John Holland, in about 1390, is an example of just such a lordly residence, with enormous windows in its great hall. An inventory created shortly after Holland's death in 1400 lists some of its furnishings. These included lavish beds with embroidered bedclothes, bed curtains, valances, mattresses and covers. There were embroidered cushions for use on chairs in the solar and on benches in the great hall. There were tablecloths, tapestries, baldequins (rich canopies that hung above the lord's chair), back cloths (tapestries that hung behind the lord's chair), and silver cups, spoons and dishes. There were silver basins, ewers and hand towels (for washing hands before and after a meal). The inventory also lists all the furnishings of the chapel, including the religious books used when services were held.[1] As this and similar documents show, when lords divided their time between just two or three houses, they could leave them fully furnished, rather than shifting their prized possessions between a large number of otherwise empty buildings.

In the fifteenth century the aristocratic innovations of the previous century were adopted by the gentry. Manor houses up and down the country were rebuilt with fine fireplaces in their halls and solar ranges, with convenient latrines and many chambers. Most had the traditional array of buttery, pantry and kitchen, accessed from a passage at the lower end of the hall which prevented draughts coming in every time someone opened the main door. Now only the servants ate and slept in the hall, while the lord's family lived privately in their solar. The lord would still take the prime position at the table in the hall on feast days but privacy was increasingly valued: it became a mark of social distinction. Private parlours were made warmer and more welcoming through the installation of wooden panelling. The plastered walls of guest chambers were often painted with scenes of knighthood or religious devotion, displaying the virtues that the lord admired and which he wanted people to identify with him and his family.

By the end of the sixteenth century, the transformation of the living space of the lordly family was complete. Where once lords had camped out in so many barn-like wooden halls, now they each owned a stately home as well as a townhouse in London. Their chambers had plastered ceilings and glass windows. Great houses like Hardwick Hall in Derbyshire, Longleat in Wiltshire and Burghley in Lincolnshire made a proud show of their glass, demonstrating status through fenestration. The design of furniture also improved, as lords and gentry sought to show off their refined taste. Long galleries were introduced for indoor exercise and amusement, and to display collections of paintings and sculptures. Gardens were reshaped and centred around squares of colourful plants. Utilitarian items were either banished to the service wings or made to look elegant. The hall diminished in importance as the great chamber became the principal social function room for the lord's family. Where once floors had been earthen and covered with rushes, now they were surfaced with squares of black-and-white marble. Every household rose and lived according to the hour of the clock. A very grand residence might have a bathroom with running water. Sir John Harington even built a flushing loo for himself at his manor house in Kelston, Somerset. Nothing could be further removed from the smoke-filled timber halls of the eleventh century than that.

Farmhouses

Eleventh-century farmhouses were far from homely. Personal possessions usually consisted of a few tools and cooking pots. The house itself was not normally the farmer's own property; it was merely allocated to him by the manorial reeve as part of his holding.

No eleventh-century farmhouse has survived to show us the living conditions that English working families experienced at the outset of our period, but excavated examples illustrate how rural houses developed over the next century or so. Wide walls of turf or cob (a mixture of earth, clay and a binding material, such as straw) were used in places that were poor in timber, while timber-framed houses with wattle-and-daub infill and thatched roofs were employed in parts where oak was abundant. A farm at Long Crendon in Buckinghamshire still retains the central part of its timber-framed aisled hall, which has been dated by dendrochronology to 1205. This single-storey aisled room, measuring about 16ft × 16ft, was heated by a central hearth and open to the rafters, with a separate chamber at one end.[2] The windows would originally have been small and closed by wooden shutters. The roof was thatched with reed or straw. In poorer and higher-altitude regions where these materials were scarce, long turves were used for roofing, draped over the ridge of the roof and pegged in place.

Only in the thirteenth century did ordinary farmers start building in stone – and then only in the areas where stone was common and timber scarce. Excavated examples from this period on Dartmoor reveal longhouses about 45–50ft long and 14ft wide with central cross passages that divide the building in two. On the lower side of the passage was the byre where cattle were tethered. On the upper side was the hall, often with an 'inner room' or chamber at the far end. There were external storehouses and barns. Some houses may have had freestanding kitchens but it seems most simply had a stone-lined cooking pit near the hearth. Foods that needed baking were placed in this cooking pit, which was heated by 'pot-boilers' (large stones transferred from the fire). In addition, a large flat stone heated by the fire served for cooking flatbread. Vegetables were boiled in earthenware vessels heated by pot-boilers, or a makeshift 'cauldron' of a hide suspended from a wooden tripod and heated in the same way. If any meat was available, it might well have been boiled rather than roasted. Milk-producing cows, sheep and goats as well as egg-laying hens were not eaten until they were old, so boiling softened the meat. It also retained all the juices and nutrients, whereas roasting was wasteful because the dripping was lost in the fire.

Entering a thirteenth-century stone farmhouse, you would have opened the door and ducked under the lintel to find yourself in near-darkness, smelling the smoke from the fire and the cow dung trampled into the straw used as bedding for the cattle. Turn towards the upper end and you'd have passed through an opening in a wattle screen to enter the dimly lit living area. The floor would have been hardened earth covered with rushes. In the middle of the living space you'd have seen the fire burning on a hearthstone and a firepit beside it. Beyond, there'd have been the door to the inner room, where the farmer and his wife kept most of their domestic possessions. This would have been the only internal door in the whole building. You would not have seen much furniture: a trestle table, a bench or two, and wooden utensils and tubs for making cheese.

One excavated stone farmhouse on Dartmoor, which burnt down in the late thirteenth century, revealed almost no metalwork and little earthenware except four small cooking pots, one green glazed jug, two charred wooden platters and one large cooking pot buried in the floor of the hall. In the inner room of this house were a pottery cistern, two yellow-glazed jugs and another cooking pot.[3] When the time came for the inhabitants to go to bed, they would have brought out straw mattresses and arranged them around the fire, using logs for pillows. In this particular house there was a wattle-and-daub smoke hood above the fire, preventing the smoke from swirling everywhere. It was one of the few domestic improvements on the earlier period, when the family would have been breathing in smoke whenever they were indoors.

Most farmhouses in the wealthier parts of England continued to be built with timber frames rather than stone. A large number of these structures survive from the fourteenth century, especially in the Midlands. The aisled hall was prevalent wherever timber was plentiful. Another common building tradition in such regions was to lean two crucks – effectively naturally curving tree trunks – together to form an arch, and then to add another two or three similar pairs, and to join them together to form a cruck house of two or three or more bays. These were still open to the rafters and had a packed earth floor covered in rushes. Many smaller farmhouses employed a hall-and-chamber arrangement which, even in the fourteenth century, may have been filled with smoke, lacking both smoke hood and fireplace. The famous description of the widow's house in the Nun's Priest's Tale in Chaucer's *Canterbury Tales* includes the line 'full sooty was her bower and eke [also] her hall', which may be taken as indicative of the comforts of such two-room dwellings.

From the late fourteenth century living standards in farmhouses began to improve. A two-storey wing was often added at one end of the hall, with the principal bedchamber on the upper floor. In the fifteenth century, many farmers – comparatively richer than their forebears, as we saw in the previous chapter – rebuilt their houses as imposing halls with a two-storey wing at each end. The earliest examples of the 'Wealden' type of house still common in Kent and Sussex fall into this category. Entering such a building by the main door, you would have found yourself in a passageway running through the house, with a screen on one side and doors to the buttery and pantry on the other, in emulation of a manor house. One bedchamber was on the floor above the service rooms and another above the room at the other end of the house. The hall in the middle still had a central hearth and would have been open to the smoke-blackened rafters and thatch. It was lit by a single large, unglazed window. Security was provided by wooden mullions or carved bars that divided the window vertically. In cold weather and at night the window was covered by shutters.

The improvement of domestic living standards continued into the sixteenth century. Farmers replaced their central hearths with fireplaces and chimneys, to remove the inconvenience of swirling smoke. This of course meant that the hall could be given a ceiling and an upper floor, as the smoke no longer needed to exit through the roof. The chimney thus created could also be employed to service a fireplace in one of the newly created chambers above the hall. From the late 1560s, glass started to become a regular feature in the houses of prosperous yeomen. So too did plaster ceilings in the upper chambers, for both decoration and warmth. Many stone staircases were built to replace the ladders that had previously led to the upper floor. Some prosperous yeomen added a grand porch to the front of the hall, both for prestige and to exclude draughts.

The furniture in a farmhouse also became more elaborate and comfortable. This can be seen in the inventory of William Hall, a husbandman of Great Bourton, Oxfordshire, who died in 1589, leaving chattels worth £106 10s. Livestock, horses, carts, ladders, sheepskins, tools, poultry and other things stored in barns and the yard amounted to just over £70 of that total. The value of his household goods made up most of the remainder. In his hall he had a fireplace, a table, two long benches and two short ones, and a chair. There was also a cupboard on which he usually stacked a dozen pewter dishes, a dozen trenchers (wooden plates), six silver spoons and various pieces of pewter tableware. In the parlour was another fireplace; a small square table and four stools; four chests of belongings; and a bedstead, a cradle and a truckle bed with their various sheets, mattresses and bolsters. Both rooms were glazed. There were four upstairs chambers as well, with another four bedsteads and chests. In the kitchen was a pair of bellows, irons for the fire, fire tongs, shovel, fire fork and gridiron, as well as other cooking apparatus.[4] He probably had a bread oven built into one corner of the kitchen fireplace. Compared to the small, turf-walled, dimly lit houses of the eleventh century, where people baked in earth pits lined with stones, farmhouses like William Hall's were large, light, well-equipped and, above all, comfortable.

What is particularly interesting is that these changes were happening so rapidly that people were conscious of how much better off they were compared to their forefathers. In 1577 the clergyman William Harrison declared that old men in his village of Radwinter in Essex had noted three great improvements over the course of their lifetimes. One was the abundance of chimneys and fireplaces, which had previously been exclusively a rich man's luxury. Another was the use of silver and pewter instead of wood – for plates, spoons, bowls and other domestic ware. The last was sleeping arrangements,

> for, said they, our fathers, yea and we ourselves also, have lain full oft upon straw pallets, on rough mats covered only with a sheet . . . and a good round log under their heads instead of a bolster or pillow. If it were so that our fathers . . . had within seven years after his marriage purchased a mattress or flock bed, and thereto a stack of chaff to rest his head upon, he thought himself to be as well lodged as the lord of the town . . . Pillows (said they) were thought meet only for women in childbed.

Now there's a benchmark of luxury that few of us appreciate today – resting your head upon a pillow. It might seem far less impressive than the latest generation of smartphone but I dare say many of us would give up quite a few modern conveniences to avoid having to sleep on a straw mattress each night, with nothing but a hard log on which to lay our heads.

Townhouses

At the beginning of our period there wasn't much difference between an urban house and one in the country. There were few settlements of any great size. Even the largest cities were not especially cramped. Excavations in Winchester have revealed small, square, timber-framed buildings with earth-fast timber uprights and walls made either of wattle-and-daub or of cob. The walls of some were covered with an external weatherboarding of vertically arranged half-trunks of wood.[5] In most cases, the floors were packed earth. Roofs were normally thatched, as in the country. The main difference between townhouses and rural dwellings at the beginning of our period was that fire often destroyed large numbers of townhouses, necessitating their reconstruction even more regularly than country houses.

It was in the late twelfth century that wealthy merchants and moneylenders started to build in stone. Their motives were greater security from fire and theft, and protection from angry debtors and, in the case of Jews, anti-Semitic crowds. Their houses consisted of two storeys with the main residential hall on the first floor, heated by a fireplace, with a vaulted undercroft beneath it and a tiled roof above. Some merchants' houses were built in wood above a stone ground floor. These could be expected to last much longer than houses with wooden foundations, which further justified the investment. Stone houses are known to have been built before 1200 in many English towns: Canterbury had at least thirty by that date, all owned by merchants and moneylenders.[6]

Around 1200, towns that had successful markets started to acquire borough rights. In some cases, the leading men of the town managed to obtain a charter from the king. In others, the lord of the manor granted his market town borough status. In both cases, spacious burgage plots were laid out in the middle of the settlement to attract craftsmen and merchants. Being freehold, these plots encouraged the purchasers to build more permanent houses on stone bases. Wealthy people built wide mansions that occupied the whole plot, facing the street, with domestic buildings constructed around a courtyard behind. However, as the population grew, and more people moved into towns, so these wide plots were subdivided into long thin strips, to give each resident the benefit of some street frontage and space at the rear for a kitchen and garden. In Stratford-upon-Avon, for example, the borough charter of 1196 fixed the size of burgage plots in the borough at 3½ by 12 perches (57¾ft × 198ft). By 1251 these had mostly been subdivided into halves, thirds and quarters.

Narrow, subdivided plots encouraged people to build taller houses, and these were much more affordable in timber than in stone. Timber also allowed householders to jetty the upper storeys out above the ground floor, thus gaining more space on the first floor and potentially even more space on the second. Jetties are known to have existed in London from the 1240s; they spread to other towns in the late thirteenth century. Normally a townhouse of this period had a shop facing the street with a chamber above it and a lofty hall open to the rafters behind the front block. To limit the risk of fire, thatch was prohibited in London from 1212 and many other towns followed suit. Instead, roofs were covered in tiles or wooden shingles. This reduced the risk of a rogue spark setting the thatch of one roof alight in high winds and thus destroying the whole town.

From the early fourteenth century, urban proprietors began to build terraces of small houses for rental. The block known as Lady Row in Goodramgate, York, was built in 1316. It is made up of ten one-up and one-down houses, with the upper chamber jettied out over the street and open to the rafters. Stonegate, also in York, was built about the same time but to a higher specification, being a row of three-storey dwellings, each floor projecting further out over the street than the one below. By the 1330s such three-storey terraces were common. Occasionally they were built with fireplaces.[7] In the south-west an architectural style developed in which substantial party walls of stone were erected at 90 degrees to the street and timber houses constructed between them, supported by these walls.

Fifteenth-century houses have survived in many towns. Some were built by merchants, some by the Church, some as almshouses, some as noblemen's townhouses and a few as inns. Two or three storeys with projecting jetties were now usual. Fireplaces too were common. Two splendid terraces of forty-two one-up, one-down stone houses can still be seen in Wells, Somerset, all dating from about 1400. They are equipped with fireplaces, chimneys, washing stations and latrines. Small gardens were added in the mid-fifteenth century. A wealthy merchant might now live in a three-storey house with elaborately carved window frames and doorways, and painted jetties and beams. Behind this street-facing frontage he might have an imposing hall with a hammerbeam roof open to the rafters, with painted fireplaces in every chamber and an impressive fireplace in the hall. The richest might even have glass in the windows facing the street – so as to give a positive impression of wealth. By 1500 a prosperous townsman could enjoy a far higher standard of domestic comfort than an eleventh- or twelfth-century king.

Over the course of the sixteenth century, town-dwellers started to enjoy all the refinements that manorial lords had previously incorporated into their houses. Chambers were panelled with finely carved and painted wainscotting. Glass windows became common. Brick started to be used regularly for fireplaces and chimneys. Separate kitchens with fireplaces and bread ovens were installed, and halls were divided vertically, creating parlours on the ground floor and bed chambers upstairs. Latrines were provided on all floors, emptying into cesspits in the basement; in turn, these were emptied at night by workers known as 'gongfermours'. In London, where the population quadrupled over the course of the sixteenth century and space was at a premium, houses were five or even six storeys tall; some now exceeded the heights of eleventh-century church towers. In every town across the country, the built horizon had risen – from single-storey dwellings to multi-storey ones.

The sophistication of townhouses was not only to be seen in their external appearance. Someone from 1000 would have been no less impressed by the range of their furnishings. Consider the home of John Newberry of Farnham, Surrey, which was a small town of between 3,000 and 4,000 people at the time of his death in 1600. He was no wealthy merchant but merely a glover – a man who cut and stitched gloves from leather and other animal skins, like John Shakespeare, William Shakespeare's father. His moveable goods were worth a total of £104, half of which was in the form of cash, debts and animals and corn in fields outside the town. His townhouse had a shop on the ground floor, wherein he kept his leather and working tools. In the chamber above his shop he stored more tools as well as large amounts of wool and a 'woollen wheel' or spinning wheel (unknown in Europe before the thirteenth century). Moving into his hall, you would have seen this had effectively become a dining room. Painted cloths and dornicks (woven woollen cloths) hung all around the walls, in the way that we might hang wallpaper. The furniture amounted to a table with two wooden armchairs and six stools, a settle and a cupboard. There were

patterned cushions on the stools; and a Bible and some other books lay
on the cupboard. Metal tools were on hand to manage the fire: and-
irons (otherwise known as firedogs), a pair of tongs and a 'fire prong'
or poker.

In the room above his hall, John Newberry kept his essential
supplies – large amounts of wheat, barley and rye. He also kept a stock-
pile of maslin (a mixture of wheat and rye). He and his wife probably
brewed their own beer as he also had sacks of malt and hops stored
here. His parlour was dominated by an oak-framed bedstead with a
painted tester and a valance around it, with a feather mattress, a feather bolster, sheets and blankets. On one side stood a cupboard and a
round table. Tablecloths, napkins and pillows were stored in a couple
of chests. The room above the parlour was the principal bedroom,
with an impressive bedstead. Downstairs in the kitchen, the family's
brassware included pans, kettles, pots, candlesticks and a mortar. Here
were stacked the plates, saucers, pots, cups, salt cellars and pottingers
(bowls to hold pottage or soup), all made of shiny pewter and looking
like silver. Here too were his fruit dishes, drying pan, dripping pan and
spits for roasting meat. There was another bedchamber above the kitchen and, outside at the back of the house, a stable and bakehouse. He
even had chamber pots in which to relieve himself if he woke in the
night and did not fancy trudging down to the earth closet. These were
a recent invention and must have made life much more comfortable in
the absence of flushing loos. All in all, the number of possessions,
utensils, comforts and implements far exceeded those to be found in
the eleventh century. And this, remember, was just the house of an
ordinary tradesman.[8]

At the very bottom of the social spectrum, among the rural labourers and smallholders, housing conditions were largely unchanged since
the fourteenth century. The poorest sixteenth-century families still
inhabited a single-storey cottage with an unglazed, smoke-filled hall
open to the rafters and a bower at ground level, with a packed earth
floor. However, even these buildings differed from the earth-fast timber huts of the eleventh century, as they were normally built to last,
with stone foundations. As for the furnishings, they differed considerably. In the sixteenth century a poor rural family might well possess
iron cooking apparatus and pewter plates and spoons, for so much had
been produced over the years that the second-hand market had redistributed it around society. Much the same can be said for some

working-class townsmen. The Teignmouth fisherman George Grosse left chattels worth just £2 6s 4d when he died in January 1592. His clothes and bedding were worth 16s 4d. A pig in the yard was worth 20d. He had very little furniture in his cottage: just a trestle table, two benches, a cupboard, two chests, a barrel and a broken tub. Like his ancestors, he had no bedstead; he probably slept on a mattress on the floor. But unlike them, he had a number of metal items: a frying pan, pewter plates, two candlesticks, two brass crocks, two brass pans, a cauldron and a skillet, and the hooks to hang the cauldron and crocks over the fire. These things would have made him the envy of many much more prosperous people in the eleventh century.[9]

Food

Such advances in domestic comfort, impressive as they are, don't take into account the physical necessity of having enough to eat and drink. Many medieval people found greater comfort in stacking their chambers with grain and cheeses rather than furniture. It is worth noting that about half of the wealth of the farmer, William Hall, and about one-fifth of that of the urban glover, John Newberry, was in the form of livestock, flitches of bacon, sacks of corn and blocks of cheese. Food was an everyday worry for many people, even relatively prosperous artisans like John Newberry. It was important to know that you and your family would have enough to eat for the foreseeable future, in case the next couple of harvests failed. Long-term food security was therefore the most important element of human comfort – as it still is today, even if we don't realise it.

As we saw in the previous chapter, food shortages were a regular aspect of eleventh-century life. First there was the Great Famine of 1005, which according to the *Anglo-Saxon Chronicle* was the worst in living memory. Further famines occurred in 1012, 1016, 1025 and 1031 before, in 1042, a dreadful period of food shortages began which was said to have lasted seven years.[10] Overall, famine affected England one year in every four in the early eleventh century. This meant towns could not easily grow, for when farmers who would otherwise have sent their surpluses to market saw their yields reduced by a half, they were forced to retain what little grain they had to feed themselves and for seed for the next crop. And this was the situation *before* the depredations of the Norman Conquest. As a result of William I's laying waste to the north of England in 'the Harrying of the North', the inhabitants 'driven by hunger, ate human, dog and horse flesh', as one chronicler put it. His reference to cannibalism is supported by another writer who declared that 'many were forced to eat horses, dogs, cats, rats and other loathsome and vile vermin; yes, some did not abstain from eating the flesh of men.'[11]

The number of famines noted by English chroniclers remained high in the early twelfth century, being recorded for twelve years in the first half.[12] In 1124 one writer noted, 'Such a famine prevailed that everywhere in cities, villages and crossroads lifeless bodies lay unburied.'[13] However, the Medieval Warm Period – that stretch of global warming between about 1000 and 1250 – gradually lessened the regularity of crisis years and the next recorded severe famine in England did not take place until 1183. Although the terrible famine of 1193–6 prompted the chronicler Walter of Guisborough to write that 'the common people perished everywhere for lack of food', this was actually the period of the most rapid population growth in England of the entire Middle Ages. Famine remained a feature of everyone's lives but chronic food shortages now occurred about one year in seven, not one in four. Moreover, new trading links meant that the grain market had become international. When famine broke out again in 1258 after a poor harvest the previous year, London merchants procured fifty shiploads of wheat, barley and bread from Prussia.[14]

From the thirteenth century, we do not need to rely on chroniclers' accounts alone for the description of food shortages; we also have prices from the earliest surviving manorial accounts. Between 1209 and 1250 these highlight four very difficult years.[15] Grain prices again hit crisis levels four times between 1250 and 1289 but then rose to uncomfortable extremes as the Medieval Warm Period came to an end. The years 1290–1 and 1293–6 were not a happy time for the peasantry. Over the thirteenth century as a whole, famine was less frequent than it had been in the eleventh and twelfth centuries but, as we saw in the previous chapter, population growth meant that many poor families did not have enough to eat even in a good year. As a result, society was still precariously balanced. When important lords and prelates made arrangements for their funerals, often they would ask that a loaf and a penny be offered to every pauper who attended. Sometimes tens of thousands of people turned up. Most cathedrals and abbeys donated

These two paintings of the Last Supper, one from the 1070s and the other from the 1540s, are ostensibly about the same thing. Yet the differences are enormous. The use of perspective in the later one is obvious – as is the absence of a halo – but note the depiction of window glass, the different clothes worn and the new pigments in the paint. The comparison illustrates how sixteenth- and eleventh-century society differed – 'like a clock from a sundial' (Chapter 1).

The geographical horizon. This simple contrast shows both the expansion of our knowledge and the increased sophistication of geographers. The upper image is a map of the world made in England in about 1030 (Britain is in the top-left corner). The lower one shows a map of the world published by Gerard Mercator in his *Atlas* of 1585.

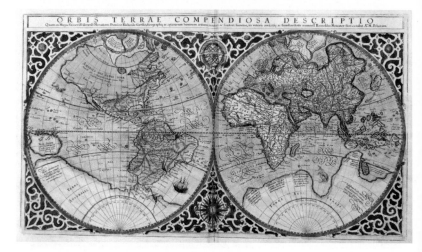

The horizon of war. The Bayeux Tapestry depicts Norman knights charging against spear-throwing Saxons in 1066. The painting of the siege of Maastricht in 1579 also shows horses and spears but war had by then wholly changed due to the development of fortifications, guns and the law. It had ceased to be an aspect of everyday feudal life and had become an occasional 'necessary evil', subject to legal limits and underwritten by national taxation.

The horizon of domestic comfort. In the early eleventh century, even lords' houses were single-storey timber structures, such as this reconstruction at Trelleborg, Denmark. Such buildings have almost nothing in common with the houses enjoyed by the wealthy in the late sixteenth century, as shown by Hardwick Hall, built by the rich widow Bess of Hardwick in the 1590s.

Internally too housing changed beyond all recognition. Few Saxon or Norse lords would have had anything more comfortable than a hall with a packed-earth floor, heated by a central hearth. This reconstruction, from Unst in the Shetland Islands, which would have been smoke-filled and dark all year round, is a world away from the High Great Chamber at Hardwick Hall, with its high ceilings, well-lit interior and lavish fireplace.

The horizon of personal liberty. In the eleventh century, English society consisted mostly of slaves and unfree peasants – men and women bound to the land. By the end of the sixteenth century, almost everyone was free to marry whom they chose and go where they wanted.

The temporal horizon. This watch, made in London in about 1600, has a built-in alarm function. Before 1330, an hour was simply a twelfth of the daylight. Our concept of time changed over the course of the Middle Ages.

The commercial horizon. The coconut in this cup, made in the Netherlands in 1533–4, would have come from the Indian Ocean – a part of the world unimagined in the eleventh century.

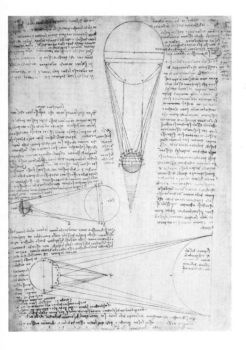

The horizon of the self. Because of the rediscovery of the mirror, everyone for the last five hundred years has known what they look like. This sets us apart from eleventh-century people, who did not. The implications for self-awareness, self-control, self-improvement and individualism cannot be overestimated. These three fifteenth-century images hint at those changes: women beautifying themselves; van Eyck's 1433 self-portrait in a turban; and Leonardo da Vinci's mirror-writing in his notebooks. The last in particular suggests that reflection is the very essence of late-medieval intellectual life.

The architectural horizon. At Beauvais you can directly compare the scale of the cathedral that stood here in 1000 with the eastern end of the colossal thirteenth-century structure that was intended ultimately to replace it.

This photograph of the eastern end of Le Mans Cathedral, built in the early thirteenth century, was taken at the spot that inspired the envoi of this book. Those who associate the word 'medieval' with backwardness or ignorance wholly misunderstand the Middle Ages.

food and clothing to the poor every week of the year, and some every day. Such charity was important, for the period 1315–23 witnessed the Great Famine: a series of harvest failures, atrocious weather events and cattle plagues resulting in more than half a million excess deaths.

The Black Death proved to be the watershed in the social history of Europe. We have seen how it broke the causal link between population growth and real wages, thereby reducing inequality. Families who survived the plague were able to eat meat and fish far more frequently than their predecessors. While poor workers continued to rely heavily on bread, it made up a declining proportion of their diet. At Sedgeford, Norfolk, bread accounted for just under half of a worker's calorific intake in the late thirteenth century; in the late fourteenth it was less than a fifth. At the same time, the proportion of meat in their diet increased from about 4 per cent to 30 per cent.[16] Still there were years of extreme food shortages and high prices, but there were relatively few famines. Chronicles more frequently talk about dearth than death.

Food shortages were recorded five times in the first half of the sixteenth century: one year in ten. In the second half, the crisis years were less frequent but worse. Large amounts of grain were imported to alleviate shortages in 1565. In 1587 another famine resulted in widespread mortality, especially in the north of England. In the 1590s harvests failed for four years in a row. However, although the north would experience chronic food shortages once more, in 1623, the famine of 1594–7 was the last time that large numbers of people in the south starved to death. One reason was improvements in agriculture; another was the maturity of the market system that allowed food to circulate from areas of high supply and low prices to those with low supply and high prices. But the key reason was the development of the Old Poor Law, to which we will return later. From 1597 it was the duty of every parish in England to set a rate for the raising of money to feed the poor. This capacity for charity, coupled with the market system, gradually brought an end to mass starvation.

Choice

Over the medieval period as a whole, the question at the heart of most ordinary people's lives changed from 'is there anything to eat?' to 'what would you like to eat?' The horizon of domestic comfort expanded to encompass greater choice. A prosperous fifteenth-century family might opt to eat meat or fish instead of cheese, and for their pottage to contain bacon or chicken as well as onions and beans. In addition to whey and weak ale it became possible to drink strong ale, mead (honey fermented in water) or cider. From about the middle of the fifteenth century, people started to brew their ale with hops, thus creating beer, which lasted a lot longer than plain ale. A century later, brewers gave their beers names such as Mad Dog, Father Whoreson, Angels' Food, Dragon's Milk and Lift-leg, in a sort of precursor to the products of modern microbreweries. The growth of the market system meant that fish, fruit and vegetables became more frequent options. How you ate your food changed too: the inventories of William Hall, John Newberry and George Grosse all mention pewterware, which was not available in the eleventh century. The first two men also had silver spoons: these similarly would not have featured in the houses of ordinary farmers and glovers in the eleventh century.

The ways in which people cooked their food also changed. Before the Black Death, when a family had only a fire and a pit in the floor, or an earthenware pot, the options were limited. In the sixteenth century, when both meat and metal pans were widely available, you might choose to roast your meat, or you could bake it in a pie or pasty, fry it in a pan, or grill it over hot embers on a griddle. This might sound like a simple matter of taste to you, but it was a matter of life and death. Meat is a good source of iron, and iron pots and pans significantly enhance the absorption of the mineral, which is especially important for women, who have a greater need of it than men on account of menstruation and pregnancy. Without sufficient iron, people become anaemic, and vulnerable to a number of diseases and ailments. It is thought that this was a prime reason why women did not live as long as men until the late Middle Ages.[17] The increase in meat consumption among ordinary people after the Black Death and the slowly growing supply of iron cooking vessels were a life-saver for many people, even if they did not know it at the time.[18]

On top of all these changes, mealtimes also became a matter of choice. Throughout the Middle Ages, ordinary people ate their main meal of the day – dinner – in the late morning. For many people, especially in the eleventh and twelfth centuries, this would have been their only meal. If they had enough food, they ate a smaller meal – supper – in the late afternoon. The only occasions on which men and women had breakfast was when starting work very early in the morning, such as during harvest time, or before setting out on a long journey. However, the introduction of clocks in the later Middle Ages meant that sixteenth-century workplaces and schools shifted to a system of set hours rather than functioning from dawn to dusk. As the hours could be very long – the 1515 Statute of Labourers and Artificers established the working day between mid-March and mid-September as running from 5 a.m. to 7 p.m. – it became usual for people in towns to have a breakfast and a midday meal instead of a late-morning dinner, and a supper at the end of the day. Had you found yourself in an Elizabethan town, therefore, you could have expected the three-meal regimen with which you are familiar: breakfast, lunch and supper. But had you visited in the eleventh century, you could have looked forward to little more than bread, cheese and a grain-based pottage made with vegetables, and that probably only once a day. And remember that in one year in every four, famine might have deprived you even of that.

It hardly needs saying that the lifestyle of the lordly class and the wealthy was very different from the hardships borne by the poor. The food they ate also changed greatly, partly as the result of international trade. Take spices, for example. It was not until the Norman invasion that spiced food started to become popular with the English nobility and, even then, spices were very hard to obtain before the trade in such exotica opened up in the late twelfth century.[19] From then on, cinnamon, nutmeg, cardamom, cloves, ginger, mace, pepper, sugar and saffron were regularly employed in the nobleman's kitchen – and the richer he was, the more of them his household consumed. Currants, raisins, dates, figs and prunes also became popular, and sweet wines from the Mediterranean arrived in the fifteenth century. New ideas about nutrition and health developed in Renaissance Italy and came to England in the sixteenth century. Men whose fathers would have scorned eating vegetables or anything green now had salads presented to them as one of the dishes in the first course of a dinner.

In the late fourteenth century, recipe books started to be produced for the first time since antiquity, circulating ideas about how to cook. Printed copies in the sixteenth century allowed any literate yeoman's wife to prepare sophisticated dishes from a text. At the same time, imported foods from the New World such as potatoes and tomatoes began to appear on the banqueting tables of the wealthy. They were joined by the edible carrot from Holland and the cauliflower from

Italy. What also mattered was that at the very end of our period, religious fasting restrictions fell by the wayside. Whereas in the thirteenth century a wealthy family would have felt compelled to eat fish instead of meat on Wednesdays, Fridays and Saturdays, and every day throughout Lent and Advent, by 1600 such limitations were observed only by the most ardent Catholic families – and then only on one day per week.

Ever since the publication of the Marquis de Condorcet's *Sketch for a Historical Picture of the Progress of the Human Spirit* in 1795, modern people have cherished the notion of progress. The basic idea is that social conditions will continually improve because it is in everyone's interests that they do. This view received something of a setback in academic circles in the wake of the First World War, when 'progress' was seen to have resulted in the destruction of human life on an unprecedented scale. In 1931 the historian Herbert Butterfield gave the concept another good kicking in his book *The Whig Interpretation of History*, in which he castigated writers who looked at the past as if it was all one long march of progress to the modern world. He strongly argued that past generations should be judged according to their own standards and not in relation to the present day. As a result, it has been popular among historians to denigrate the very idea of progress in social history; they loftily dismiss such ideas as 'whiggish' and outdated. However, there can be no doubt that in terms of domestic comfort there was genuine progress between the eleventh century and the sixteenth. In the eleventh century an illiterate farmer slept on a straw mattress in a dark, turf-walled hut on an earth floor by a smoky fire with his head on a log; five hundred years later his descendant could have laid his head on a feather pillow in a feather bed in an upstairs chamber heated by a fireplace. Similarly, a sixteenth-century gentleman sitting comfortably beside a glazed window and reading a book in his warm chamber would not even have been aware of his illiterate distant ancestor of 600 years earlier, riding between his smoke-filled halls.

An adequate food supply is even more essential to human well-being, and it cannot be denied that there was progress in this respect too. The tortuous cycle of hunger and misery was slowly brought to an end over the course of the Middle Ages. The regularity of famine declined and the capacity of the market system for distributing food increased. Even though the climate worsened from about 1290, the numbers who died from starvation gradually diminished. What's more, the fact that more people lived beyond the age of fifty in the later Middle Ages – despite the advent of plague, sweating sickness, influenza, smallpox and many other fatal diseases – can only be explained by the general improvement in diet and the introduction of iron cookware. And a better diet for mothers meant a better diet for babies, which resulted in lower infant mortality. This is why life expectancy at birth is arguably the best all-round measure of the prosperity of society. By 1600 it was not far short of forty years of age – a level it would not exceed until the late nineteenth century.

This should not be taken to mean that *everyone* in the sixteenth century was more comfortable than *everyone* in the eleventh. As we saw earlier, levels of inequality in both the late thirteenth century and the late sixteenth forced the very poorest people back into a state of destitution that may be compared with living conditions in the early Middle Ages. In Elizabethan England orphaned youths and homeless men and women were camping in barns. But they were exceptions. While standards of living were appalling, even the homeless were spared the regular famines and poor living conditions that eleventh-century slaves and serfs had had to endure. No one in 1600 would have wanted to turn back the clock – least of all the poor.

5

Speed

How Fast Did People and Information Travel?

'Speed' is not a word we usually associate with the medieval period. We can imagine a messenger on horseback, his tunic emblazoned with his lord's livery, galloping towards a manor with some urgent news. But who travelled faster than him? No one. Consequently it is widely assumed that there was no increase in the speed with which news could be transmitted until the advent of steam locomotives in the early nineteenth century. 'A speed of twenty to thirty miles per day was usual' is a line that appears regularly in history books about the Middle Ages. Very few historians have noticed that the speeds attainable increased significantly over the period and none have written about the matter in any depth. No one to my knowledge has considered how the change impacted on society. These, then, are the key themes of this chapter: the discernible increments in the fastest speeds possible between the eleventh century and the sixteenth, the degree to which people shared in those benefits, and the changes in thinking that resulted.

The Contexts of Speed

The word 'speed' is a relative term. When I run for a bus I might run 'fast' but I am not moving as fast as I am when driving at 30 mph. Likewise when I am driving 'fast' at more than twice that speed on the open road I am not travelling as rapidly as a high-speed train. Such relativity may appear obvious, but it is a necessary starting point because there were many different contexts to medieval speed. When men went about routine business they did not move anywhere near as fast as when they needed to outmanoeuvre an enemy army. And being a messenger bringing urgent news was something else again. Indeed, of all the factors that affected how fast someone travelled, the most important was *why* they were travelling in the first place. Why travel by night if you are merely planning to survey your estates? It doesn't matter how much moon there is: a bed is always going to be more comfortable than a saddle. If, on the other hand, you are desperate to see your dying brother, you will press on through the darkness, even if there is no moonlight.

Then there is the question of cost. Wealthy people who could afford changes of horses were obviously able to sustain far greater speeds than those who could not. Having the fastest messengers at his disposal, a king who needed to be told of an imminent invasion was likely to be informed far more rapidly than someone expecting an update on a manor's productivity. The key was being able to change horses regularly. It is therefore necessary to look at three different kinds of speed: first, that of people going about their ordinary business; second, that of wealthy and powerful people who needed to take decisive action and therefore had to travel swiftly in person; and third, that of important information. Let's start with routine travel – for if we do not know what was routine, it will be that much harder to determine what counted as fast.

Ordinary Speeds of Business

The individuals whose movements are easiest to trace are, inevitably, kings. From the development of the records of Chancery and the Exchequer in the 1190s, we can follow them on an almost daily basis around their realms. Almost no other secular figures can be traced in such detail. However, their 'routine' business was hardly typical of people in general. In addition, they tended to be accompanied by hundreds of attendants, perhaps as many as five hundred in the thirteenth and fourteenth centuries, which slowed down their travels. These people required huge amounts of food; in some places, temporary kitchens had to be constructed. On a single day in 1292, Edward I's household consumed 'four and a half oxen, four calves, seven pigs, ten and a half sheep, eighteen lambs, five gallons of blood, six goats, six rabbits, one pheasant, a dozen partridges, eighteen ducks, three dozen woodcock and 2,200 eggs, plus unmeasured amounts of milk, butter, herring and cod'.[1] To transport the entire apparatus of the royal household a large number of carts and wagons were required – rising from twenty or thirty in the thirteenth century to more than two hundred in the late sixteenth.[2] It required lots of horses too – which in turn needed large quantities of oats, which also had to be carried (as oats bought on the road were more expensive). You get the picture: royal travel was a massive enterprise. The routine journeys undertaken by the royal household therefore do not reflect the journeys of ordinary people in medieval England.

Nevertheless, royal itineraries are worth considering for their habitual speeds. This is because medieval kings were almost constantly on the move. In the eleventh century, like all great lords, they had to shift between their many estates for the sustenance of their household. But monarchs also had to counter military threats. Even when not at war, they were required to demonstrate their authority throughout the realm. King John moved his household every single month of his reign except one – when he was besieging Rochester Castle.[3] Although the development of markets in the twelfth and thirteenth centuries lessened the need to travel for sustenance, kings were still peripatetic, overseeing their estates on the Continent as well as in Great Britain. Edward I's usual travelling speed can be appreciated from his journey from Bamburgh to Windsor in January 1300, when he covered 360 miles in twenty-five days, resting on six of them.[4] His speed was thus in the region of 19 miles a day, despite dragging with him several dozen wagons and carts and hundreds of men and it being the depths of winter. In the course of a normal year, he stopped at over a hundred towns and villages, even when in his sixties.[5] Today, we may picture kings in their castles but we should also imagine them on horseback, surrounded by their servants and courtiers, cursing the English rain and muddy roads.

Edward III was easily a match for his grandfather, with regard to both the distances and the speeds at which he travelled. He too regularly visited more than a hundred places a year.[6] But he often travelled much faster. Between 4 and 29 August 1333, he rode from Newcastle upon Tyne to Westminster.[7] He covered the 76 miles south to Knaresborough in four days and spent eight days there before setting out on the 16th for Navenby in Lincolnshire (85 miles away), arriving on the 18th. After leaving Navenby on the morning of the 19th he passed through Wisbech and reached Little Walsingham (87 miles from Navenby) on the 21st. The next day he did 29 miles on his way to

Wymondham, where he stayed overnight. He then rode another 29 miles to Great Yarmouth and remained there for two days before starting out on 26 August to travel the 135 miles to Westminster via Redgrave, Bury St Edmunds, Long Melford and Chelmsford. He arrived at Westminster on the evening of the 29th. He had covered a total distance of 441 miles and he was on the road for only sixteen of the twenty-six days of the journey; this makes an average speed of almost 28 miles per travelling day. In March 1338 he covered as much ground even faster, travelling from London to Newcastle in less than seven days, and completing the whole journey from London to Berwick and back, a distance of more than 700 miles, in less than nineteen.[8]

Bishops also routinely travelled around the country. They had smaller households than kings and fewer political obligations but their spiritual responsibilities kept them on the move. When touring their dioceses, they travelled only short distances, from parish to parish. Their journeys further afield, however, give us a much better idea of their usual speeds. On 2 November 1000, Bernward, bishop of Hildesheim in Germany, set out for Rome on the most direct route, via Trento – a distance of 875 miles. It seems that he was delayed by snow in the Alps, for it took him until 4 January to get there: a journey of sixty-three days, averaging about 14 miles per day. He wisely chose to return by a much longer route of 1,018 miles via the abbey of St Maurice d'Agaune in present-day Switzerland, which took fifty-three days – a speed of just over 19 miles per day.[9]

Bishop Bernward's rate of progress was not uncommon for a travelling prelate. As the historian R. L. Poole tells us: 'A message from Rome might reach Canterbury in a little less than five weeks, and a traveller, as distinguished from an express courier, was expected to spend about seven weeks on the journey.'[10] Thus a twelfth-century bishop going to Rome normally travelled at 21 miles per day. It seems that this remained the standard for centuries. A systematic check on the bishops of Exeter reveals that on ordinary trips between Exeter and London and between London and Paris they averaged around 20 miles per day until the fifteenth century.[11] Occasionally we come across bishops keeping up a faster long-distance speed but such haste was not routine for a man of the cloth.

Twenty miles per day for an important personage and his household accords with the distance established for the 'legal day' in fifteenth-century England (the distance someone might be legally required to cover in twenty-four hours).[12] But is this an underestimate of other people's ordinary travel? The accounts of thirteenth- and fourteenth-century noblewomen suggest that journeys of significantly more than 20 miles were unusual at any time of year, unless there was a particular reason to travel quickly. On 1 June 1265 Eleanor de Montfort set out from Odiham to Portchester, 33 miles away, but the fact she did so *after* she had eaten dinner (usually served around 10.30–11 a.m. and lasting a couple of hours) suggests that this was a sudden departure. Almost all medieval upper-class journeys began in the morning.[13] In this case, her long trip to the coast was almost certainly a response to the news of the escape of her husband's enemy, Prince Edward, from Hereford Castle on 28 May. A more reliable indication of a noblewoman's ordinary speed is given by the progress of Joan de Valence, who travelled forty-seven times in the period 21 May 1296 to 12 September 1297, covering 735 miles in total, or roughly 16 miles per day. Every day's journey was less than 23 miles except for two: one of 28 miles and one of 32.[14]

Those of lesser status and wealth did not necessarily travel much more slowly. With only about 350,000 horses in late-thirteenth-century England, and perhaps half of them in the possession of manorial lords, many ordinary people did not have a mount.[15] However, while noblemen and noblewomen were obliged by their high status to ride or, in the case of a few elderly countesses, to take a carriage, ordinary people could walk without loss of dignity. If they were fit, they could easily cover 20 miles in a day – and this may well also have been a factor in designating 20 miles as a 'legal day'. For those who had the need to walk further, obviously they could. They were not constrained by the necessity of looking after their horses.

Extraordinary Circumstances

The expectation that anyone could travel 20 miles per day was by no means a limit. Many people could travel much further and faster. Roman troops were expected to march 30–35 miles a day on campaign and it is likely that Harold's army advanced at a similar speed on the way south from Stamford Bridge to face the Norman invaders in 1066. But those who could obtain the use of more than one horse per day were able to cover considerable distances. Three envoys sent from Rome by Pope Gregory VII to the Holy Roman Emperor, Henry IV, at

Goslar in December 1075 took twenty-three days to cover the journey of about 900 miles, travelling at roughly 39 miles per day.[16]

One example of the speed with which twelfth-century knights could cross long distances, even in winter, relates to the killing of Thomas Becket, archbishop of Canterbury, on 29 December 1170. The story goes that the four murderers heard Henry II speak of his desire to be rid of 'this low-born clerk' at Christmas at Bur-le-Roi, near Bayeux, 'probably on Christmas Day'.[17] They travelled separately, having agreed to meet at Saltwood Castle in Kent on the evening of the 28th.[18] They must have planned to reach Calais by about noon on that day, leaving them enough time to cross the Channel and ride the 12 miles to Saltwood. If they left Bur-le-Roi after dark on Christmas Day, they had about sixty-six hours to complete the 214-mile journey. Allowing eighteen hours for sleep and stoppages over that period, this equates to approximately 4½ miles per hour. However, they probably could not avail themselves of many changes of horses, which was the key to fast travel. Also, only about twenty of their forty-eight hours travelling time would have been in daylight. Had they kept this speed up for twenty-four hours, they could have covered 100 miles in a day.

Unfortunately, we cannot be certain about the timing of Henry's speech nor the knights' departure, so the above performance is conjectural. In addition, it is difficult to find examples of knights travelling anywhere near 100 miles per day before the fourteenth century. Famous thirteenth-century dashes include King John's remarkable advance on Mirebeau between 30 July and 2 August 1202, when his whole army covered 80 miles in forty-eight hours to capture his nephew, Prince Arthur.[19] Another is the return of the friar and traveller William of Rubruck from the Mongol camp of Karakorum, when he claimed to have covered almost 70 miles per day.[20] Neither of these is directly comparable with Becket's murderers.

In the fourteenth century we have more reliable examples of people travelling fast. One occurs in connection with the arrest of Roger Mortimer and Queen Isabella in Nottingham Castle on the night of 19 October 1330. The pope heard news of this event on 3 November. The distance from Nottingham to Avignon via London is 795 miles, including the 30-mile sea crossing, indicating that the messenger travelled at an average speed of 53 miles per day. However, the pope wrote to Edward III on 7 November to say he had that day received further information about the arrest from a merchant who had been in

England at the time. Presuming the merchant in question heard the news in London on 22 or 23 October, he must have travelled the 671 miles to Avignon in fifteen days: a speed of 45 miles per day.[21] This was fast for a merchant. The usual speeds for long-distance commercial travel were described by Giovanni di Antonio da Uzzano in the mid-fifteenth century. Examples include fifteen to sixteen days for Avignon to Paris (25–27 miles per day) and twenty-five to thirty days for Florence to London (31–36 miles per day).[22]

Edward III's own itinerary includes a number of instances when he travelled in excess of 40 miles per day. It is possible that he rode the 68 miles from Eltham to Dover with a small number of companions in disguise on 3 April 1331.[23] In 1336 he took six or seven days to cover a 380-mile route from Perth to Nottingham.[24] In August 1342, he returned from Gloucester to London (103 miles) in less than two days.[25] Mayors might also travel quickly when the need arose. The lawyer Nicholas Radford was murdered at his house in Poughill, Devon, on the night of 23–24 October 1455. The following day John Shillingford, mayor of Exeter, rode to London with the news, arriving late on the night of the 27th and seeing the Chancellor the next morning, thereby managing at least 42 miles per day.[26] Even bishops might record speeds in excess of 40 miles per day. In January 1401 Edmund Stafford, bishop of Exeter, made the 177-mile journey from Bishop's Clyst to London in less than three days (more than 60 miles per day), which is impressive for a fifty-five-year-old cleric at that time of year. But he went on to repeat the feat in his sixties, in 1406 and 1409. On 31 January 1410, aged sixty-five, he rode the 190 miles from Crediton to London in three days. Returning from London in 1416, then aged seventy-two, he left London on 8 July and was at his manor of Bishop's Clyst in Devon on the 10th.[27] It seems that you did not necessarily have to be young to travel at a speed of 60 miles per day in the fifteenth century: you only had to be able to afford it.

The Speed of News: Benchmarks

It was of course news that travelled fastest in the Middle Ages. However, historians have spent less time investigating its actual speeds and more pointing out that medieval news was very slow compared to the *Cursus Publicus* of the Roman Empire, which is often said to have been capable of 160 miles a day. They have also regularly observed that it was even slower in relation to the messenger service set up by Genghis Khan for the Mongolian Empire in the thirteenth century. In his book *The Medieval Traveller*, Norbert Ohler tells us that 'In twenty-four hours the well-organised relay courier service in the Mongolian Empire was supposed to cover 235 miles (the Roman state post, the "cursus publicus", did only 190–210 miles).'[28] But are these figures accurate? Can we use them as benchmarks? It is worth scrutinising them both to see whether they are reliable or not before looking at medieval European examples to check how they compare.

The original blueprint for the *Cursus Publicus* was the postal system of the Persian Empire. A series of stations for horses was created along the major routes to Rome at intervals of 25 Roman miles (23 statute miles – a Roman mile of 1,000 paces being about 1,620 yards). Fresh horses were maintained at each station for the exclusive use of imperial messengers. The principal difference between the Persian system and the Roman one was that the Persians used a sequence of relay riders to transfer a message, whereas the Romans insisted on a single rider who changed horses at each station. The advantage of the Roman system was that, on arrival, the rider might impart further information in addition to the written message. The drawback was that he would inevitably grow tired on the way and slow down.

One of the best sources for the speed of the *Cursus Publicus* is Procopius's *Secret History*, written in the sixth century. He says:

> As a day's journey for an active man, they decided on eight stages in some places, in others less, but hardly ever less than five. Forty horses were kept for each stage, and grooms in proportion to the number of horses. By frequent relays of the best mounts, couriers were thus able to ride as long a distance in one day as would ordinarily require ten, and bring with them the news required . . .

Thus, when necessity demanded it, the *Cursus Publicus* could require riders to travel at speeds of up to 200 Roman miles (184 statute miles) in twenty-four hours.[29]

Were Roman soldiers actually capable of such speeds? The short answer is yes, at least on occasion. Valerius Maximus recorded how the future emperor Tiberius rode 200 Roman miles in a day and a night to reach his brother Drusus on his deathbed in the summer of 9 BC. This demonstrates that his readers believed such rapid journeys were possible. Evidence that they were accomplished lies in a report of the mutiny of two legions at Mainz, Germany, on the morning of 1 January 69. The messenger covered the 1,253 Roman miles from Mainz to Rome via Cologne and Rheims in less than ten days, showing that speeds of more than 120 Roman miles per day were possible even in winter.[30] But in January there are only nine hours of daylight in that part of Europe. Had such a messenger been riding for twenty-four hours in summer, in northern Italy, where there are approximately seventeen hours of daylight, he would have been able to cover 198 Roman miles (182 statute miles) in twenty-four hours.[31] This supports Tiberius's reputed speed, riding to see his dying brother.

When it comes to the Mongolian postal system, we should expect greater speeds than this, for two reasons. One is that the Mongolians used riders in relays, like the Persians. This meant the message kept travelling on a twenty-four-hour cycle. Second, Mongolian saddles had stirrups – invented in Hungary, probably in the seventh century – which allowed riders to balance themselves more securely and thus ride faster. Unsurprisingly, therefore, greater speeds are indeed claimed for the khan's riders. Although these claims are based on the testimony of Marco Polo, whose reputation for exaggeration is well founded, his account is partially supported by several other writers, including the more reliable Franciscan friar, Odoric of Pordenone, who visited China about fifty years later.

The Mongolian system depended on two forms of messengers: runners and horsemen. Posthouses, called yams, were situated every 25–30 miles along the major roads; these provided accommodation for both sorts of messenger. In the mountainous regions yams were located every 35–45 miles. Every three miles between them was a fort from which runners would pass on messages in a relay. This system allowed the khan to receive messages from ten days' journey away in a single day. Marco Polo clarifies this by stating that 'in the fruit season many a time fruit shall be gathered one morning in Cambaluc [Beijing] and the evening of the next day it shall reach the Great Khan at Chandu [Shangdu, near Dolon-nor], a distance of ten days' journey'.[32] The 'day' to which he refers is thus actually a day and a half. This is quite feasible. The distance is about 224 miles. If a team of seventy-five runners were to cover their respective three-mile stints in an average of twenty-four minutes each – an easy pace for a fit young man, even when carrying a bag of fruit – and allowing up to six hours of darkness when no running took place, then fruit picked at 9 a.m. in Beijing could indeed have been delivered to Shangdu by 9 p.m. the following evening.

With regard to the horsemen, Polo's account of the speeds they could attain is as follows:

> There are also at those yams other men equipped similarly with girdles hung with bells who are employed for expresses when there is a call for great haste in sending despatches to any governor of a province, or to give news when any lord has revolted, or in other such emergencies, and these men travel a good 200 or 250 miles in the day and as much in the night. I'll tell you how it stands. They take a horse from those at the station which are standing ready saddled, all fresh and in wind, and mount and go at full speed, as hard as they can ride, in fact. And when those at the next post hear the bells they get ready another horse and a man equipped in the same way, and he takes over the letter or whatever it be, and is off full speed to the next station, where again a fresh horse is found all ready, and so the despatch speeds along from post to post, always at full gallop, with regular changes of horses. And the speed at which they go is marvellous. By night they cannot go so fast as by day because they have to be accompanied by footmen with torches, who could not keep up with them at full speed. Those men are highly prized and they could never do it if they did not bind hard the stomach, chest and head with strong bands.[33]

By Polo's own admission, speeds of 200 miles or more in a day were only undertaken when there were emergencies. It also should be noted that he contradicts himself when he states that the messengers travelled 'as much in the night' as they did in the day because he adds that they could not go any faster at night than pedestrians with torches. We should bear in mind too that Marco Polo's estimate of riders' performances 'per day' may actually have been a day and a half, as noted above with regard to the runners. However, the speeds he claims were not impossible in summer. On a day with sixteen hours of daylight (based on the dawn-to-dusk figures for Beijing in June), a message could have been carried 224 miles in twenty-four hours.[34]

To sum up, Ohler's figures are only slight exaggerations. Two important clarifications are that fast messages were only despatched when there was a need for great urgency and that the greatest speeds were only possible in summer. The Roman postal system allowed messengers on imperial business to cover up to 182 miles in twenty-four hours in ideal conditions but their greatest speed in winter was only two-thirds of this and usually they travelled at only about 50–60 miles per day. The Mongolian system, when presented with a crisis, was capable of carrying a message even faster, perhaps as much as 220 miles per day when conditions were ideal. However, it is important also to remember that the Roman system was designed to transport a *messenger* as fast as possible, whereas the prime purpose of the Mongolian one was to convey a written message.

We may now compare these speeds with a more modern benchmark. On 5 November 1831, in response to a wager, the English sportsman George Osbaldeston saddled up twenty-seven racehorses at Newmarket and rode 200 miles around the Round Course in eight hours forty-two minutes.[35] The ground was flat and the going good; the forty-five-year-old man in the saddle was short (5ft 1in) and of moderate build (11 stone). The horses had been bred for speed: Osbaldeston himself estimated that it would have taken him an hour longer if he had used good hunters rather than racehorses. And each racehorse only had to gallop for 7½ miles, not the 23-mile stages of the Romans or the 25 miles of the Mongols. Nonetheless, it is astonishing how much faster he could travel than both the Roman and Mongol riders. Had Tiberius been able to travel as fast as this to see his dying brother, he would not have taken twenty-four hours to cover the 200 Roman miles but eight hours exactly. This requires us to question the assumption that there was no change in the maximum speed that news travelled before the railways, mentioned at the start of this chapter. Is there any evidence that speeds of over 100 miles per day were possible in England before 1600? And if they were, what difference did the increased speed of news make to society?

The Speed of News: The English Evidence

In the early thirteenth century the English royal household had two categories of messenger. One was the *nuncius regis* or royal messenger, who would ride his own horse in England and hire horses and boats on the Continent. The other was the *cursor* or foot messenger. Neither sort travelled very fast: usual speeds were around 20 miles per day which, as we have seen, was routine at the time.[36] The requirement for the *nuncius regis* to be mounted had more to do with his higher status than the need for speed. However, messages could be delivered much more quickly. To return to the murder of Becket, news of the killing in the early afternoon of 29 December 1170 reached the king at Argentan, in France, on 1 January.[37] The distance from Canterbury to Dover is 16 miles and the crossing would have taken four hours at the very least. Then the messenger would have had to ride another 204 miles along the winter roads. Even if he crossed the Channel on the same evening as the murder, his speed must have been at least 70 miles per day.

In the thirteenth century the king's messenger service became more efficient. Men carried special pouches bearing the royal arms that allowed them to hire horses in the king's name and to pass through ports without paying tolls. Older men were recruited, who had often been messengers in other noble households – to take advantage of their experience, their knowledge of the routes, their language skills and their diplomatic tact. Being a messenger abroad could be dangerous, as you could be suspected of spying. By the fourteenth century, most messengers crossing the Channel were accompanied by a second man, in case they were attacked or arrested. This also allowed the second man to learn the routes from the senior messenger.

One of the messenger's most under-appreciated skills was being able to find the intended recipient. When kings were writing to peripatetic lords and bishops, it was not always possible to send a letter to a particular location. The messenger had to work out where his addressee was likely to be and refine his destination as he drew closer. This perhaps accounts for the slowness with which some information was transmitted. The register of Roger Martival, bishop of Salisbury, reveals that of 768 individual official letters sent to him, 621 (81 per cent) travelled at 10 miles per day or less. Only nine (1 per cent) travelled at more than 40 miles per day.[38] The fastest were two royal writs that covered the 69 miles from Westminster to his manor house at Ramsbury, Wiltshire, on the same day they were written.

Important messages did travel fast – and few were as important as news that the king had died. Therefore these events are interesting indicators of maximum speeds. Edward I breathed his last at Burgh by Sands near the Scottish border at about 3 p.m. on 7 July 1307 and his son and heir, then in London, was informed on the 11th.[39] This entailed a journey of more than 300 miles at between 72 and 78 miles per day.[40] Edward II's death supposedly took place on 21 September 1327 in Berkeley Castle, Gloucestershire. Lord Berkeley's letters to this effect were carried by Thomas Gurney to the young king and his mother at Lincoln, by way of Nottingham, and arrived during the night of the 23rd.[41] This distance is 156 miles. If Gurney set off on the afternoon of 21 September itself, this equates to about 62 miles per day.

It was Edward III who introduced a system of stations throughout England, where royal messengers could change horses.[42] It is therefore not surprising that it is in his reign that we have our first confirmed journeys of 100 miles per day. In 1343 the king ordered one of his senior messengers, Jack Faukes, to travel with an assistant to the pope at Avignon and to return within eighteen days 'on pain of life and limb'. The distance from Westminster to Avignon was 674 miles by the shortest route, including the sea crossing, so this amounted to an expectation that Faukes and his assistant would cover at least 75 miles per day. Fortunately, the detailed account of their route has survived.[43]

On the first day, 26 July, Faukes and his companion made their way via Rochester and Canterbury to Dover, a journey of 75 miles. They stayed in Dover for the morning of the next day – possibly waiting for the wind to change direction – and crossed the Channel that afternoon. As soon as they set foot in France they rode on to Saint-Riquier and Pois, reaching Paris on the evening of the third day, where they rested. No doubt they slept well after covering the 165 miles from Calais in a day and a half. On the fourth day they rode to Dourdan, and, having paid 7d to have their hired horses taken back to Paris, they proceeded by way of a 'chariot' to Ouzouer-sur-Loire, thereby completing a day's journey of 93 miles. Day five saw them travel along the Loire to Cercy-le-Tour where, after another 93 miles, they halted for the night. On the sixth day they rode to Chalon-sur-Saône and then followed the River Saône downstream to Lyons, completing 145 miles. On the seventh day, they hired a boat to take them the last 137 miles to Avignon, arriving the following day (2 August) at the hour of vespers (about 6 p.m.). The whole journey of 730 miles, including the Channel crossing, had taken seven and a half days. That is an average speed of more than 97 miles per day. After concluding their business, Faukes returned alone by a different route, taking twelve days. His relatively slow return – albeit at a speed in excess of 60 miles per day – meant he failed to meet his expected eighteen-day journey time by a day and a half.

Faukes's account shows that an experienced messenger could travel with exceptional speed in the mid-fourteenth century. It has some-times been presumed by historians that speeds of 100 miles per day could not have been achieved without relays.[44] Faukes's mission shows that they could. However, we should note that, although such speeds were possible, they were extremely rare, even when it came to infor-mation of the greatest importance. News of the capture of Richard II in 1399, for example, took at least three days to make the 180-mile journey from Chester to London.[45] News of the battle of Agincourt, fought on 25 October 1415, does not seem to have reached Bordeaux, 450 miles away, until 23 November, four weeks after the event.[46]

The journeys in all these examples involved one messenger travel-ling the entire distance, in the style of the *Cursus Publicus*, but relays started to enter the picture in the fifteenth century. Frederick III, the Holy Roman Emperor, established a limited relay system between Feldkirch and Vienna in 1443; by 1479 Louis XI had a similar postal sys-tem for France. These initiatives seem to have inspired Edward IV to establish a relay system in 1482, when he was fighting the Scots.[47] It consisted of ten messengers stationed along the road from Berwick to London. It was said that they could bring news south at a rate of '200 miles per day'.[48] The new infrastructure proved its worth in the year of its establishment when it transferred the news of the capitulation of Berwick to London in less than forty-eight hours: a speed of more than 170 miles per day.

The above relay is the only known instance of such rapid informa-tion transfer in fifteenth-century England. It was therefore probably not a permanent system. A study of the speed of news at the time of the Wars of the Roses suggests that urgent information normally trav-elled at about 70 miles per day.[49] However, Edward IV's example had proved the value of postal systems for specific purposes. Another relay was organised between Plymouth and London in 1501 in order to inform Henry VII of Catherine of Aragon's arrival in England. News of her landing travelled at more than 100 miles per day.[50]

By 1509, the position of Master of the King's Posts had been set up to oversee information relays on the routes from London to Dover in the south and Berwick in the north. Speeds definitely increased. On 1 April 1515 the English envoy in Scotland, then at Stirling, wrote a letter to Henry VIII beginning: 'this Friday, when I came home to dinner, I received your most honourable letters by post, dated at your mansion, Greenwich, 26 March.'[51] As 'dinner' would have still been served in the morning, this means the king's letter had covered the 435 miles in five days, at a speed of 87 miles per day. The northern route seems to have been a little erratic, however, for the Master of the King's Posts, Sir Brian Tuke, wrote to Thomas Cromwell in 1533, stating that

> It may [please] you to understand the King's Grace hath no more ordinary posts [nor] of many days hath had, but between London and Calais . . . and [since] October last, the posts northward . . . For, Sir, you know well that, except the hackney horses between Gravesend and Dover, there is no such usual conveyance in post for men in this realm as is in the accustomed places of France and other parties.[52]

Two years later Tuke wrote to the governor of Calais assuring him that 'wheresoever the king be, there be ever posts laid from London to his grace, and between London and Dover be always posts ordinary'.[53] It seems that certain routes were still only temporary. This may have been the case for some decades. Although the postal route from London to Ireland, by way of Holyhead, was established in 1572, and that from London to Bristol and Plymouth in 1579, they were only officially funded on an occasional basis. At other times, they were kept going privately, with government approval, so they could be made official again at short notice.[54]

In its early days, the post was exclusively for the benefit of the king and his government. Gradually, however, its remit widened as other people used it to carry private letters. They also started to use it as a means of personal transport. In his 1535 letter, Tuke refers to people paying to ride with the post between London and Dover. This route had four intermediary stations – at Gravesend, Sittingbourne, Rochester and Canterbury – so riders could have fresh horses approximately every 15 miles, which was crucial for maintaining rapid speeds. As time went by, this private element of the postal service became accepted. It was formalised in the 1560s or 1570s, when Thomas Randolph was the Master of the King's Posts, with a charge of 2d per mile being levied on every person riding with the post in a private capacity.[55] Minimum speeds were established, of 7 mph in summer and 5 mph in winter. The regulations also laid down maximum journey times of forty-two hours from Berwick to London in summer and sixty hours in winter. These imply minimum average speeds of 8.1 mph in summer and 5.6 mph in winter, by night as well as by day.[56] Whereas Edward III had expected his messengers occasionally to travel at 75 miles per day, now private citizens could pay to ride more than twice as fast.

Did the post reach these speeds? As with the *Cursus Publicus*, the answer is yes, occasionally. Sometimes we can piece together exactly how fast a letter was travelling at any given point in its journey. Letters sent to the Privy Council were endorsed by postmasters with the time and date when they passed through their offices. Hence we may track a letter in much the same way that modern parcels are tracked. For example, a letter from the commander of the garrison in Plymouth to the Privy Council in London was posted at 7 p.m. on 25 July 1599: it passed through Ashburton at 2 a.m., Exeter at 6 a.m., Honiton at 8 a.m., Crewkerne at 11 a.m., Sherborne at 1 p.m., Shaftesbury at 4 p.m., and so on until it arrived in London at about 11 p.m. on 27 July, fifty-two hours after it was despatched. That was slow for this 216-mile route. If a letter travelled at the greatest possible speed for each stage of that journey, it could have reached its destination within twenty-seven hours of posting: a speed of 192 miles per day. The average was forty-six hours (113 miles per day).[57]

These times are for letters but they also indicate how fast those who rode with the post could travel. The fastest time on record would appear to be that possibly achieved by Richard Boyle, the future earl of Cork (and father of the scientist Robert Boyle). In a short review of his life, he remarked on one particular experience:

As clerk of the council [of Ireland], I attended the lord president in all his employments, and waited upon him all the whole siege of Kinsale, and was employed by his lordship to [go to] her majesty with the news of that happy victory, in which employment I made a speedy expedition to the court; for I left my lord president at Shannon Castle, near Cork, on the Monday morning about two of the clock, and the next day, being Tuesday, I delivered my packet, and supped with Sir Robert Cecil. Being then principal secretary of state, at his house in the Strand; who after supper held me in discourse till two of the clock in the morning; and by seven that morning called upon me to attend him to the court, where he presented me to her majesty in her bedchamber, who remembered me, calling me by my name, and giving me her hand to kiss, telling me, that she was glad that I was the happy man to bring the first news of that glorious victory.[58]

Travelling from Cork to London in about forty-two hours is nigh on incredible. Even if we allow just seven hours for the sea crossing between Dublin and Holyhead (66 nautical miles) – and surely it must have taken longer than that – Boyle must have ridden the 155 miles from Cork to Dublin via Kilkenny and then the 269 miles of the Holyhead postal route in thirty-five hours. This equates to an average of over 12 mph, day and night, or 291 miles per twenty-four hours. Even more remarkable is that he did it in late December.[59] His speed per day was thus more than twice that of the *Cursus Publicus*. Although there are some reasons to doubt his claim, the attention he gives to this one event in an extremely brief account of his life suggests he set great store by it and we should not dismiss it.[60] And such a journey was not impossible. There were eighty horses laid on at every posthouse between Holyhead and London in 1598 and, had this provision been maintained in December 1601, Boyle should have been able to take advantage of the best mounts available.[61]

Another impressive long-distance journey was completed just a year later, when Sir Robert Carey carried the news of the death of Elizabeth I to Scotland. The queen died at Richmond Palace in the early hours of 25 March 1603. Carey set out between 9 and 10 a.m. and rode 162 miles to Doncaster that same day. As there was a modest amount of moonlight (33 per cent) he probably pushed on for three or four hours after dusk, before resting. On 26 March he rode another 136 miles to his own house at Widdrington, in Northumberland, where again he rested. At midday on the third day he was approaching Norham Castle, having completed 49 miles, when he fell off his horse and badly injured his head. Thus he had to ride the last 50 miles to Edinburgh slowly and did not get there until after the king of Scotland had gone to bed.[62] Nevertheless, he still did the 397-mile journey in about sixty-two hours, and his average progress over the first two days was 149 miles per day, including two nights' sleep. Thus news of Elizabeth's death was taken *to* Scotland twice as fast as the news of Edward I's death was brought *from* Scotland, three hundred years earlier.

Both Boyle and Carey were engaged on royal business. However, the improved postal system in England did not benefit just the government but everyone who could afford to pay the necessary fees. In 1600, private individuals could send a letter through the post and expect it to travel at over 100 miles per day. If they could afford to, they could ride with the post. On 20 October 1599, after lunch in London, the Swiss physician Thomas Platter and five friends took the ferry down the Thames to Gravesend, where they spent the night. The following morning they took the ordinary post to Rochester (7½ miles), changed horses, rode to Sittingbourne (10½ miles), changed horses again, rode to Canterbury (16 miles), changed horses again and rode 16 miles to Dover. The 50-mile trip took them 'about five hours'.[63] It seems that they did not enjoy the journey as they found English post saddles far too small for their backsides, but that is not the point. These young men were able to travel along the roads of Kent in autumn at 10 mph – a speed that compares very favourably with the *Cursus Publicus* and even with the famed Mongol relay riders. What's more, they took it so much for granted, they could complain about their discomfort.

It may seem preposterous today to describe a 5 mph increase in the maximum land speed as revolutionary. It sounds like someone pointing to a hillock and calling it a mountain. But it *was* revolutionary, for a number of reasons. Like a one-degree rise in average global temperature, it represents a huge change. This is because it is not a one-off event but a permanent doubling of the maximum potential speed. By 1600 the fastest riders could cover 150 miles in a day and individual letters carried by teams of riders could travel at speeds of up to 200 miles per day. This significantly reduced the time it took to inform the government about the goings-on in the realm. If the Scots attacked Berwick when the king was at Winchester, and the news came south at 40 miles per day, as it is likely to have done in the eleventh century, it would have taken nine days to arrive. After the king had deliberated what to do, if only for a day, the response would have travelled back at the same speed – so the north of the kingdom would have been without royal instructions for almost three weeks. If, however, the post could carry the news at 200 miles per day, the king and his advisers could decide on a response in less than two days. After a day's discussion, the king's instructions would have been back in the Berwick area less than five days after the danger had arisen – two weeks faster than in the eleventh century.

It is hard to exaggerate the political and social implications of such a change. The rapid delivery of information allowed a king far greater control of his realm. When communications were very slow, a rebel leader could raise an army and rampage through an area without the king knowing what was happening. This placed the burden of policing the far-flung parts of the kingdom on the shoulders of local lords. In return, kings had to trust the said lords completely. This often involved giving them a great deal of autonomy in their lands, in order to retain their loyalty. Hence the Marcher lords on the borders of Wales and Scotland were given rights and privileges that went well beyond those granted to ordinary English lords. When rapid communications kept the king informed about distant events, central government could take control of the further-flung regions. Local lords lost their political authority. The rise in travelling speeds subtly shifted the balance of power away from territorial lords and towards central government. This is a trend which has continued to affect governments and nations ever since.

The speed of information thus created a demand for *more* information. There is not much value in having a spy at a foreign court if all the news he gives you is out of date by the time you receive it. If, on the other hand, your spy can send you a letter by way of a relay that will tell you of a planned invasion before it sets out, you can take measures to defend yourself. Of course, that applies not only to military attacks but to initiatives of any sort. It also relates to opportunities such as trade links, potential alliances and scientific and geographical discoveries. Whether you call them agents or spies, there were few such men in Europe in the eleventh century. There were hundreds in the sixteenth. Every major European state had its agents in the major cities of its neighbours, all of them writing to their masters back home on an almost daily basis. What made their letters valuable was not just their insight but how up to date their news was. This is why by 1600 the English government not only had agents all over Britain and Ireland but also maintained thirteen spies in France, ten in the Low Countries, five in Italy, five in Spain, nine in Germany and three in Turkey.[64]

Another reason why that small increment in the maximum speed is important is what it says about society. It shows people working together for the common good. Once horse relays had been recognised as providing maximum efficiency, horse stations were developed and financed, with rules for their use. Specialist horse breeding allowed stronger and faster mounts to be employed.[65] The conditions of the roads were improved, especially as a result of the Highways Act of

1555, which introduced parish surveyors to oversee the repair of damaged stretches. Handbooks and charts started to be produced to inform people of the fastest routes by which to travel. Most significant of all, the state's postal infrastructure was made available to its private citizens. Today we take it for granted that the state provides us with services but, outside the legal system, this was rarely the case before 1500. From the 1530s, private individuals could ride with the post or use it to send letters, and everyone who had the wherewithal to pay for fast transport had an interest in making the system work.

Looked at simply as a statistic, an increase in speed of 5 mph is not very impressive. In terms of the cultural horizons explored in this book, however, it is profoundly important. Imagine the rings spreading out from where you are now – the first ring marking the limit of how far you can travel in one day, with a further ring beyond it marking two days, and then a yet further ring marking three days. Now imagine all those moving further and further outwards, each one twice as far. As mentioned in chapter one, you haven't just doubled or trebled the area you could cover in one, two or three days, you've increased it exponentially. If you can only travel 20 miles in a day, your total range is theoretically 1,257 square miles. If, however you can travel 100 miles in a day, it is 31,416 square miles. With the collective horizon also increasing exponentially, you can see how a doubling of the distances people could travel in a day had a huge impact on the nation's understanding of itself and what was going on within and beyond its borders.

There is one other subtle shift implicit in all this, and it takes us right back to a point made at the start of this chapter, about the contexts of speed. Why travel in the first place? For most of the Middle Ages, the only people who needed information to be delivered rapidly were those who had a political responsibility or a personal commitment. The vast majority of non-political information exchanges were not urgent. You might have wanted to travel fast if you needed your physician's advice but most ordinary people had very few reasons to rush anywhere. As Bishop Martival's register indicates, only 1 per cent of high-status messages moved at more than 40 miles per day. But this changed over the period. Why?

The clock.

You may recall Thomas Platter and his friends rushing to Dover in 1599 at a rate of 10 mph – the sort of speed at which a Mongol emperor would hope to hear of a rebellion in one of his provinces. Why were they in such a hurry? To catch a boat. Or, to be exact, to make sure they had time to conduct some business before they caught a boat to cross the Channel. They were organising their days according to a timetable. This was in complete contrast to eleventh-century slaves and serfs working in the fields, who did not care what time it was. Unfree workers did not need to be anywhere else. Their days were controlled by the daylight and the movement of the sun across the sky. Even in the fourteenth century, when bells tolled the hour in the larger towns and cities, the gates were shut at dusk. By the sixteenth, people were making arrangements to meet friends at 'three of the bell' or hear a sermon at 'two of the clock'. Acts of Parliament laid down times at which people should be available for work. Local laws stipulated the hours when markets should open and close. Our sense of urgency in daily life developed alongside our adoption of clock time and the speed with which we could travel. In the case of ports, the time that the tide would permit a boat to sail could be estimated in advance, allowing people to know when they needed to embark. We see the results in Thomas Platter's journey in 1599. The faster you could travel, the longer you could spend over your lunch in London before having to ride to Dover to catch your boat for Calais. As an attitude, you have to admit, that does seem familiar.

6

Literacy

The Cultural Impact of Tyndale's Translation of the Bible[1]

In 1526 a little book was published in the German city of Worms. The reason it was small was because owning a copy was illegal in England, so its size meant its owner could conceal it more easily. The print run was substantial for the time: 3,000 copies. However, almost all of them were bought up by one man, Cuthbert Tunstall, the bishop of London. Then, on 27 or 28 October 1526, he burnt them at St Paul's Cross in London.[2] The book in question was William Tyndale's translation of the New Testament. Although today only three copies survive, it has a good claim to be regarded as the most influential book ever published in the English language.

The reason why Tyndale's little book is so important is not because it was the first English translation of part of the Bible: John Wyclif and his acolytes had produced a translation of the whole Latin Vulgate Bible in the late fourteenth century, initially with the approval of members of the English royal family.[3] Its importance rather lies in the quality of the translation, the fact that it was mass-produced and – above all else – the timing of its publication. If Tyndale had been born in the tenth century and had translated the New Testament into Old English, his legacy would have been no greater than that of Aelfric of Eynsham, whose Gospel of Mark was quoted in the introduction. Obviously, the limitations of producing such a work before printing was possible would have stymied attempts to circulate his translations. In addition, the Norman Conquest, which introduced French as the language of government, would have swept away the demand for an English Bible. Tyndale's impact on literacy, language and society in England was thus very heavily determined by the time in which he lived.

The English were late to the game of publishing vernacular Bibles compared to several other European nations. By 1526, the Germans had had a printed Bible in their own language for sixty years, in the form of Johannes Mentelin's translation of 1466. They had also accumulated thirteen further editions in High German and four in Low German.[4] Martin Luther's own translation of the New Testament had appeared in 1522. The first Italian Bible was printed in Venice in 1471. The New Testament appeared in French in about 1474, in Czech in 1475 and in Dutch in 1477. A complete Catalan Bible hit the stationers' shelves in 1478 and a complete Czech one in 1488.[5] Ideas arising from reading vernacular Bibles were circulating internationally. By translating the New Testament and then parts of the Old Testament, Tyndale brought England into a series of world-changing debates about how people should practise religion – whether as a matter of personal faith, collectively as a Church, or in obedience to the pope.

Most of the cultural horizons we have so far considered in this book were formed by forces far beyond the control of a single individual. Tyndale's story, however, shows that one person could have enormous influence – although it needs to be acknowledged that much of it was indirect. Tyndale's translation had an impact on hundreds of thousands of his contemporaries, and over the following centuries billions of people, as a result of the international spread of the English language and English culture. As a result, he arguably shifted our cultural horizons as profoundly as any medieval monarch.

That is quite a claim of course. But Tyndale's legacy is not just that of a translator. If we think in those terms, we are likely to forget *what* it was he was translating, when he was translating it, and the world in which he was living. We are similarly likely to forget the people whom he inspired and what *they* achieved. Instead, we should open our eyes to a whole series of cultural horizons that expanded in the wake of the publication of the English Bible. Some of these were the direct result of Tyndale's translation. Others were due to the work of translators whom Tyndale had inspired and encouraged. Still others related to the fact that Tyndale and his fellow reformers provided spiritual guidance to those trying to find their way as religion was transformed. This chapter focuses on six such horizons to demonstrate the far-reaching significance of the translation: the importance of the Bible; the growth of responsible citizenship; increased levels of literacy, especially among women; the standardisation of the English language; the primacy of the vernacular; and the questioning of authority. But first, before we examine these, we need to get to know Tyndale, his collaborators and their work a little better.

Tyndale and the Development of the English Bible

William Tyndale was born around 1494 in Gloucestershire and educated at Oxford University. A gifted linguist, he eventually mastered six
languages besides English: Latin, Ancient Greek, Hebrew, German,
Spanish and French. He graduated in 1512 and entered the priesthood
in 1515. He was thus still young when he came across Erasmus's 1516
edition of the New Testament in Ancient Greek. This set him on the
path he was to follow for the rest of his life. As he himself is alleged to
have said, when a learned Gloucestershire man suggested people
would be better off without God's law than without the pope's: 'I defy
the pope and all his laws; if God spare my life ere many years, I will
cause a boy that driveth the plough shall know more of the Scripture
than thou dost.'[6]

When Tyndale originally envisaged translating the New Testament
from Ancient Greek into English, he did not imagine it would be such
a controversial project. Initially he saw it as a straightforward exercise –
albeit an arduous one – and sought Bishop Tunstall's support. When
this was not forthcoming, however, it would have dawned on him that
he was treading a very dangerous path. He accordingly decided to produce his book overseas, leaving England for Germany in April 1524. Yet
even on the Continent he could not publish his translation with impun-
ity. In Cologne in 1525, he started to produce a quarto edition of the
New Testament in English, based on Erasmus' third Greek edition
of 1522 and including translations of Luther's commentary. It was
stopped in the press after only the prologue and the first twenty-two
chapters of the Gospel of Matthew had been printed. It was seen to
pose enormous political danger. Henry VIII feared that England might
be brought over to Lutheranism through the democratisation of the
Bible. Indeed, it was no coincidence that the Reformation was most
fervently supported in Germany, where vernacular Bibles had been
available longest.

Tyndale fled to the city of Worms to start over again. This time he
produced that pocket-sized edition of 1526, which bore no prologue or
Lutheran notes, just the English translation of the Greek original.
Copies were smuggled into England and Scotland in bales of cloth.
The authorities were horrified to realise that, despite their best efforts
to prevent it, the New Testament was now available in English for

anyone to read. Bishop Tunstall forbade its circulation in the diocese of London and started to buy all the copies he could find. Tyndale printed more in Antwerp. The archbishop of Canterbury wrote to all the bishops urging them to donate money to acquire the books so they could be burnt. Booksellers were warned against selling them. Bishop Tunstall had his bonfire. But no one could burn the knowledge of what Tyndale had done.

After the publication of the New Testament, Tyndale worked on further religious texts and translations in secret locations in and around Antwerp. His *Obedience of a Christian Man* (1528) taught English readers that the Catholic Church was corrupt and that the pope was guilty of 'selling for money what God promiseth freely'. He followed Luther's example in publishing a translation from the Hebrew of the Pentateuch (the first five books of the Old Testament) in 1530. The following year he published his *Exposition on the First Epistle of St John*. Of course, any of his work that appeared in England was immediately banned and burnt. So too were the people who were caught in possession of the texts. A priest called Thomas Hitton was arrested in Kent with a copy of Tyndale's New Testament and, having been condemned to death by both the archbishop of Canterbury and the bishop of Rochester, was burnt at the stake in February 1530. He was just the first of more than a dozen men and women who were burnt alive for heresy connected with the New Testament in English in the early 1530s.[7]

Although Tyndale remained in hiding abroad, Sir Thomas More took on the job of attacking him in his absence as a heretic, declaring him to be worse than Luther. Tyndale responded by pointing out that More was defending a Church that put its own interests above the teachings of Holy Scripture. While More eventually wrote half a million words castigating him, Tyndale replied with publications demolishing the authority of the Catholic Church. These too were deemed heretical. Several times Henry VIII tried to tempt him to return to England, but Tyndale feared a trap. He insisted that he would not return until the king had granted his subjects the right to hear the word of God in their own language. Henry's reluctance to do so suggested that he set greater store by his prelates' corrupt practices than his people's salvation. That put the king too on the wrong side of scriptural authority.

Tyndale produced a new edition of his English New Testament in 1534 and his translations of the historical books of the Old Testament were brought to completion, as far as the Second Book of Chronicles.

He also translated the Book of Jonah. But then disaster struck. His location was betrayed for cash by an impecunious young Englishman and Tyndale was arrested on 21 May 1535. He was charged with heresy, interrogated and, after sixteen months in prison, executed on 6 October 1536. His last words were: 'Lord, open the king of England's eyes.'

Shortly after Tyndale's arrest, a complete English Bible was produced in Antwerp by his friend and collaborator, Miles Coverdale. Coverdale had worked closely with Tyndale on the translation of the Old Testament texts – one contemporary English commentator refers to him as Tyndale's 'disciple' – but he was no match for Tyndale when it came to understanding Greek and Hebrew. He wisely used Tyndale's New Testament and his Pentateuch, completing the rest of the Old Testament with his own translations from Latin sources and the German texts of Martin Luther and Huldrych Zwingli.[8] However, although Coverdale lacked Tyndale's facility with foreign languages, he was similarly gifted when it came to finding lyrical phrases in English. The versions of the Psalms we know today owe much to his translations from the Latin. You will almost certainly recognise parts of his version of Psalm 137:

By the waters of Babylon we sat down and wept, when we remembered Sion.

As for our harps, we hanged them up upon the trees, that are therein.

Then they that led us away captive, required of us a song and melody in our heaviness: sing us one of the songs of Sion.

How shall we sing the LORD's song in a strange land?

The fact that his words would be turned into the lyrics of a worldwide hit single in the twentieth century testifies to his contribution in shaping modern English as a lyrical language.

In England, even as Tyndale died, there were stirrings about producing an official English Bible. Some bishops remained firmly set against the idea. Others realised that, unless they took the initiative, the reformers would steal a march on them. The king was coming around to the latter point of view. In 1537 Coverdale and John Rogers – another erstwhile collaborator and 'disciple' of Tyndale's – produced the second complete English Bible. Tyndale's name could not be mentioned in connection with it, so it was published as having been 'translated into English by Thomas Matthews'. An early copy found its way to Thomas Cromwell, who arranged for it henceforth to be published with royal approval. 'Set forth with the Kinges most gracyous lycence' appears at the foot of most of the surviving copies. In the year after Tyndale's death, therefore, it became legal to own an English Bible. In 1539, Coverdale revised the 'Matthews' translation and published it with royal approval as the Great Bible. A copy was ordered henceforth to be placed in every church in the country. Tyndale's dying wish had come true.

All subsequent translations of the Bible have built on this foundation. The New Testament of the King James Bible, first published in 1611, is 84 per cent Tyndale's work. About 76 per cent of his Old Testament translations were retained by King James's team of editors. Overall, just over half of the whole King James Bible can be directly attributed to Tyndale.[9] Almost everyone, therefore, who has heard the Bible read aloud or has read it for themselves has encountered Tyndale's poetic prose. Anyone who has ever sung a psalm in church has recited Coverdale's lyrics. Given that more Bibles have been printed in English than in any other language – and bearing in mind that even today about a third of the American population still use the King James Bible – there cannot be many people whose words have been repeated more times in world history – if any.[10]

The Importance of the Bible

Tyndale paved the way for the biblical culture that shaped how people thought for the next three hundred years. This is not to say that no one had paid attention to the Bible before him. The fact that the first book printed in Europe was a Bible underlines its relevance to Christian thinking. However, we need to remember that the Bible was neither as ubiquitous nor as pervasive before 1500 as it was afterwards. For a start, it was in Latin, which only a small percentage of the population could understand. In the words of the historian Christopher Hill, it was 'the private property of the clergy'.[11] Even if that is a slight exaggeration, it was definitely the preserve of the highly educated and the wealthy. Printed Bibles were only available from urban booksellers, and the book-distribution network in Britain was rudimentary compared to that on the Continent. Manuscript Bibles were even harder to obtain. They were especially laborious to produce and consequently expensive. Those in English were also very dangerous to own. Archbishop Arundel's *Constitution against Gospellers*, issued in 1409, did not ban the English Bible *per se* but made it illegal to own a copy without permission, or indeed for any individual to produce his own translation of the scriptures. This meant that possessing or copying any existing English Bible could result in you being charged with heresy and burnt at the stake. Consequently, even those who owned a copy were very cautious as to whom they lent it.

In this relatively non-biblical world, religious experience was largely sensory. Men and women connected with God through images, smells, sounds and, above all, the mystery of the Sacrament. Given the dullness of rural workers' daily lives, and the darkness of their homes, it would have been a transformative experience for them to enter a church with its colourful wall paintings, stained glass and painted rood screen. The sweet smell of herbs, incense and beeswax candles; the blue and red light; the ringing of bells; the sound of music and the rhythms of the Latin Mass – taken together it would have amounted to a delicious assault on the senses. And high up above the nave, the rood depicted the crucifixion, the ultimate focus of the Christian faith. You didn't need a Bible to relate to the dying Christ when you could see him there, bleeding, before your very eyes.

Reference to such imagery makes the process of worship sound largely reactive: confronted with images and smells, the illiterate peasant was induced to think holy thoughts. However, we should not see imagery working purely in this way. Medieval worship was just as much about performance. First, there was the sacred music. Many more psalters and antiphonals for singing survive from medieval libraries and churches than Bibles. Then there were the processions on feast days, and religious cavalcades in towns when guilds and fraternities needed to mark special occasions. Mystery plays based on biblical stories remained popular throughout the fifteenth century. There were baptisms and churchings, marriages and burials. There was confession. There were periods of enforced fasting and chastity. Men and women formed fraternities to keep candles burning on their altar in the local church. Church ales were regularly enjoyed by all the parishioners. People found guilty of moral crimes were required to perform public penances, either in the parish church or the marketplace. Many people went on pilgrimages. And everywhere there was prayer. Images of

Christ and the saints could facilitate such acts of devotion and provide a focus for them. The sensory world of the church was not just about seeing, smelling and hearing but also about taking part in enactments of faith. It was a dance to the music of God.

Tyndale had no time for any of this. As he put it in his *Exposition on the First Epistle of St John*,

> To speak of worshipping of saints, and praying unto them, and of [making] them our advocates . . . yet it is as bright as the day to all that know the truth how that our fasting of their eves, and keeping their holy days, going bare-foot, sticking up of candles in the bright day, in the worshipping of them to obtain their favour, our giving them so costly jewels, offering into their boxes, clothing their images, shoeing them with silver shoes with an ouch of crystal . . . are with all like ser- vice plain idolatry, that is, in English, image-service. For the saints are spirits and can have no delectation in bodily things.

Nothing, he emphatically declared, had greater authority than scrip- ture. As he put it in his prologue to the Pentateuch, 'the Scripture is the touch-stone that trieth all doctrines, and by that we know the false from the true.'[12]

This vision of religion, enshrined in the English Bible, challenged the old forms of worship in the most powerful way. Tyndale did not just *tell* people that reading the word of God was better than praying to the saints, he *showed* them. If previously your purpose in going to church to pray and perform rituals in accordance with a series of mys- tical clues had been to smooth your path to Heaven, the English Bible cut through the uncertain mysteries and showed you exactly what to do. 'God hath appointed in the Scripture how we should serve him and please him,' Tyndale wrote in his *Obedience of a Christian Man*. To employ a modern analogy, he wasn't just giving his readers hints and clues as to how they might win the lottery of everlasting life: he was giving them the winning numbers.

As a result of Tyndale's work, the Bible became central to the reli- gious experience of ordinary English people. Despite the fact that almost the whole print run of the New Testament was bought up piecemeal and destroyed in 1526, Tyndale continued to produce more copies. It has been suggested that as many as 16,000 had been shipped to Britain by the time he died in 1536.[13] Cuthbert Tunstall and the

other book-burning bishops might well have served to advertise his
work with their literary pyres. The mere news that such books existed
marked a conceptual shift. If you could not obtain a New Testament in
English, the impetus was nevertheless there to look for other works by
Tyndale and his followers. And people who could gain even temporary
access to a copy could memorise large sections. It is easy for us in the
modern world to forget how important memorisation was, when we
have so many ways of recovering information and texts.[14] But for Tyndale's contemporaries, learning passages from the English Bible was
inexpensive, spiritually moving and incredibly exciting. It was also
much safer to carry the word of God in your memory than it was in
the form of an illegal book.

The biggest advance came in 1539, when the government ordered
that a copy of the Great Bible be placed in every church in the country.
Within two years, 9,000 had been printed.[15] Those who could afford to
do so bought their own for private devotion. The illiterate heard it read
to them by the minister in church and by their employers in the houses
in which they worked as servants. It was quoted by magistrates and
civic authorities as well as by clergymen. For the first time, large numbers of people heard Christ's teaching in their own language. And
everyone knew they were participating in the same mass experience –
just as people did in the mid-twentieth century when they all watched
the same TV programmes because there was only one channel. At the
same time, it allowed each listener to develop his or her own personal
relationship with God. As we have seen, hitherto most people had
experienced religion collectively. Now, for the individual who wanted
to better his or her life, or to live a more godly one, the Bible became
an additional channel of revelation alongside the church service. In
fact, it swiftly took over from the priest's sermon. If you could read the
Bible, you could study and interpret the word of God for yourself. You
could determine your own path to redemption: you did not need the
intervention of a priest.

All this was bound to divide people. The new understanding that
the Bible provided the foundations of the Christian faith opened the
door to fundamentalism, setting common religious practice against a
holier-than-thou approach justified by biblical sources. In England this
developed into Puritanism. It is salutary to remember, therefore, that
the English Bible had negative as well as positive consequences. For a
start, it permitted religious zealots to criticise aspects of daily life that

were *not* in the Bible. *The Anatomy of Abuses* (1583) by Philip Stubbes shows just how vitriolic and splenetic the Puritans were against their fellow men – and how full of unholy bile. Stubbes railed with the greatest scorn against any form of self-indulgence, from the pride of men to the quality of their shirts, their wearing of ruffs and jewellery, and what they chose to eat. He would cheerfully have seen every person who cherished the slightest luxury cast into Hell. And while his intolerance was extreme, he was not alone. Twenty years earlier, in 1563, England had come within a hair's breadth of becoming a fundamentalist state, when a Bill to enact a full Puritan agenda failed to become law by just one vote. We need to remember that the excessive Puritan demands of the seventeenth century – such as the death penalty for adulterers and blasphemers – also have their roots in the biblical culture that arose in the wake of Tyndale's translation.

The enhanced authority of the Bible thus was of prime importance in the development of English culture. It resulted in the destruction of a sensory manner of approaching God through ritual and performance. It imbued people with a greater sense of individualism. It encouraged the questioning of long-standing traditions. But it also led to extremist religious views and persecution. Hence it is the first reason for supposing Tyndale's influence on English history was as great as that of any medieval monarch. Can you imagine a world in which the Bible is only available to you in Latin? Would you be able to quote it if it was? Today, when we hear evangelical preachers speaking about what we should do to save our souls, we don't hear them saying we should go on this pilgrimage or pray at that shrine: they tell us to read the Bible. It has been that way in England for the last 480 years. The English Bible rapidly became the prime authority for directing Christian life. But it achieved this position not by being imposed on congregations from the pulpit or from Rome but by being translated into the vernacular so it could be sought out by individual worshippers who soon gave it precedence over all other instruments of worship.

Responsible Citizenship

The biblical culture that emerged after the publication of the English Bible made people more responsible for the well-being of their fellow human beings. As one commentator put it in 1607, 'the Bible taught magistrates how to govern and teachers how to teach'.[16] It was also instructive to many men and women who did not fall into either of these two categories – from masters of households and their wives to medical men anxious that the healing power of God should work through them. Generally, biblical texts codified how members of society should aim to please God by helping one another, following the teachings of Christ.

It is not hard to find evidence of this new emphasis on responsible citizenship. The increase in charitable giving and the foundations of schools from around 1540, for example, both have to rank high on any such list. But perhaps the clearest measure of responsibility is to be seen in the development of the Poor Law.

Between 1500 and 1600, the population grew from about 2.3 million to over 4 million, without there being any provision for the extra people to work or live, so the problem of unemployment became ever more acute. The government initially opted for a policy of repression. In 1531 an Act was passed stipulating that vagabonds be whipped and returned to their place of birth; those who were unable to work were to be licensed to beg in their native town or parish. In 1547 the law became even harsher in that vagabonds were to be enslaved for two years; children were to be put into service; the elderly poor were to be put to work; and only the impotent poor were to be supported by voluntary donations. The enslavement of Christians was too much for most people and this element of the law was repealed two years later. Then, in 1572, all the earlier statutes were replaced with a new Act. Parishes were empowered to establish overseers of the poor to make local collections for their relief. Repression was still a key feature of the law: vagabonds were to be whipped and have holes burnt through the gristle of their ears. But in 1597 an Act was passed that introduced what we today call the Old Poor Law. The overseers of the poor in each parish were required to raise money to look after the poor by setting a compulsory parish rate. With these funds, they were expected to relieve the impotent poor and set pauper children to work or to bind them as apprentices with more prosperous households within the community. This legislation might not have been as dramatic as the defeat of the Spanish Armada a few years earlier but it stands as one of the greatest achievements of Elizabethan England. It saved people from starving to death.

You could say that the various Poor Law Acts eventually succeeded in their principal aim, which was to alleviate suffering. However, that was not the initial aim at all. The early legislation sought to reduce the number of down-and-outs by relegating them to a desperate obscurity. So why did policy change? The simple answer is that society became more aware of its responsibilities. In 1545 the London mercer Henry Brinkelow wrote, 'I thinke in my judgement under heaven is not so lytle provision made for the pore as in London, of so ryche a Citie?'[17] Two years later, the London authorities took action. A tax was levied for the 'sustenance and maintenance' of the city's poor. This accompanied the re-establishment and endowment of four hospitals, St Bartholomew's, Christ's Hospital, Bedlam and St Thomas'. Other towns soon followed London's example. The authorities in Bristol and Canterbury started to buy corn for the relief of the poor. In 1557, the profits from Stourbridge Fair were handed over for the benefit of paupers in Cambridge. Ipswich joined London in taxing its citizens for the benefit of the poor that same year. Norwich surveyed all its poor citizens in 1570 with a view to assessing the levels of relief necessary. Increasing numbers of Bible readers had realised that, like Daniel in the lions' den, who was saved by the angel because he was 'blameless', the impotent poor did not deserve their fate. Social problems which previously had been ascribed to the will of God were no longer seen in that light. They were increasingly regarded as the consequences of the failure of members of society to follow the teachings of Christ – in particular, with regard to helping their fellow men in their hour of need.

When famine killed thousands in 1594–7, Parliament could no longer ignore the situation. A Christian sense of duty directed the legislators. The charitable relief of the poor – in which the giving was primarily to benefit the donor's soul or reputation – was replaced by a tax, a social duty undertaken for the benefit of the sufferers. The historian Paul Slack has argued that 'the crucial factor was a new conception of what governments could and should do for the poor, inspired by humanism'.[18] I would add that you cannot separate this humanism from the sense of responsibility engendered by the reading of the Bible. In 1596, the anonymous author of *Three Sermons or Homilies, to Moove Compassion towards the Poore and Needie in these times* told its readers:

> When thou meetest a poor man in the streets, consider that he is a man, created after God's image: though he be poor, naked and miserable, yet beware thou despise him not, such as he is; take heed thou smite him not, take heed thou drive him not away.[19]

Henry Arthington was even clearer about this civic responsibility being a Christian duty in his *Prouision for the Poore*, published the following year. He begins with a paraphrase of the Beatitudes – 'Blessed is he that considereth of the poor; the Lord will deliver him in the time of his trouble' – before laying down precisely why civic responsibility is a Christian virtue:

> The first consideration, for all able persons to thinke vppon, is how the poore may and must be releeved, if we will shew our selves to be true Christians, or euer looke that Christ should comfort us at our last ending, when death shall arrest us.[20]

In many towns, the wealthy bequeathed money or stocks of wool and other raw materials to provide work for the poor. In places where they founded almshouses, the inmates were invariably expected to be both moral and pious. Humanism may well have inspired the new understanding that governments should try to help the poor and not simply whip, enslave and brand them but it was the new biblical culture that informed it in almost every aspect. As Professor Slack adds, 'it is difficult to find a municipal scheme [of poor relief] unsupported by Puritan or godly rhetoric'.[21] Such rhetoric would not have existed if there had been no English Bible.

This, then, is the second reason for supposing Tyndale's influence on English history was as great as that of any medieval monarch. The reason why people in southern England ceased to starve to death in large numbers after 1597 was largely this acceptance of civic responsibility, which in turn depended on the new biblical culture. If you want to understand why 10 per cent of northern Europe – including 2 million people in France – died in the terrible famines of 1690–1710, yet England saw almost no casualties, at least part of the answer lies in the establishment of the Old Poor Law a hundred years earlier and people's sense of responsibility towards their fellow men that followed the publication of the English Bible.

Increased Literacy

The cultural change most commonly associated with the translation of the Bible is the increased level of literacy. If you had access to a book in your own language, you could teach yourself to read by following the letters and training yourself to recognise the words. Or someone in your family could teach you. You did not need to go to school to become literate. And while a printed Bible might still cost 3s or more, that was far cheaper than the 2s *per week* you might have to pay in school fees for a boy to learn Latin so he could read the Latin Bible. Moreover, it was significant that the most widely available book in English was the Bible – this was the book that most people wanted to read. Had the English not had their scripture in the vernacular until the eighteenth century, levels of literacy would have remained far lower in subsequent centuries. The Bible did not appear in Portuguese until 1753; this was no doubt one of the reasons why, in 1900, only 36 per cent of Portuguese men and 18 per cent of Portuguese women were literate (compared to UK figures of 98 and 97 per cent respectively).[22] The fact that Tyndale created a core text that remained central to English culture for so many centuries can only have attracted more people to read it. Seen in this light, he was without doubt the most successful teacher the English-speaking world has ever had.

Having said this, the benefits of people learning to read were not universally appreciated in the early sixteenth century. The preamble to the Great Bible of 1539 carried the following line:

> Here all manner of persons, men, women, young, old, learned, unlearned, rich, poor, priests, laymen, lords, ladies, officers, tenants, and mean men, virgins, wives, widows, lawyers, merchants, artificers, husbandmen, and all manner of persons, of what estate or condition soever they be, may in this book learn all things.

This looks very much like an exhortation for everyone to hear the Bible read in English, if not to read it themselves. However, the consequences of this philanthropic initiative seem to have shocked the government. Indeed, it felt the need to withdraw the invitation to all and sundry in an Act of Parliament just four years later:

> There shall be no annotations or preambles in Bibles or New Testaments in English. The Bible shall not be read in English in any church. No women or artificers, apprentices, journeymen, servingmen of the degree of yeomen or under, husbandmen, nor labourers shall read the New Testament in English.[23]

The cat was out of the bag, however. The very fact that it was necessary to pass the second Act suggests that a large number of people
were indeed looking into the Bible for themselves in these years. The
restrictive legislation was repealed in 1547 and two years later the *Book
of Common Prayer* was published, which incorporated parts of Tyndale's translation that had been absorbed into Miles Coverdale's Bible.
From now on, everyone was exposed to, and becoming familiar with,
the word of God in their own language on a regular basis.

The educative ghost of Tyndale can also be found in the context of
what used to be called 'the Tudor revolution in government' – a massive increase in the nation's bureaucracy. Parish registers were created
from 1538 and churchwardens' accounts were kept in ever greater
numbers, alongside an immense amount of other written business. It
became clear to anyone who wanted to get ahead in society that he
needed to be able to read and write. Many would have started with
chapbooks, or similar black-letter scripts, but before long most would
have felt it necessary to put their reading skills to the ultimate good use
by reading the Bible. Whereas in 1500, about 10 per cent of the male
population of England could read and write, 30 per cent could do so
by the 1640s. By that time, a million Bibles had been printed in
England.[24]

So much for male literacy. What about women and girls? If anything, here we see an even more dramatic increase, for the simple
reason that there were relatively few educational opportunities open to
females in the fifteenth century. Only wealthy families could afford to
teach their daughters to read, and not all saw an advantage in doing so.
There *were* literate medieval Englishwomen but not many. While more
than a hundred of the 1,000 plus letters in the fifteenth-century Paston
collection were from women, most of them were composed on behalf
of Margaret Paston, who was illiterate. We find a similar picture if we
look at the three other important pre-1500 letter collections: the Stonor
Letters contain twenty-seven items (about 10 per cent) written by or
on behalf of women; out of 247 letters in the Cely family collection
just one is from a woman; and the Plumpton correspondence contains
just two out of the 143 dated before 1500. All these families were of
high status and able to afford private tutors, so the small number of
letters is significant. Female signature literacy across the country
was less than 1 per cent in 1500. By 1600, however, it had risen to 10
per cent.[25] Since the number of girls' schools did not increase in

proportion, the first tranche of literate women were either taught by private tutors or self-educated. With regard to the latter, the majority of those who learned to read must have done so by studying the book most widely available: the Bible.

The reason why the rise in female literacy was so important is that it allowed women to have a public voice for the first time. Some of the ensuing works were hugely important. In 1560 Anne Locke published her translation of sermons by the French Protestant theologian Jean Calvin. Four years later, Anne Bacon published a translation from the Latin of John Jewel's *Apologie of the Church of England*, the founding theological tract of the English Protestant Church. Already in 1554, John Standish could declare that 'women have taken upon themselves the office of teaching'.[26] Women began to create literature for other women, circulating ideas that could be read aloud to those women who could not read. In 1582 Thomas Bentley published *The Monument of Matrones*: a two-volume anthology of religious writing by women for women. By the end of the sixteenth century women were writing and publishing on a vast array of subjects. Several published their own poetry. For the less literary sorts, there were self-help books with advice ranging from the correct arrangement of a banquet to medical recipes and directions for self-beautification. And literate women were now able to engage with books written by men, so male authors could no longer presume that they were communicating with an almost entirely male audience. For the first time in history, knowledge and debate were not an exclusively male privilege.

A mass of new ideas emerged from this greater level of literacy. Growing numbers of readers made it commercially viable to produce large print runs of medical and legal books, as well as geographical, historical and theological treatises. To pick one subject, hundreds of printed medical self-help titles were available by the end of the sixteenth century, and many of these would have been lent out many times. Professor Slack has estimated that the total readership of such works at the end of the sixteenth century was in excess of 100,000.[27] Many people now had more information at their fingertips than those who provided nursing care. Overall, the number of books grew considerably. In the first three decades of the sixteenth century, 1,828 titles were published in England; in the last three decades, that figure swelled to 9,788. It simply comes down to intellectual economics: if the demand for new texts remains high, they will be produced in ever-increasing numbers. And so they are, to this day.

Standardisation of the English Language

Fifteenth-century English is not difficult to understand once you get used to it. But it is not harmonious: every sentence is an irregularly shaped peg that does not fit smoothly into the round hole of our understanding. There is also a lot of variation and irregularity. Apart from the odd line of Chaucer, little pre-1500 English has stood the test of time. The language from the reign of Elizabeth, on the other hand, is quite familiar to us. Most educated people today can quote dozens of lines of late-sixteenth-century literature, whether they be from Shakespeare's plays and sonnets, Marlowe's plays and poems or the works of the many poets whose individual images and metaphors are more famous than their authors. The key reason for our familiarity with English literature from the late sixteenth century is that the language was heavily influenced right at the outset of popular printing by the English Bible. The rhythms of Tyndale's prose became the common drumbeat of the English language. It is no exaggeration to say that without Tyndale, there would have been no Shakespeare.[28] Even today, we all speak a little bit like him. In 2011 an examination of the King James Bible revealed that it contained 257 idioms still in daily use. Only eighteen of them originated with the team of more than sixty translators and editors appointed by King James. Almost all the rest came from Tyndale.[29]

It was not so much Tyndale's vocabulary that made English what it is but his way of speaking, the pattern of his words. To illustrate this, compare the Beatitudes – the first ten verses of chapter 5 of the Gospel of Matthew – as translated by John Wyclif and his followers in the late fourteenth century with the same text translated by Tyndale in his revised New Testament, published in 1534:

Wyclif Bible, circa 1390

1. And Jhesus, seynge the puple, wente vp in to an hil; and whanne he was set, hise disciplis camen to hym.
2. And he openyde his mouth, and tauyte hem, and seide,
3. Blessed ben pore men in spirit, for the kingdom of heuenes is herne.

4. Blessid ben mylde men, for thei schulen welde the erthe.

5. Blessid ben thei that mornen, for thei schulen be coumfortid.

6. Blessid ben thei that hungren and thristen riytwisnesse, for thei schulen be fulfillid.

7. Blessid ben merciful men, for thei schulen gete merci.

8. Blessid ben thei that ben of clene herte, for thei schulen se God.

9. Blessid ben pesible men, for thei schulen be clepid Goddis children.

10. Blessid ben thei that suffren persecusioun for riytfulnesse, for the kingdam of heuenes is herne.

Tyndale New Testament, 1534

1. When he sawe the people he went vp into a mountayne and when he was set his disciples came to hym

2. and he opened hys mouthe and taught them sayinge:

3. Blessed are the povre in sprete: for theirs is the kyngdome of heven.

4. Blessed are they that morne: for they shalbe conforted.

5. Blessed are the meke: for they shall inheret the erth.

6. Blessed are they which honger and thurst for rightewesnes: for they shalbe filled.

7. Blessed are ye mercifull: for they shall obteyne mercy.

8. Blessed are the pure in herte: for they shall se God.

9. Blessed are the peacemakers: for they shalbe called the chyldren of God.

10. Blessed are they which suffre persecucion for rightwesnes sake: for theirs ys the kyngdome of heuen.

There is a greater simplicity of phrasing and a gently pressing rhythm in Tyndale's version. It seems cleaner, more elegant and less encrusted with superfluous syllables. But perhaps most of all – and this is something over which he had no control – his and Coverdale's version became *the* Bible. Had their wording been discarded in later versions, the standardisation of the English language would have depended on the rhythms and cadences of a different set of translators. The consistency with which all later Bibles reproduced Tyndale's simple sentences and Coverdale's lyricism meant that their words were constantly repeated and became familiar to generation after generation. As a result, all the variant forms of English that had previously existed up and down the country were forgotten. If you have any doubt about the significance of this in the long term, just imagine this book being written in the English of John Wyclif.

The Primacy of the Vernacular

To the modern mind it is simply a matter of common sense that, if most people speak English and few speak Latin, it is better to publish a book in English. But that presumes you want people to read it, and that it is better that more people can and will read it, regardless of their background. As we have already seen, that was not the case in 1500. Knowledge was religiously guarded – literally – and kept locked up in Latin. It is therefore hugely significant how far and how fast Latin gave way to English in the wake of the production of the English Bible. Of the 1,828 books mentioned above as being published in England between 1501 and 1530, only half were in English. That proportion rose to 85 per cent for those appearing between 1571 and 1600. The tipping point was the 1530s, which saw the number of titles in the vernacular increase from 47 per cent to 76 per cent.[30] As English became a fitting language in which to publish the word of God, it became a suitable vehicle for any and every other text that could appear in print.

This shift from Latin to the vernacular is a major development in itself. Imagine going into a bookshop today and half the books on sale being in Latin. But the implications at the time went far further than just ease of reading. Latin was the language of social control. Although Edward III had allowed people to plead in court in their own language since 1362 – and this included English, which was recognised in that year as 'the tongue of the nation' – court records were still written in Latin. Many other official documents were too. Therefore it is significant that Tyndale did not suggest that people eager to read the Bible should learn Latin – which one might have expected of a brilliant linguist – but that the Bible should be available in the tongue of the people. The lowest common denominator came first. And that tipped the balance. Publishing something in Latin after the 1530s could only be justified as an attempt to reach a specific international audience, for which Latin remained the *lingua franca*. It is no coincidence that when the Puritans finally obtained control of the government in the mid-seventeenth century, one of the first things they did was to abolish the official use of Latin.

The decline of Latin as the language of power is one side of the equation; the other is the rise of English as the voice of the people. If we were to tell the story of England over the last thousand years, a major theme running through the entire narrative would be the democratisation of society. We would perhaps begin with Magna Carta and Simon de Montfort's first parliament and similar early attempts to hold the king to account. But we could also represent this as a series of efforts to make kings and other authority figures listen to the people. Kings increasingly did listen, especially Edward III and Henry IV, who both worked closely with Parliament. They understood that a common language was essential if there was to be a meaningful dialogue and collaboration between ruler and ruled. When Henry IV claimed the throne in Parliament in 1399, he did so in English, not French or Latin. By the mid-fifteenth century, English had become the day-to-day language of the aristocracy and nobility. And by 1540, when almost every English citizen spoke English, the vernacular Bible not only provided final confirmation that English was the national tongue, it also defined the form that the language should take. It thus became a linguistic and cultural cornerstone of English national identity.

Questioning Authority

The publication of the English Bible meant that prelates and clergy-men could no longer claim to have unquestionable authority in religious matters. Their decrees needed to be underwritten by scrip-ture. As Tyndale put it,

> God's word should rule only and not bishops' decrees, or the pope's pleasure . . . [they ought] not to expound the Scriptures carnally and worldly, saying, 'God spake this to Peter, and I am his successor, there-fore this authority is mine only.'[31]

The English Bible was thus revolutionary in that it sought to replace ecclesiastical hierarchy with people's own interpretation of 'God's word'. It encouraged ordinary people to examine the religious basis on which clergymen justified their positions and power. And in many cases they found it lacking.

Tyndale himself was not interested in the secular implications of this process, only the spiritual benefits, but his challenge to leading clergymen inevitably cast doubt on the acceptability of other forms of authority too. Most prelates were temporal as well as spiritual lords; what's more, they only enjoyed their worldly power by virtue of their ecclesiastical positions. If the lord of your manor was a bishop and you paid rent to him, and if he wielded authority in a way that was contrary to the teachings of Christ – by selling pardons and indulgences, for example – then by paying him rent you were in effect supporting a sinner. Doubting his religious standing also cast doubt on a prelate's secular position. This gave the English Bible a revolutionary flavour.

Another revolutionary aspect of scripture in the vernacular was that it allowed people to see the disjuncture between Christ's message of universal equality and their own experience of inequality. In the Gospel of Matthew, they could read about the wealthy young man who had never sinned but who nevertheless was unable to give up his riches in accordance with Christ's instruction and therefore would not enter the kingdom of Heaven. In Tyndale's 1534 edition, this reads as: 'It is easier for a camell to go through the eye of a nedle then for a ryche man to enter into the kyngdome of God.' It followed that storing up great wealth was ungodly – and people naturally thought that also applied to secular lords, lawyers and merchants as well as to bishops and abbots. Why, then, should any of them be obeyed? When Tyndale spelled out a revolutionary passage in words of one syllable – 'Soo the laste shalbe fyrste and the fyrste shalbe laste' – anti-authoritarian sparks flew.

Despite the revolutionary character of his work, Tyndale, like Luther, was staunchly opposed to social revolution. He wrote *The Obedience of a Christian Man* specifically to explain to his readers that there was a difference between exposing religious corruption and questioning secular rule.[32] As far as he was concerned, Christ had taught people to love their enemy. If you were oppressed by the king or a lord, you should show your devotion to God though accepting your oppression, even if the king threatened you with death and seizure of all your property.[33] Unsurprisingly, not everyone agreed. 'If princes or rulers will deny [the scriptures] when they will be taken for faithful, the said people may deprive them their kingdoms and lordships,' argued a

French writer whose work was translated into English in 1536.[34] As for the lords of the realm, by what right had they been appointed? According to Clement Armstrong, an evangelical London grocer writing in the 1530s, the lords had wrongly appropriated the trees and fields that God had given to the people. They had also unjustly appointed their relatives to enjoy the benefit of tithes exacted from farmers. Parliament was not mentioned in the Bible; therefore it should have no authority over the Church. Armstrong's questioning of the religious basis for the social order was in each case a direct attack on that order itself. You could not separate the two. Tyndale's and Luther's shared reluctance to endorse revolutionary ideas was irrelevant. In giving ordinary people access to Christ's teaching on equality, both men had inevitably promoted those ideas.

Previously the leaders of working-class revolts in Europe had rarely sought to eliminate the hierarchies prevalent in society: they had merely attempted to put an end to bad practices and policies. The only notable exception in England was the renegade priest, John Ball, who preached during the Peasants' Revolt of 1381 that 'all men were created equal by nature, and that servitude has been introduced by the unjust and evil oppression of men, against the will of God'.[35] He used an old proverb to hammer his point home: 'When Adam delved [dug] and Eve span [spun] / who was then a gentleman?' But as a priest, Ball had access to the Bible and was ahead of the game. Once they were able to read the Bible in translation, many more people began to question the old social order. In some places they took up arms. This was especially the case in Germany, where the Bible had been available in the vernacular for the longest time and serfdom was still widely prevalent. From the 1490s, peasants who took part in the Bundschuh uprisings were threatened with being drawn, hanged and quartered. Those who sheltered them were to be outlawed. These punishments were harsher than those hitherto imposed. As the justification for them made clear, it was specifically because the peasants

had joined . . . in an assembly, conspiracy, and common understanding against all authority, including the highest authorities, with the intention to free themselves from their subordinate position, which would lead to the destruction of all divine, human, spiritual and temporal law, all authority [or] government of the princes, nobles, and city councils.[36]

Such local uprisings were just the start. After Luther's translation of the New Testament, some leaders roused the disaffected German peasantry to revolution. The German Peasants' War broke out in 1524. In Swabia, the Twelve Articles, widely promulgated as a manifesto, included the demands that clergymen be elected from their congregations and only preach the Bible, with no additions; that only the great tithes of wheat and corn, mentioned in the Bible, be exacted, and that only one third of these was to go to the minister, with the rest going to the poor; that serfdom was to come to an end, in line with the teaching of St Paul, 'be not ye the servants of man'; that everyone was to have the right to hunt and fish wherever he liked, and take freely what he needed from woods and forests; and so on. It may sound like a moderate set of demands to us today but at the time it was a revolutionary challenge to the social order.

As the German Peasants' War progressed, more dangerous forces were unleashed. Thomas Müntzer led a working-class takeover of the town of Mühlhausen, calling for all property to be held in common and exhorting his followers with an Old Testament-like splenetic fervour to murder the rich and powerful. 'I say with Christ that ungodly rulers should be put to death,' he wrote.[37] The war resulted in the killing of thousands of people, most of them peasants. But for many sympathisers, challenging authority was simply the logical extension of what they had read for themselves in the Bible. Understanding the word of God had given the peasantry something they had never previously conceived of and something they would never forget: the idea of social revolution.

England did not witness a similar uprising. Nevertheless, here too men and women felt compelled to question authority. Most prominent among these was, paradoxically, the king himself. In 1533 Henry VIII renounced his loyalty to the pope and separated England from the Roman Catholic Church. As we all know, he decided on this course of action so he could divorce Catherine of Aragon and marry Anne Boleyn. What is less frequently appreciated is that Anne's appeal was not merely sexual (although it certainly was that): the young Protestant lady came with her own copy of Tyndale's *Obedience of a Christian Man*. In the margin she marked the passages that might interest the king, telling him it was 'a book for all kings to read'. Tyndale's denunciation of papal authority and his exhortation to put Christ's teaching above everything else can only have inspired Henry. When the time came to provide a new formulary for his Church, the official text he issued, *The Institution of a Christian Man* (1537), owed much to Tyndale's *Obedience*.[38] Therefore, when we talk about Tyndale's legacy including the questioning of authority, we are touching on some of the most significant and long-lasting changes in English history, namely the English Reformation and the Dissolution of the Monasteries. Tyndale didn't cause them to happen but his work certainly influenced those who did.

If the king could shrug off his obedience to the pope, why couldn't ordinary people deal with their superiors in a similar manner? As we have already seen in the case of Clement Armstrong, some reckoned they could. Others thought that the Bible could be used to bring about legal reform. In the 1540s William Turner called for the overthrow of all the laws that were not contained in the Bible. He refused to accept that Parliament could legitimise any non-biblical law. He even went so far as to deny flatly that the king had any authority to legislate in ecclesiastical matters.[39] The more moderate Henry Brinkelow declared in 1542,

> Study the scriptures and there shall ye see that judges and rulers, yea even the kings sat in judgment in the open gates, as appeareth in the second [book of] Kings the 19th chapter, Deuteronomy the 16th, the second of Esdras the third chapter. And why sat they in the gates, but that the people, yea even the poorest, might come and open unto the king his own cause?[40]

Brinkelow was a political nobody yet here he was, telling the king how he should make himself accessible to his lowliest subjects. Armed with the English Bible, some people felt that, if scripture was on their side, God was also on their side. They believed it gave them the right to tell their social superiors how they should behave, even kings and queens. In every walk of life, therefore, the English Bible led to the questioning of authority with a conviction that had never been seen before.

No other publication in history has had as great an impact on England as the English Bible. With regard to biblical culture, it caused many people to swap their old performative ways of worshipping for the teachings of Christ. That in turn led to a deeper and wider sense of civic responsibility. It led to the willingness to question authority in all its forms, from the rights of bishops and the authority of the pope to the government of the realm. Tyndale himself, through the poetic prose of his Bible translation, did more than anyone else to create the standardised language we speak today. His prioritisation of the vernacular contributed to the decline of international, elitist Latin and the confirmation of English as the voice of the people. In extending the horizon of literacy, he helped bring about improvements in education and greater equality between the sexes. The broadcaster John Humphrys claimed in 2003 that BBC Radio 4 was '*the* civilising influence in this country'; it would be hard to find a better contender than Tyndale for the title of '*the* civilising influence in this country' over the last five hundred years. He remains to this day the only writer in the English language more influential than William Shakespeare.

What is truly tragic about Tyndale's achievement is that he was judicially murdered for it on Friday 6 October 1536. Although the offence for which he was eventually strangled and burnt at the stake was that of heresy, it was his translation of the Bible and demands for religious reform that led to the authorities plotting his arrest and execution. His death goes beyond mere poignancy, and even beyond martyrdom. For a martyr dies for his or her own faith; Tyndale suffered and died as part of a collective quest for greater learning and spiritual understanding among men and women. There have been many martyrs in the course of English history but none who consciously sought to improve the lives of his fellow countrymen on so many levels, in both this world and the next.

7

Individualism

The Horizon of the Self[1]

Earlier chapters have highlighted many dramatic changes in people's attitudes and behaviour. But what did they think about themselves? To what extent were they aware of being individuals as opposed to members of a group or a crowd? And what difference did it make? In addition to the *external* cultural horizons we have already examined, there was also an internal one – that of the self – which undoubtedly developed over the centuries as people became more self-focused and more independent.

It hardly needs to be pointed out that it is not easy to investigate this aspect of the medieval past. Unlike modern psychologists, we cannot interview the people we are talking about to discover what they thought. Instead, we have to infer their mental processes and emotional responses from manuscripts and artefacts – rather as we would reconstruct the behaviour of an extinct animal from the fossil record. But the difficulty should not dissuade us from the duty, for the inner horizon is no less important than the others we have encountered. In fact, it is arguably even more significant – not only because it is the key to answering the fascinating question of whether the human character has changed over the centuries but also because it helps us to understand many of the other cultural developments described in this book.

In 1939 the sociologist Norbert Elias published the original German edition of his classic study, *The Civilising Process*. In the book he suggested that those forms of behaviour that we would consider rudimentary and rough – violence, insulting language, poor eating manners, dirtiness, public performance of bodily functions, sexual impropriety and so forth – were gradually suppressed by the adoption of higher standards of behaviour. Crucial to his argument was the concept that pride and shame forced people to exercise greater self-control to measure up to social expectations. Being ashamed of breaking wind or urinating in public meant people did these things more discreetly; while being proud of their high-quality clothes meant that individuals flaunted their wealth and taste.

Elias's study appeared in English in 1969. Three years later, Thomas Shelley Duval and Robert Wicklund provided the psychoanalytical foundation for the self-controlling mechanism that Elias had postulated when they published *A Theory of Objective Self-Awareness*. In summary,

> Self-Awareness Theory holds that, when people are self-focussed or self-aware, they compare the self with standards of correctness that specify how the self ought to think, feel and behave. The process of comparing the self with standards allows people to change their behaviour and to experience pride and dissatisfaction with the self. Self-awareness is thus a major mechanism of self-control.[2]

This concept is now universally accepted by psychologists. The more self-aware people are, the more thoroughly they assess their own behaviour and the more likely they are to conform to norms of social conduct. Identifying changes in self-awareness over the centuries therefore allows us to see why people generally stopped being violent and vulgar. But it also explains why many of the previously outlined horizons shifted as they did. Master masons, aware of the praise won by the builders of a 120ft-high cathedral tower, no doubt felt the pressure to exceed expectations when commissioned to construct one that was even taller. Slave owners, noticing a growing moral objection to slave markets, no longer wished to be seen buying and selling human beings. Men and women, ashamed of their illiteracy, taught themselves to read. This is why the 'mechanism' of self-awareness, self-evaluation and self-control is so important. It is intrinsic to all human decision-making beyond the basic requirements of day-to-day living. Self-awareness is therefore a factor in most aspects of cultural change – arguably all except those directly resulting from external pressures, such as plague, pestilence and the weather.

The title of this chapter is 'Individualism', however, which goes far beyond self-awareness. Self-awareness is being conscious of one's character, appearance, emotions and reputation. Individualism means independence of action and reasoning. The two are related in that increased self-awareness not only encourages people to *conform* to society's standards of behaviour – to avoid shame, as Elias states – but also to attempt to *surpass* social expectations in order to feel good about themselves, and so feel pride. This inspires them to act with greater initiative, to take risks and question orthodoxy, as other psychological studies have shown.[3] Growing self-awareness thus transformed the medieval personality in two ways. One was Norbert Elias's 'civilising process', in which individuals were incentivised by pride and shame to conform to ever higher standards of behaviour. The other, outlined here, was the 'individualising process', in which the expectation of pride incentivised individuals to take the initiative more often and behave more independently.

The Early Eleventh Century

At the outset of our period, as described in the early chapters of this book, people were largely defined by their function. There were those who fought, those who prayed and those who worked. What they *were* was less important in the eyes of contemporaries; it was what they *did* that mattered. But although the bishop of Laon regarded all three groups as mutually supportive, the reality was that the priests and the workforce functioned in prescribed ways in support of the decision-makers, the warriors. This group did not have to obey the others except perhaps the leading members of the clergy, who set the religious rules for the whole of society. As a result, there were significant differences in the range of choices available to each group and therefore in their scope for individual behaviour.

To begin with those who worked. It is difficult for us in the modern world to appreciate how few individual decision-making opportunities there were for ordinary people in 1000. The peasants who made up the vast majority of the population lived and worked communally. This was because cooperation often meant the difference between life and death. No one in the early eleventh century could have afforded to share Erasmus's opinion that 'the most disadvantageous peace is better than the most just war'. If you didn't fight an invader, you and your family were likely to be killed. Everyone had to obey his or her lord without question to maximise the chances of survival – by fighting as a single cohesive unit. The same applied to food production. At a time when harvests regularly failed, working as a team and obeying instructions maximised your chances of survival.

Individuals did not matter; it was the well-being of the community that was important.

In northern Europe, this communal way of living was due in no small part to the widespread adoption of the heavy plough in the ninth and tenth centuries. While it was the most efficient way of farming in areas with rich soils, the downside was that a heavy plough required a team of eight oxen to draw it. As a result, peasants were required to take collective responsibility for the cultivation of the land. Workers lived in close proximity to each other and shared the manor's assets. Everyone ploughed, sowed and harvested together in the fields. Even marriages were integrated with the production of food. Every peasant was required to marry in order to produce the next generation of the workforce. Single or widowed men or women who did not choose a marriage partner for themselves were allocated one by the manorial reeve. Brides were expected to marry young to maximise the number of children they could produce to work on the manor. No one among the workers was literate. Education was communal and practical. Children started work as soon as they were old enough to be useful.

Even when not working, peasants lived homogeneous lives. On Sundays and holy days they worshipped together. On feast days, they ate together. If someone hurt a member of the community or stole something from a house, the hue and cry was raised and all the men were expected to go in pursuit of the offender. If someone caught a disease, the chances were that everyone else would catch it too. Personal appearance and hygiene were a communal enterprise. Mothers wiped their children's faces, combed their hair and picked their lice; married women might attend to their husbands and their female friends in similar ways. There was no *self*-fashioning. People had no mirrors, so how they looked was down to their neighbours and relatives. All the clothes were homemade. And everyone was known by a single name. Peasants didn't need to be identified outside their community – where everyone knew each other – so there was no need for surnames. Nor was there any need to remember people from the past. When those who remembered them died, all trace of their existence was extinguished. A peasant's ancestry was simply the manor. There was no sense of family longevity.

With regard to status, no peasant owned his land: the lord did. Such a community was somewhat akin to the Society A we hypothesised in chapter three, in which everyone except the lord was equal. There *were* differing levels of peasant standing, of course, with some having the use of more land than others. An estate-management manual written in the Somerset area shortly after 1000 lists the types of serf on a manor as the *geneat* (the highest-status farm worker), cottager (lower-status farm worker), *gebur* (labourer), beekeeper, swineherd, oxherd, cowherd, shepherd, goatherd, cheesemaker, barley-keeper, wood-ward and hayward.[4] They all had differing duties to perform but otherwise their lives were equally governed by the decisions of the lord's reeve. All their homes would have looked more or less the same, made with local materials. If one of them needed help building his house or making a barn for his crops, he called on his kinsfolk and neighbours. He didn't need to pay anyone for such work but would help them in return. Most everyday items were created on the manor, so everybody's possessions were made of the same locally produced materials. They might have been able to barter or buy an earthenware crock, but peasants at this time owned very few objects. Many of them would have had only a single tunic and a cloak or other overgarment. Jewellery was quite out of their reach: most women would have fastened their clothes with a pin of animal bone, not metal. Their individualism was restricted to their performance of specific skills and their behaviour in relation to their families and other members of the community. Personality was largely a matter of physical appearance and strength, and natural traits like their voice, quick-wittedness and sense of humour.

All this means that the 'self' of which most peasants were conscious was less personal than communal. This implies less individual self-evaluation, which would have resulted in less ostentation and less self-control. Peasants were susceptible to the passions of everyday life, of course – and were more liable to resort to violence, vulgarity and sexual misbehaviour – but they would have felt greater shame in being accused of offences that threatened the productivity of the manor, such as idleness and negligence.[5] Unless a man broke his bonds and ran away, he was little more than a worker on a farm that carried on producing food for centuries for the benefit of the community and the lord's household. People did run away from time to time, to become a free labourer in a town or to embark on a life of crime. But although we may read of peasants lamenting how hard they had to work, we do not come across them rising up against their lords in this period. Robin Hood-like stories of rebellion belong to the fourteenth century and later. Peasants accepted their lot because they simply did not know any different.

Very few country people fell outside these parameters. There were a few farmers who owned their own fields outright – who were independent of the control of a manorial lord – but their freedom was curtailed to a large extent by the cycles of the farming year and the vicissitudes of the weather. They had the freedom to travel to a market and buy objects to denote their status but, beyond that, they had little scope for exploring or demonstrating their individuality. They had relatively few decision-making opportunities. They could never leave their farms for long.

Things were different for the families of 'those who fought'. They were required to travel and make important choices on a regular basis. They were responsible for the administration, good governance and defence of their households and estates. They often had the power of life and death over anyone who committed crimes on their land. They also had control over any churches they had built and the priests they appointed to serve in them. All the decisions these roles entailed would have given rise to processes of self-evaluation. Moreover, they had wealth and power. They bought fine tunics, knives, cloaks, furs, rings and brooches for their families and their followers. They proudly displayed the symbols of their status – from weapons, armour and riding horses to tapestries, tablecloths and precious ornaments. They had the means and liberty to take themselves on long pilgrimages – in some cases as far as Rome or Jerusalem.

Having said this, even the wealthy did not enjoy unlimited individual freedom. They were expected to obey the king and any intermediary overlord. They were obliged to lead men into battle. Even if they could afford more food, the markets offered few exotic or luxurious items, so they were forced to eat the same things as everyone else of their class. Being constantly surrounded by servants, tenants, messengers, retainers, priests and visitors, they enjoyed little privacy. As for their children, their sons had only two options: either to take up the sword or the cross. Their daughters could choose to marry or enter a nunnery – if, that is, their parents gave them the choice.

Men and women who opted to go into the Church fell somewhere between the other two groups. Abbots, bishops and other senior clergymen had many decision-making opportunities. These arose from their wide range of responsibilities, which included supervising monks and nuns, and managing their estates, as well as giving spiritual advice to the king and his nobles. Priests at the bottom of the ecclesiastical

ladder had fewer choices. Young people who entered a monastery had
no possessions of their own. They too knew little privacy – sleeping,
praying, eating and working as a community. What would have filled
them with pride? Doing their duty to God, bringing honour to the
abbey, pleasing its senior officers, working hard on the estates, singing
well at Mass and copying out and illuminating a page of a text beautifully. Again, their sense of self would have been more communal than
personal.

With regard to the free townsmen, civic leaders had more independence and thus more scope for individualism. They oversaw the
markets and administered local justice. In times of war, they arranged
for the defence of the walls. The wealthy could adorn themselves and
their families with status symbols. London was a trading town for merchants from as far as Norway, Denmark, Germany and northern
France; York too was full of Danish traders. However, only a tiny proportion of the urban population travelled long distances. Similarly,
there were many fewer craftsmen than in later centuries. Most townsmen were bound to accept the orders of their employer. They would
have been more familiar with money than their country cousins but,
having little of it themselves, they would have purchased relatively few
items other than food. And although they would have met more
strangers – and thus been more conscious of the differences in people's
dress, language and customs – this would have had little impact on
their individuality and personal freedom, which was limited by the
necessary functions they needed to perform to stay alive.

1050–1200: Religious Self-awareness and Individualism

When we look at the development of individualism after about 1050,
it is best to consider the religious and secular elements separately. This
is because pride and shame were not the sole motivating factors in the
pursuit of religious activities. Spiritual aspects, such as the hope of
heavenly rewards or earthly miracles, played a major role. People went
on pilgrimages primarily for the sake of their soul or to cure a particular ailment. Of course, pride would have given them a further incentive
to visit far-off places but we should not presume the same mechanism
was at work in both religious and secular undertakings.

As we saw in chapter one, there was a marked increase in obedience to the Church in the late eleventh century. Successive popes imposed their control on the moral behaviour of the whole of Christendom. This included emphasising the sanctity of marriage. As the pope lacked coercive power to force kings and lords to accept such standards, we should read their widespread acquiescence as indicative of greater religious self-awareness and self-control. Kings saw value in encouraging their subjects to accept these standards and took pride in doing so themselves. And of course there were direct spiritual benefits in following the pope's directives. The overall result was greater religious conformity.

Papal authority was not the sole cause of the improvement in spiritual standards in the late eleventh century. It seems that a greater religiosity was generally pervading society. Take, for example, this list of penances imposed on the Normans who had fought at Hastings issued by Ermenfrid, bishop of Sion in Switzerland, when he came to England in 1070:

> Anyone who knows that he killed a man in the great battle must do penance for one year for each man that he killed. Anyone who wounded a man and does not know whether he killed him or not must do penance for forty days for each man he thus struck (if he can remember the number), either continuously or at intervals. Anyone who does not know the number of those he wounded or killed must, at the discretion of his bishop, do one penance for one day in each week for the remainder of his life; or, if he can, let him redeem his sin by a perpetual alms – either by building or endowing a church. The clergymen who fought, or who were armed for fighting, must do penance as if they had committed these sins in their own country, for they are forbidden by canon law to do battle . . .[6]

This may well strike you as astonishing. You would not expect Norman warriors to do penance for killing men in a battle. Penance for *not* killing them, perhaps, but not for doing their job. Nevertheless, herein we see them being instructed to accept a senior clergyman's moral judgement on their behaviour, even though fighting was their *raison d'être*.

This widespread uplift in spiritual self-awareness was accompanied by an enhanced desire for self-knowledge. This was expressed in the ancient Greek imperative 'Know thyself', which was remembered in medieval times on account of it being mentioned in Plato's

Dialogues. A similar phrase appears above the door of the church of Sant'Angelo in Formis, southern Italy, which was carved about 1070: 'You will climb to heaven if you know yourself.'[7] The theologian and early memoirist Guibert of Nogent wrote in 1108 that 'No preaching seems to me more profitable than that which reveals a man to himself.' Peter Abelard gave his *Ethics*, written in the 1130s, the alternative title of 'Know thyself' because understanding your own intentions was the key to living a moral life. Aelred of Rievaulx would have agreed. 'How much does a man know if he does not know himself?' he asked in his *Mirror of Charity*, written about 1142. The emphasis on self-knowledge appears over and over again in the works of twelfth-century theologians: people should approach God inwardly, through self-discovery and, by implication, self-evaluation.[8]

Some men readily embraced this exhortation to explore their individual personalities. One early example is the memoir by Otloh of Saint Emmeram, a prolific composer of saints' lives and theological works, who died about 1070. This is the first sustained piece of European autobiography since St Augustine of Hippo wrote his *Confessions* at the end of the fourth century. Otloh was a remarkable self-analyst, even going so far as to declare that he had had personal doubts about God's existence:

> For a long time I found myself tormented by a compulsion to doubt altogether the reliability of Holy Scripture and even the existence of God himself . . . I was altogether enveloped by complete doubt and darkness of mind, and I thoroughly doubted if there were any truth or profit in the Bible or if Almighty God existed.[9]

Otloh made this admission to show that even someone as imperfect as he was could be redeemed. In other words, he evaluated his own life and used it as an example of divine providence.

The most famous autobiographer of the period, the theologian and philosopher Peter Abelard, followed suit. He goes into extraordinarily frank detail in his *Historia Calamitatum* (History of Calamities), written in the 1130s. He holds nothing back from his account of his passionate love for Heloise – a young woman he was tutoring – and the subsequent birth of their child, their secret marriage and the savage removal of his private parts one night by hired thugs. He discusses just as

honestly and fully the persecution he suffered at the hands of orthodox
leaders of the Church, principally Bernard of Clairvaux, and the public
condemnation and destruction of his works:

> Thus did it come to pass that while I was utterly absorbed in pride and
> sensuality, divine grace, the cure for both diseases, was forced upon
> me . . . First was I punished for my sensuality, and then for my pride.
> For my sensuality I lost those things whereby I practised it; for my
> pride, engendered in me by my knowledge of letters . . . I knew the
> humiliation of seeing burned the very book in which I most gloried.
> And now it is my desire that you should know the stories of these two
> happenings, understanding them more truly from learning the very
> facts than from hearing what is spoken of them, and in the order in
> which they came about.[10]

Although Abelard's purpose in writing was to show how one might
deal with any adversity by trusting in God, his pride in his own intellectual brilliance and his shame in being castrated – and his readiness to
write about such things – are all revealing of his heightened self-
awareness and individuality. The principal difference between his
perspective and our modern one is that an author's religious views
today would be considered subservient or irrelevant to the human
story, whereas in Abelard's case, his relationship with God was his principal purpose in writing. As he states at the end of the book:

> We should endure our persecutions all the more steadfastly the more
> bitterly they harm us. We should not doubt that even if they are not
> according to our deserts, at least they serve for the purifying of our
> souls. And since all things are done in accordance with the divine order-
> ing, let everyone of true faith console himself amid all his afflictions
> with the thought that the great goodness of God permits nothing to be
> done without reason, and brings to a good end whatsoever may seem
> to happen wrongfully . . . Whosoever grows wrathful for any reason
> against his sufferings has therein departed from the way of the just,
> because these things have happened to him by divine dispensation.

People's increasing levels of self-awareness were boosted even further in the 1140s by the development of the concept of Purgatory.
Until then it had been widely believed that when you died you went

directly to Heaven or to Hell. But the idea began to spread that while a few saints did go straight to Heaven and some awful sinners were immediately despatched to Hell, most people found themselves in Purgatory. Prayers said by the living could considerably shorten the length of time the soul of the dead person had to stay there. As a result, wealthy lords and ladies founded religious houses in greater numbers than ever before to facilitate the singing of Masses for their souls. In England, the number of monasteries more than quadrupled between 1100 and 1216, from 151 to 728. Any parish that did not already have a church quickly acquired one. Worshippers of all classes could pray therein for the souls of their kinsfolk and friends, as well as those of the family of the lord who had built the church.

Purgatory could only have amplified people's self-awareness – and not just in religious terms. Previously, they had only needed to deal with their fellow parishioners in *life*; now they also had to consider their relationships with them after death. 'How will people think of me after I am gone?' they would have wondered. 'Will the other people in this church pray for me after I am dead?' Peasants necessarily began to consider their posthumous reputation among their fellow manorial workers. Trying to imagine how other people saw them, they were forced to concentrate on the image they would leave behind in other people's minds when they died. Whereas the attributes that had previously made up their identities were largely beyond their control – appearance, skills and so forth – now they had to be mindful of their general behaviour in order to avoid the recriminations of others. This no doubt encouraged them to aim for higher standards in daily life, in line with the expectations of their communities. Elias's civilising process was already underway.

Another possible consequence of this heightened religious self-awareness was the growth in the numbers of domestic and international pilgrims. More and more relics appeared in Europe, attracting the devoted and the medically desperate. Freemen started to travel regularly to pray at distant shrines. Whole churches were rebuilt with the income generated. After the killing of Thomas Becket in Canterbury in 1170, for example, pilgrims to his tomb brought in an average of more than £400 per year, which was more than most lords received.[11] People felt pride in meeting their religious obligations and knew that such devotion increased their social standing. But not everyone went on a pilgrimage and few could afford – or dared – to go as far as Rome,

Santiago or Jerusalem. Therefore, although we might see the large numbers of pilgrims as being indicative of crowd behaviour, it was actually a winnowing out of the faithful from the mass. The pilgrim was doing something individualistic, identifying himself with a saint's relics. Simply by making a journey to a shrine, he or she became one of the few, not the many.

Education also allowed people to define themselves in new ways. From the late eleventh century, some cathedrals and leading monasteries had maintained schools to prepare well-born students for positions in the Church. A few individuals had gone on to study further, becoming scholars at the forefront of the expansion of knowledge, rediscovering ancient Greek and Roman texts in Arabic translations in the libraries of Spain and Italy. There they also encountered the mathematical, medicinal and astronomical works of Arab writers, which they translated into Latin. In turn, these men and their reputations inspired other scholars and students. A small but significant body of learned men emerged who occupied a distinct position in European society: their works form the core of what historians now call the Twelfth-Century Renaissance. At the same time, ground-breaking theologians and philosophers presented new ways of seeing the world – men like Anselm of Laon, John of Salisbury and Peter Abelard. The combination of the new philosophy and theology and the rediscovered works of classical wisdom gradually led to the development of the earliest universities. Paris became an especially important seat of learning. At Bologna, scholars advanced the science of jurisprudence. Medicine was the speciality at Salerno. Men of great ability started to be appreciated not just for their high birth and their leadership skills but for their minds.

1050–1200: Secular Self-awareness and Individualism

When we turn to the secular side of life, we find people increasingly identifying with smaller and smaller groups, hiving themselves off from the mass of other people by adopting signs and signifiers that were unique and personal to them. Nowhere is this more apparent than with the growth of the family as an institution. Today we take it for granted that medieval families passed on their titles, manors and castles according to the rules of primogeniture. But this had not always been the case. Not until the eleventh century did inheritance patterns become firmly established, so that eldest sons could expect to inherit their father's estates as a matter of course. Only after that could they start to dignify their ancestral seat by adopting its name as their own. Very few families of knightly rank and above had a hereditary surname before 1050; almost all did by 1200, and it was more often than not the name of their principal manor.

The certainty of a landed inheritance and the dignity of a family name provided the bedrock on which landowning families could build stronger and longer-lasting identities. One essential element was heraldic design. Around 1150, knights started to have individual patterns painted on their shields so their followers could recognise them in battle, when their features were obscured by their war helms. By the end of the century, it was generally accepted that the sons of a knight inherited the design. In addition, lords transferred their coats of arms to their seal matrices, linking the design with their personal authority. Most high-ranking families now also founded an abbey to serve as their family's special place of worship, often within a mile or two of their principal seat. Priests in the abbey compiled family chronicles. They sang Masses for their patrons' souls and said prayers for the living members of the family. Very often, the abbey was where family members were laid to rest. With a unique ancestral seat, a unique spiritual home, a unique coat of arms and a unique seal, a twelfth-century landed family – headed by a single lord – had many ways of asserting its identity and its independent standing. Those who went on crusade brought honour to the family. So too did those lords who took leading roles in politics or war. Such families were still classifiable as 'those who fought' but now they were clearly identifiable subsets of that group.

At the same time as the growth of the family, socially elevated people were becoming more sensitive to their secular reputations. The clearest evidence for this is the series of guides to courtly behaviour that appeared at the end of the twelfth century.[12] The most popular example, *The Book of the Civilised Man*, written by Daniel Beccles, was based on the court of 'old King Henry' – that is, Henry II of England, who reigned from 1154 to 1189. It instructs young courtiers how to do such things as sing in chapel, manage servants and greet a lord. It also offers practical advice, such as 'Don't mount your horse in the hall' and 'At night, the doors, windows and ways into the house should be closed. Hidden inside there should be fire, candles and lamp oil, weapons and able young men, and the hall will be safe enough.' It also touches on a number of sexual matters, such as not sleeping with your godmother or your goddaughters, and when feeling the need to visit a prostitute, to 'look for one who is not visited by absolutely everyone, drain your testicles and leave quickly'. Much of the guidance concerns table manners: 'When you pick up food with your spoon, do not shovel it on board with your thumb. Two guests should not share one spoon. Do not take the spoon you were provided with at dinner home with you.' The section dealing with bodily emissions directly refers to feelings of shame:

> Do not spring vengeance upon a defecating enemy and do not disturb him . . . it dishonours you to harm someone in that condition . . . In public, your bottom should emit no secret winds past your thighs. It disgraces you if other people notice any of your smelly filth.[13]

Of course, such books of advice were only for the wealthy and literate. But what the social elite did, everyone else tried to emulate. And evidently people did try to follow these guidelines because this text and others like it were widely copied and revised until the sixteenth century.

The significance of people adopting such codes of behaviour is that, unlike compliance with the law, etiquette was not backed up with the threat of force. Therefore, the popularity of these works suggests an increasing sensitivity to personal criticism of behaviour and a general heightening of feelings of pride and shame. This is in line with the mechanism of self-awareness, self-evaluation and self-control outlined at the start of this chapter. The question we now need to answer is whether this new social self-awareness contributed to the individualising process as well as the civilising one.

The Book of the Civilised Man contains many references to sexual relations, moral problems and how to behave at court. Thus it is closely aligned with codes of chivalry, which also developed in the twelfth century. Knights were supposed to be pious, honest, loyal, brave and respectful of the weak, especially women and children. At the same time, they were expected to excel in feats of arms, bravery and Christian fortitude. Heroic stories of crusaders taking on vast numbers of Muslim warriors were the tales of individualism promoted by this supposedly conformist code of conduct. And while knights were required to be utterly loyal to their lord, there was a romantic element in which each one also served the lady who had accepted him into her service as her champion. Thus, ironically, in order to conform, knights had to stand out from the crowd. In later centuries, chivalric ideas spawned an extensive and varied literature, including the famous tales of Arthur and his Knights of the Round Table, many of which celebrate individual prowess. In the fourteenth century, Edward III deliberately used the Arthurian myths to inspire his most ambitious warriors to feats of extraordinary courage in fighting the French. There is no doubt that pride and shame were the principal levers of the mechanism encouraging men to take such risks and, indeed, to live up to all the many expectations of a chivalric knight.

At the same time as chivalry was developing, courtly poets known as troubadours or trouvères were beginning to emerge in France – the Occitan-speaking troubadours in the south-west, the French-speaking trouvères in the north. They soon inspired the minnesingers in Germany and Austria. Some of them were of the highest social rank: William IX, duke of Aquitaine, was one of the very first troubadours, while the Holy Roman Emperor, Henry VI, and several margraves and dukes appear among the ranks of the minnesingers. Indeed, their high status goes a long way to explain the remarkable individualism that the troubadours displayed from the outset. William IX was excommunicated twice and had a picture of his mistress painted on his shield, explaining that 'he wished to bear her in battle as she had borne him in bed' – only a high-ranking lord would have been able to get away with things like that.[14] (His wife was not impressed and stomped off to live in Fontevraud Abbey.) Not all were high born – the troubadour Marcabru, for example, had been left as a baby on someone's doorstep – but most were of relatively high social status and so were their audiences. Many of those whose works have been preserved sang or recited a life story as a prelude to their performances. Unfortunately for historians, these were often exaggerated or wholly fictitious. Nevertheless, the troubadours' depiction of themselves as personages with unique life experiences reveals a heightened sense of individualism in twelfth-century society.

The troubadours' poems were mostly about courtly love, sexual desire and chivalric ideals (although the Germans in particular liked to throw in a few good drinking songs). In choosing such themes they were deliberately flouting the religious expectations of the age. They were joined in this by another group of highly individualistic poets, the goliards, most of whom were young students writing in Latin. As many of them were noblemen's younger sons who had been sent off against their will to study in Paris and similar cathedral schools, their works were satirical and often deeply mocking of the Church. Thus, being intellectual renegades, they created a body of truly original and individualistic literature. One of the most popular writers was known as the Archpoet, whose *Confession*, written in the 1160s, was copied many times. It is so spirited, irreverent and timeless that it is worth quoting several verses from Helen Waddell's inspired 1929 translation:

> Since it is the property
> Of the sapient
> To sit firm upon a rock,
> It is evident
> That I am a fool, since I
> Am a flowing river,
> Never under the same sky,
> Transient for ever.
>
> Hither, thither, masterless
> Ship upon the sea,
> Wandering through the ways of air,
> Go the birds like me.
> Bound am I by ne'er a bond,
> Prisoner to no key,
> Questing go I for my kind,
> Find depravity.
>
> Never yet could I endure
> Soberness and sadness,
> Jests I love and sweeter than
> Honey find I gladness.
> Whatsoever Venus bids
> Is a joy excelling,
> Never in an evil heart
> Did she make her dwelling . . .

Down the broad way I go,
Young and unregretting,
Wrap me in my vices up,
Virtue all forgetting,
Greedier for all delight
Than heaven to enter in:
Since the soul in me is dead,
Better save the skin . . .

For on this my heart is set:
When the hour is nigh me,
Let me in the tavern die,
With a tankard by me,
While the angels looking down
Joyously start singing:
God, may you show mercy to
One who loves his drinking.

Good my lord, the case is heard,
I myself betray me,
And affirm myself to be
All my fellows say me.
See, they in thy presence are:
Let whoe'er hath known
His own heart and found it clean,
Cast at me the stone.[15]

The backdrop to all the above developments was an improving and expanding economy in the wake of the Medieval Warm Period. The milder climate permitted unprecedented levels of trade. By the mid-twelfth century, the six Champagne Fairs held annually in north-eastern France were underway. These saw Italian merchants come north over the Alps with dyes, furs, silks, drugs and spices and other such exotica. Other traders arrived from England, northern France, Germany and the Low Countries with leather, fleeces and woollen and linen cloth. Wealth flowed from city to city and with it came new styles, fabrics, foods and consumer objects.

All these new luxuries allowed the rich to mark themselves out from the poor. This was especially the case in a large city like London, where everything was on offer, as William FitzStephen explained in 1173:

> In London, on the riverbank amidst the ships, [there is] wine for sale from the wine vaults and a public cookshop. On a daily basis there, depending on the season, can be found fried or boiled foods and dishes; fish large and small; meat – lower quality for the poor, finer cuts for the wealthy – game and fowl (large and small). If friends arrive unexpectedly at the home of some citizen and they, tired and hungry after their journey, prefer not to wait until food may be got in and cooked, or till servants bring water for hands and bread, they can in the meantime pay a quick visit to the riverside, where anything they might desire is immediately available . . . Those with a fancy for delicacies can obtain for themselves the meat of goose, guinea-hen or woodcock – finding what they're after is no great chore, since all the delicacies are set out in front of them. Middlemen from every nation under heaven are pleased to bring to the city ships full of merchandise . . . crimson silks from China; French wines; and sable, vair and miniver from the far lands where the Rus and Norsemen dwell.[16]

Cities offered a smorgasbord of choices and ways to enhance your appearance and display your personality. When Eleanor of Aquitaine – granddaughter of the troubadour William IX – arrived in Paris to marry Louis VII of France in 1137, she brought all the fashions of the south with her, and self-aware people would have felt bound to try to emulate them. Aristocratic women's clothing started to be tailored to fit the body, particularly in the long dress known as the *bliant* and the figure-hugging corsage. These were not convenient clothes – you had to be stitched into them every time you put them on – but women like Eleanor were prepared to suffer for the sake of fashion. Their hair, which previously would have been totally covered in a headdress, was now allowed to fall naturally or in plaits. Self-fashioning had arrived. Once upon a time, heroines had been presented in literature as stout, capable wives and mothers who could run an estate while their husbands were away fighting. Now, in the days of troubadours and trouvères, what mattered most was that they were young and beautiful – and ready to fall in love.[17]

Unsurprisingly, the churchmen of the time did not approve. But, from a historical point of view, thank heavens they didn't because their castigations provide rare evidence of otherwise ephemeral behaviour. This, for example, is what Bernard of Clairvaux wrote to a young woman called Sophia who had taken a vow of chastity:

> Silk, purple and paint have their beauty, but they do not impart it. They show their own beauty when applied to the body, but they do not make the body beautiful . . . The comeliness which goes on with clothes, comes off with clothes, it belongs to the clothes and not the clothed . . . Consider it wholly beneath you to borrow your appearance from the furs of animals and the work of worms [silk], let what you have be sufficient for you . . . The ornaments of a queen have no beauty like the blushes of natural modesty which colour the cheeks of a virgin.[18]

The references to 'silk' and 'purple' are striking enough – purple being an extremely costly dye to obtain, and traditionally reserved for Roman emperors. However, the really remarkable word is 'paint'. Bernard died in 1153, so this passage indicates that makeup was being used in the first half of the twelfth century. A troubadour called Pierre de Vic, who was writing at the end of the century, has left us an entire song in the form of a discussion between a monk and God about 'ladies who paint themselves . . . who heighten their complexion and make their skin shine with paint that should be used on statues'.[19] These are among the first European references to the use of makeup since the days of ancient Rome. What's more, de Vic's song also suggests that these women were using mirrors – they 'painted *themselves*'.

Mirrors have existed since prehistoric times. Several decorated Celtic bronze examples have survived, as have many ancient Roman examples – some of which were made of silver but others of glass. There are references to mirrors in both the New Testament (in the Epistle of James) and the *Confessions* of St Augustine. But after the fall of the Roman Empire, they vanish from literature. They also disappear from the European archaeological record. It appears that the knowledge of their manufacture was lost. This is perhaps why the rediscovery of the mirror has not been appreciated by historians. Since they were invented in ancient times, people tend to presume they have always been around. At the start of the Middle Ages, they simply weren't.

Mirrors reappeared in Europe during the early twelfth century. The only European-made example from this period that I have come across is the bronze case that once contained a small silver mirror, 11 cm in diameter, which is now in the Metropolitan Museum of Art in New York.[20] In addition, it is possible that some similarly sized bronze mirrors made their way to Europe from Asia and the Middle East at about this time.[21] But despite their rarity today, we can be confident they were widely used in noble circles on account of the number of works entitled 'The Mirror of . . .' that were composed in the early twelfth century. Authors would not have chosen this metaphorical title if the intended readers had no idea what a mirror was. One of the earliest instances is a book by Honorius of Autun entitled *Imago Mundi* – literally, 'Image of the World' – in which the author states he has tried to describe the universe 'as if it were seen in a mirror'.[22] Honorius, who lived most of his life in present-day Switzerland and died in about 1156, also produced a book of sermons which he called *Speculum Ecclesiae* ('the Mirror of the Church'). Similar titles were given to works created at this time in a variety of places. An anonymous *Mirror of Virgins* was written in Germany in about 1140. Aelred of Rievaulx composed his *Mirror of Charity* in Yorkshire in about 1142. William of Saint Thierry, who lived in Rheims and died in 1148, wrote *The Mirror of Faith*. There is no doubt that mirrors were known across Europe by 1150 – at least among the highly educated and wealthy members of society.

With regard to people's self-awareness, the importance of the mirror cannot be overstated. When men and women first looked at their faces in a mirror they would have seen themselves more or less as other people saw them. It is not surprising that the introduction of the mirror coincided with the development of Purgatory and the codes of courteous behaviour. All three led to greater self-awareness and self-evaluation. But whereas the other two prompted people to reflect on what they *did*, the mirror prompted them to reflect on what they *were*. Although the men and women who could afford a mirror at this time were already among the most independent members of society – having greater decision-making powers than anyone else – the mirror confirmed their individuality, enhanced their self-awareness, and gently urged them to obey the ancient imperative 'Know thyself'.

By the end of the twelfth century, you could still describe people in terms of their function. The three original groups – 'those who fought', 'those who prayed' and 'those who worked' – were still easily recognisable. But there were many people who did not fall into one of these categories. Some could be described as 'those who traded', others as 'those who judged', 'those who studied' or 'those who entertained'.

Even the ranks of workers were not what they had once been. For example, there was now a considerable body of skilled architectural masons and carpenters building the castles, cathedrals and churches for which the Middle Ages are famous. More and more sectors were being hived off from the collective grouping of 'those who worked'. Although peasants still made up the majority of the population and remained locked into traditional communities, the wealthy began to pride themselves on their independence and defined themselves in new ways: family, chivalry, duties, education, status symbols, fashion and so forth. The biggest difference between their individuality and that of the modern world was that their identity was still a subset of their faith. Every aspect of their lives was linked to religion. As we have seen, a noble family did not just have its ancestral seat but also a spiritual home in the form of its chosen abbey. For those who embarked on their autobiographies, God was still at the centre of their lives, as He had been for St Augustine in the fourth century. Even those like the goliards, who criticised the self-righteousness and prim morality of supposedly holy men, did not doubt God or the divine order of things. The spiritual umbilical cord was still attached to the whole of society.

1200–1345

These patterns of individual behaviour broadly continued in wealthy circles throughout the thirteenth and early fourteenth centuries. But they also began to filter down to the lower classes. Minor landowners who saw a mirror knew that they too wanted one. Townsmen who noticed that the educated younger sons of noble families could achieve high positions of authority in the Church or the law similarly wished their own sons to benefit from a comparable education. People have always tried to emulate their social superiors: in the Middle Ages, it was just a question of whether you could afford to do so – and whether the authorities would allow you.

While the wealthy were learning how to express themselves in the ways mentioned above, peasants were beginning to discover individualism through a range of new economic opportunities. These gave them choices and the ability to distinguish themselves – in many cases, for the first time. Key to the change was trade. Over 1,600 English markets were given permission to start up between 1100 and 1300. In addition, there were about a thousand annual fairs by the early four-teenth century. These developments resulted in a sudden and massive increase in ordinary people's ability to buy things that they could not make for themselves. In the 1150s, when relatively few individuals in England were using coins on a daily basis, the kingdom's money sup-ply amounted to about 6d per head of the population; by 1320, that had grown to 10s. And that doesn't take into consideration the amount of credit available.[23] The population doubled but the money supply increased approximately forty times. For those who could now sell their products in a market, this amounted to the chance to distinguish themselves from their neighbours in ways not previously possible.

As we have already seen, the root cause of this change was the Medi-eval Warm Period. However, the process was not as simple as better weather allowing farmers to produce more crops and trade their sur-pluses. Eleventh- and twelfth-century peasants were not free to leave their manors to go to market. Nor could they simply set up trading centres without royal permission. Instead, manorial lords set up the markets that facilitated the growth of the economy and the develop-ment of lower-class individualism. Often they had no choice. As the amount of available land ran out in the early thirteenth century, they could either carry on subdividing tenements into smaller and smaller livings, as we saw in chapter three, or they could let their peasants head off to a market town. The first strategy resulted in tenements too small to support a family. The second lost the lord his peasants' service. There-fore a third option had to be considered: establishing a new market within his own manor. This was potentially in everyone's best interests. It meant a lord could retain his workforce while attracting more busi-ness. If one of his tenants learnt how to make shoes, for example, and if he sold those shoes in the new market, he no longer needed any land to feed his family: he could buy everything he required. The lord would continue to benefit from his service and, at the same time, he would gain from the rents the man paid on his house and market stall. If the market then became a borough, all sorts of traders might come and buy the small plots of freehold land around the marketplace and set up shops, bringing the lord yet more money in rent and market tolls.

Mention of freehold land draws attention to another important fac-tor underpinning the economic prosperity and individualism of the rural peasantry at this time. Before 1150, it would have been difficult to disentangle English land ownership from its feudal tenure. But after

Henry II's accession in 1154, the common law was revised to accommodate a man or woman owning freehold land within someone else's manor.[24] Some lords offered smallholdings to their men-at-arms in return for loyal service. For those who owned perhaps ten or twenty manors totalling 30–60,000 acres, giving away farms of 50–100 acres to each of a dozen worthy followers was a good investment: the beneficiaries would forever be grateful and loyal. Other lords sold off portions of land freehold or leased it to free tenants. In so doing, they laid the foundations of a rural middle class.

By the early fourteenth century, most manors were a hotchpotch of ownerships and titles. On top of the old-style unfree peasantry you had freeholders and leaseholders, market traders and borough freemen. Some yeomen had 100 acres or more; some labourers had nothing but their cottage garden. In addition, at the heart of the manor, there were now fifty or sixty houses arranged around a market square, where people would gather once a week to buy and sell and socialise. The peasantry had become stratified. They still did many things as a community – from attending the manorial court to responding when someone raised the alarm – but they were now living more diverse, individual lives, with different prospects and different futures. They were buying things at markets and fairs that set them apart from their neighbours: iron pots, finer cloth, ivory combs, cushions, silver rings and belt buckles – perhaps even a set of silver spoons, in the case of a prosperous yeoman. And some boys and young men received an education. Social mobility was greater than it had ever been. In the cities and towns, working men could define themselves as members of a guild, as freemen of the town, as belonging to a religious fraternity or as parishioners – or all these things. They also adopted surnames, like their social superiors. Some took the name of their birthplace; others called themselves after their trade or adopted a nickname. And their surnames, like those of aristocrats, soon became hereditary. For all but the poorest families, the multidimensional process of self-definition was well underway by the time of the Black Death.

1345–1500

It is impossible at this distance in time fully to appreciate the psychological impact of the Black Death. What is clear, however, is that it acted as an accelerant on many aspects of life. United in their faith in God when the disease hit, people were forced to ask 'why me?' or 'why my spouse, my child?' And just as the question was rooted in religion, so too were the answers. Some people started thinking heretical thoughts. Had their sins been so numerous that God wished to punish them? Or did the tragedy actually have nothing to do with God's will? Was it the result of rotten meat being sold in unregulated markets, as some physicians believed? Was it the result of a conjunction of the planets, as scholars from the University of Paris maintained? Had God perhaps been unable to stop it? Whereas up to this point religious belief had generally brought people together, now it started to divide them.

The plague acted as an accelerant on economic individualism too, as we saw in chapter three. The deaths of approximately 40 per cent of the population left the survivors with considerable additional resources. Livestock was inherited, the furniture and tools in the houses of the deceased were shared out, and farmland was allocated to new tenants. Serfs found themselves free to leave their manors and sell their labour to other lords, thereby replacing their feudal bonds with financial obligations. Others moved into the towns to become craftsmen. All these developments enhanced the standing, the wealth and the independence of the common man and woman. Those who had made money ate meat regularly and wore furs and dyed clothes, distinguishing themselves from their neighbours. Edward III was so disturbed by the display of such status symbols among the lower classes that he introduced sumptuary laws limiting what they were allowed to wear and eat. He also enacted the 1351 Statute of Labourers, which sought to prevent peasants from leaving their manors to seek higher wages. But there was no holding back the tide. Those who remained put and did *not* make money found their lack of self-improvement – their poverty – started to define them as much as liberty and wealth started to define their more enterprising ex-neighbours.

At the same time as peasants' standards of living began to rise rapidly, ordinary Englishmen found they were able to devastate enemy armies with the massed use of the longbow, as mentioned in chapter two. When a peasant earning perhaps £3 per year could bring down and kill a knight whose horse and armour alone were worth £50 or more, it was only natural that he and his kind should question the social order: they could take pride in having become 'those who fought' themselves. Such military prowess, combined with far greater economic power, encouraged working people to think differently about their social superiors. It is no coincidence that from this point on, stories of the rebel Robin Hood, robbing from the rich to give to the poor, started to grow in popularity. Peasants had gained a new sense of their individual worth.

The consequences are easily dismissed as crowd behaviour but in fact they were of great importance for the development of individualism. Demonstrating your individuality by wearing exotic furs or brilliantly dyed cloth is one thing, but doing so by questioning the entire social order is quite another. And this is precisely what happened. Revolts broke out across Europe. The French *Jacquerie* of 1358 saw an unprecedented explosion of violence against the nobility. It began with the well-planned assassination of nine noblemen at a village called Saint-Leu-d'Esserent, which is about twenty-three miles south-east of Beauvais. Within weeks, it had engulfed the whole of northern France. Many lords and ladies were killed. Several towns were briefly taken over. Although the stories of the atrocities told by contemporary chroniclers exaggerate the offences – Jean le Bel describes a knight being roasted on a spit and his wife being raped and then forced to eat his flesh before having her brains bashed out – their tone conveys something of the chroniclers' shock that the peasantry could revolt. This, for example, is from Jean Froissart's chronicle:

> Some of the inhabitants of the country towns assembled together in the Beauvais region, without any leader; they were not at first more than one hundred men. They said that the nobles of the kingdom of France, knights and squires, were a disgrace to it, and that it would be a very meritorious act to destroy them all; to which proposition everyone assented, and added, 'shame on him that saves the gentlemen from being destroyed'. They then, without further counsel, collected themselves in a body, and with no other arms than the staves shod with iron which some had, and others with knives, marched to the house of a knight who lived near, and, breaking it open, murdered the knight, his lady, and all the children, both great and small; they then burned the house.
>
> After this, their second expedition was to the strong castle of another knight, which they took, and, having tied him to a stake, many of them violated his wife and daughter before his eyes; they then murdered the

lady, her daughter, and the other children, and last of all the knight himself, with much cruelty. They destroyed and burned his castle. They did the like to many castles and handsome houses; and their numbers increased so much that they were in a short time upward of six thousand . . .

These wicked people, without leader and without arms, plundered and burned all the houses they came to, murdered every gentleman, and violated every lady and damsel they could find. He who committed the most atrocious actions, such as no human creature would have imagined, was the most applauded and considered as the greatest man among them.[25]

To hear such stories – let alone witness the violence – must have been deeply disturbing. No one had seen a peasant uprising on this scale before. But the *Jacquerie* was not to be the last such outbreak of class-motivated destruction. In 1378 the *Ciompi* broke out in Florence, when workers demanded better representation among the political guilds that ruled the city. Three years later, the Peasants' Revolt took place in England. Each of these events shows a new sense of purpose and carries with it a strong flavour of the new recognition of individual self-worth among the lower classes. All were swiftly suppressed and the protagonists slain or hanged. Nevertheless, workers across Europe realised they had not only been enriched by the Black Death but also empowered by it, with far-reaching consequences for their self-importance and identity.

The accelerant effect of the Black Death amplified many other individualistic trends already underway in the late thirteenth and early fourteenth centuries. No longer did people have to accept the manorial compulsion to marry. Similarly, manorial lords gave up trying to prevent any remaining unfree peasants from marrying someone from outside the manor. Selling or leasing land to its occupiers or intermediaries now became the norm, ending the direct management of manors by their lords. Any families who did not yet have a hereditary surname acquired one by 1400. Noble families developed their own family mottoes and had family livery made for their retainers, further emphasising the family's identity. And as we saw in chapter four, everyone – nobles and farmers alike – started to seek greater privacy. Lordly castles were built with bedchambers in every tower. From the late fourteenth century lords gave up eating with their servants in the great hall and had meals separately with their families in their solar. Yeomen enlarged their old hall-houses by building upstairs floors, bedchambers and parlours, allowing each member of the family greater seclusion. All these served to imbue people with the sense of their individuality, as opposed to seeing themselves as members of a crowd or an anonymous workforce.

Few things confirmed this individualism quite as powerfully as the gradual spread of glass mirrors among the lower classes. Invented – or rather, rediscovered – at the end of the thirteenth century, probably in Venice, glass mirrors replaced those of polished silver and bronze in the households of the aristocracy in the fourteenth. Large numbers of carved ivory cases that once held small glass mirrors are to be seen in museums today. In the fifteenth century, the mirror became an icon of the Renaissance, as we can see from Brunelleschi's famous experiment with perspective, undertaken in the 1420s. Using a box containing two mirrors facing each other, he was able to sketch the Baptistry in Florence and compare it with how it appeared in his device, enabling him to copy the perspective view exactly. In 1433 Jan van Eyck painted the earliest surviving self-portrait, *Portrait of a Man with a Turban*, which must have involved the use of a mirror. Indeed, a round mirror occupies a prominent position in the background of *The Arnolfini Marriage*, which he painted the following year. Leonardo da Vinci wrote in back-to-front script, requiring people to use a mirror to read his words and thereby emphasising the importance of reflection. In fact, all these artists were turning a mirror on mankind. Whereas humanity had once been studied as part of God's Creation, now it became worthy of examination and representation in its own right.

The greatest impact of the mirror, however, was on the common man and woman. Almost everyone could afford one by 1500, when they might cost as little as 6d. Small glass shaving mirrors were found on the wreck of the *Mary Rose*, for example. Between the twelfth century and the sixteenth, looking glasses spread from the private chambers of aristocrats to the bedchambers of farmhouses, and with them spread the standard visual image of the 'self'. If you're asked today to draw a picture of yourself, you will probably attempt to depict your face. Such a self-image relies on the existence of a mirror. If a peasant had had a self-image before 1350, it would have taken the form of a picture or symbol which indicated his occupation or social standing. A blacksmith had his anvil, a priest his cross, a miller his millstone.

Such self-images relate to what these people did. When a medieval peasant saw himself in a mirror, therefore, he acquired a new awareness of himself *without* the accoutrements that he had previously associated with his 'self', such as his plough or the piece of land that his family had tilled for generations. For a miller, his new facial self-image might have revealed to him that he was not necessarily born to be a miller: he might 'see himself' as an explorer or a builder – or someone destined to better things.

Seeing themselves for what they *were* rather than what they *did* thus set people apart from their early-medieval ancestors. An objective view of their faces became their normalised self-image. Moreover, they knew that everyone else who had access to a mirror saw themselves in the same way. Whereas in 1100 our proverbial miller thought of himself as a man created by God to grind corn – and knew that everyone else saw him as a grinder of corn in the divine order of things – now he saw himself as a man with a receding hairline and a scar on his face, and he understood that this was how everyone else perceived him too. In addition, our miller realised that the people he met knew that he thought of himself in that way, because they thought of themselves similarly. They could not presume any longer that it was his God-given role to be a miller. In fact, they should not even presume he *was* a miller. He could be whatever he wanted. If he went to a new town, no one would necessarily know he had ever been a miller. He was at liberty to choose a new career path. You could say that the mirror helped set people free.

By 1500, no one was wearing the tunics and hoods of the mid-fourteenth century. Buttons had revolutionised clothing, allowing everyone to wear garments cut to fit the body closely. Shoes with ridiculously long toes – known as krakows – had come and gone. So too had men's tights worn in conjunction with short tunics that revealed the buttocks. Before long the codpiece would arrive. Across Europe, people sought out new dyes to make their clothes stand out. In the south of France, merchants in towns like Toulouse and Albi became rich from the long-distance trade in blue pastel dyes, made from woad. Red dyes made from brazilwood and kermes gave people the chance to wear red clothes that were brighter than their neighbours'. Self-fashioning was now a matter of personal choice for almost everyone. Men no longer needed to rely on their wives to shave them or dress their hair; a mirror allowed them to do these things for themselves. For the wealthy, the image of their own face became something they wished to preserve. From the late fourteenth century we have detailed portraits of kings – such as those of Jean II of France and Richard II of England – and from the fifteenth we know the faces of many aristo-crats, prelates and merchants and their wives. Effigies were sculpted to record the actual appearance of the deceased. More and more aspects of self-definition had been introduced into people's lives. Although people still belonged to their family, manor, parish, fraternity or town guild, they now had a personal identity that transcended all such groupings.

The Sixteenth Century

Into this increasingly self-aware and individualistic world stepped Luther, Tyndale and the other Bible translators. As we saw in the pre-vious chapter, many people were prompted thereby to reconsider their relationship with God. If you could read, and you had a Bible, you could study and interpret the scriptures for yourself. You could deter-mine your own path to redemption; you did not need the intervention of a cleric. You could think as an individual rather than as a member of a congregation. In fact, you *had* to start thinking individually, for you yourself were responsible for your salvation. More people learnt to read. More people put forward their religious opinions. By the end of the century certain writers could criticise organised religion as vehe-mently as the goliards in the twelfth century, but with the important difference that they and their audiences now saw faith as a personal matter, dependent on their individual reading of the Bible.

In the late sixteenth century, we start to come across accusations of non-belief. Physicians were often labelled atheists because they seemed to be trying to stop God from punishing someone with an illness, which logically meant they were deliberately acting against God's will. Whether there were many irreligious physicians is not the point: the key issue is that the concept of atheism now existed. *The Dialogue against the Fever Pestilence* by William Bullein, published in 1564, illus-trates as much by introducing the figure of the *nulla fidian*, the 'nothing believer'. As a merchant is lying sick of the plague, a physician recites a line of scripture to him inaccurately. When the merchant points out the fault, the physician replies, 'I care not for I meddle with no

scripture matters.' The merchant admits that he too pays little attention to the Bible. The conversation then carries on as follows:

> Physician: Herke in your eare, sir, I am neither Catholike, Papiste,
>   Protestante, nor Annabaptiste, I assure you.
> Merchant: What then: you have rehearsed choyce and plentie of
>   religions. What dow you honour? The Sonne, the Moone, or the
>   starres, Beast, Stone, or Foule, Fishe, or Tree?
> Physician: No forsothe. I doe none of them all. To be plain, I am a
>   Nulla fidian, and there are many of our secte.[26]

Similarly, the surgeon John Read wrote in 1588 that

> Some moreover papists are,
> Some *nulli fidians* likewise be,
> Some atheists temporisers, and
> Some machivells a griefe to see . . .[27]

The accusation of being an atheist was also levelled against men
who had nothing to do with medicine. Christopher Marlowe is perhaps the most famous example. He not only mocked the Christian
faith in his play *Doctor Faustus* but – according to the testimony of his
fellow playwright, Thomas Kyd – even went so far as to suggest Christ
had a sexual relationship with St John the Evangelist. Marlowe was directly accused of being an atheist by a government spy, whose report on
him survives.[28] There is no doubt that, by 1600, while Puritans in England might put God at the centre of everything, others felt that religion
played a very small part in their lives and a few felt it played none at all.
The idea that as individuals we might be spiritually and morally alone,
without the constraints of God's will but also without his guidance, is
a product of the Middle Ages.

As the foregoing passages indicate, by 1600 there was a spectrum of
faith. A few people believed there was no god; some paid little attention to God; many were ordinarily religious; some were firm believers;
and some were ardent to the point of being fanatical. This spectrum
was as complete and as varied as the stratification of wealth. Everyone
in society could be placed at some point on it. Therefore, like wealth,
it defined people. Indeed, the further towards the fanatical end of the
spectrum you were, the more likely it was that you would rail against

the fripperies and luxuries with which people had started to bedeck themselves. By this time, people were importing lace from Italy, Flanders and France. They were wearing fashionable starched ruffs. Some were wearing clothes dyed bright red with cochineal. Many of those who took a hard-and-fast line against such ostentation self-consciously wore black and white to indicate their views. Either way, people could now define themselves and express their individualism in what they wore, the way they decorated their houses and what they did for enjoyment – whether attending the theatre, listening to musical concerts or going to see bear-baiting. They could equally express their political beliefs. Were they supporters of the social order or believers in greater egalitarianism? Were they in favour of the state being run on religious lines or against the notion? People were able to question almost anything – even the way the monarch governed, as we saw in the previous chapter. It all adds up to the very opposite of the situation in 1000, when the vast majority were living, working and praying together, and not free to do as they chose.

This brings us to the last element of this huge shift in individualism – namely, people's *consciousness* of their developing individuality. This is most clearly to be seen in the rise of autobiographical writing in the sixteenth century. Of course, writing about the self was not a completely new phenomenon. We have already noted autobiographical works by Otloh of Saint Emmeram in the eleventh century and by Guibert of Nogent and Peter Abelard in the twelfth. We have also seen the troubadours' stories of their lives, some of which were at least partly true. We might add a handful of later confessional works, such as Petrarch's *Secretum* ('Secret Life') and Henry of Lancaster's *Livre de Seyntz Medicines* (The Book of Holy Medicines), both of which were written in the mid-fourteenth century, and *The Book of Margery Kempe*, written in the early fifteenth. But these are fundamentally spiritual texts. What we see in the sixteenth century is something different: an attempt to find an inner voice that is not primarily about God or salvation but about human experience – for as much or as little as it was worth.

Sixteenth-century autobiographical writing of a secular nature falls broadly into three categories: lyric poetry, diary-writing and formal autobiography. You are probably already acquainted with some of the autobiographical English poetry of the time, examples of which include the poems of the elder Thomas Wyatt (published posthumously in

1557) and Isabella Whitney (published between 1567 and 1573), and Shakespeare's sonnets (which were not published until 1609 but were being circulated in manuscript before 1598).[29] These all include seemingly autobiographical reflections, even if some of the moments they describe are a deliberate blurring of fact and imagination. To such a list we might also add certain speeches and soliloquies from the great dramas performed and published in England from 1587, which meld outward actions with layers of inward reflection and self-expression. These clearly demonstrate that not only had self-awareness reached a new intensity by the end of the sixteenth century but also that it was widely understood by many of those in the audiences who were far less capable of expressing themselves than Christopher Marlowe, Thomas Kyd and William Shakespeare.

The rise of the personal diary is another indication of the developing instinct for self-reflection. As a literary genre, it didn't exist before 1550. A handful of fifteenth-century men had kept day-by-day accounts of public events and of diplomatic missions; a few more in the early sixteenth century had kept daily records of pilgrimage routes, journals of specific military campaigns, and personal chronicles of public events. The duchess of Savoy had kept a monthly record of important dates between 1501 and 1522. However, every example before the mid-sixteenth century is an outward-looking account drawn up to provide information of practical use to other people. Only in the late sixteenth century do we start to come across diaries as personal records kept by an individual for his or her own benefit. One example is the journal of the London astrologer and physician Simon Forman. This was partly an autobiography drawn up for posterity and partly a journal compiled for his own personal reference. To give a flavour of the personal sections, here is an extract from the entry for 1595:

On Mundai the collectors cam to me P.M. at 6. The 4. of Feb. Tuesday, A.M. Mrs Floware and Elisher Cosin cam to me. I and a gentleman wer lik[ely] to fall out for standing at the garden by a gentellwoman. The 5. dai Wednesday, ther came at afternon an old quent marchaunte unto me, that was the confederat with Mrs Floware that came on Mundai. The 6. Dai abought 8. of the clocke in the morning cam Heugh Fort to me from A. Y. and divers gentlewomen cam to me that dai. That afternone at 4. cam Mrs Jhonson to me at the Red Crose in Watling Strete to com and see her child, and I went to her, et osculavi illam in domu sua [I kissed the woman in her house]. This 6. dai at nighte Mrs Al. sent for me to supper, and I went not, wherupon she toke great griefe and was sick.

The document is clearly not composed for anybody else's benefit – there's no explanation of who's who, for example, and no style in the writing. Like his famous fellow diarist Samuel Pepys, Forman uses Latin to conceal an immoral act in case a servant should get hold of the book. Overall, it shows the man's mind at work, reflecting on what he had done – even if he himself was not setting down what he thought and felt about those events on remembering them. This is typical of the earliest diaries. Another one, composed by the Devon farmer William Honnywell in the 1590s, records mundane things like buying 'twine to cord my peas' and selling lambs. But it also describes a trip to London in 1596 to purchase several luxury items:

19 January.—I took my journey towards London. On the 24th I came to London, and in my journey upwards I spent xvs. I paid unto my brother Christopher xls., which xls. he laid out unto Mr Nicholas Smith for a watch. On the 30th I received my watch from the dyal maker, and paid him for the mending of him vs., and I bought a purse to keep him in, which stood me as followeth: for the velvet iiijd.; for the two yards of ribbon iiijd.; the making iid.

Feb. 7.—I bought 3 pair of shoes, two of them are edged with velvet, which stood me iis. viiid.; the other stood me iis. ijd.; so the 3 pair stood me viis. vid . . .

Feb. 12.—I bought xxx gold buttons for a hat band, which xxx buttons did weigh 3 quarters, two pennyweights, 3 grains, at 50s. the oz. I paid for the making and fashioning of them vd. the piece . . . so the whole cost me lixs. vid.

A watch was quite an extraordinary thing for a sixteenth-century farmer to own. Yet neither these entries nor the rest of his diary contains anything of his inner feelings – such as the pride and joy he might have felt in purchasing such items. That element of diary-writing is generally not to be found before the seventeenth century. Nevertheless, you cannot help but suspect that Honnywell was quietly proud of these acquisitions and the satisfaction he took in recording them for posterity was one of his motivations for setting pen to paper.

The fullest literary expression of sixteenth-century individualism is, without doubt, the autobiography. One early example is the *Mémoires* of the French diplomat Philippe de Commines, published in several volumes in the 1520s. However, this is not so much a life story as a work of national history in which de Commines described public events that he had witnessed himself or knew about from first-hand informants. Another early example is Giorgio Vasari's entry on himself in the third and final volume of his *Lives of the Most Excellent Painters, Sculptors and Architects*, published in 1550. Again, this is not exactly an autobiography but a first-person account of his artistic output. In England, the form is not known before the poet Thomas Whythorne wrote his verse autobiography in 1576. Therefore the laurels fall to two Italians – the Florentine artist Benvenuto Cellini and the Milanese physician and mathematician Girolamo Cardano – for giving us the earliest proper autobiographies of the sixteenth century.

Benvenuto Cellini's autobiography was written between 1558 and 1563. It displays all the individuality, passion and inner revelations a modern reader could wish for. The whole work is imbued with a brutal honesty that is both exciting and slightly alienating. This, for example, is his description of how he sought out and murdered the soldier who had killed his younger brother in a fight:

> The fellow lived in a house near a place called Torre Sanguigna, next door to the lodging of one of the most fashionable courtesans in Rome, named Signora Antea. It had just struck twenty-four, and he was standing at the house-door, with his sword in hand, having risen from supper. With great address I stole up to him, holding a large Pistoian dagger, and dealt him a back-handed stroke, with which I meant to cut his head clean off; but as he turned round very suddenly, the blow fell upon the point of his left shoulder and broke the bone. He sprang up, dropped his sword, half-stunned with the great pain, and took to flight. I followed after, and in four steps caught him up, when I lifted my dagger above his head, which he was holding very low, and hit him in the back exactly at the juncture of the nape-bone and the neck. The poniard entered this point so deep into the bone, that, though I used all my strength to pull it out, I was not able. For just at that moment four soldiers with drawn swords sprang out from Antea's lodging and obliged me to set hand to my own sword to defend my life. Leaving the poniard then, I made off, and fearing I might be recognised, took refuge in the palace of Duke Alessandro, which was between Piazza Navona and the

Rotunda. On my arrival, I asked to see the Duke who told me that, if I was alone, I need only keep quiet and have no further anxiety, but to go on working at the jewel which the Pope had set his heart on, and stay eight days indoors.[30]

There is no doubting the viciousness of the man when provoked. But nor is there any questioning his honesty. There are many other passages that reveal aspects of his personality that are clearly not to his credit, such as his seduction of teenage girls, at least one of whom he got pregnant and then abandoned. Overall, it is a full and fascinating depiction of the thoughts and actions of an individual who is both independent-minded and self-aware. Most significantly for our topic, there is no one in his story more important than himself, not even God. Indeed, so powerful was his egotism that reading his account of his life leaves you with the impression that he did not believe the Earth went around the sun but rather that both were in orbit around *him*.

The other great autobiography to emerge from Italy at this time is of a more introspective nature. Girolamo Cardano was in his seventies when he started writing. He displays an enormous talent for self-reflection and his life had indeed been full of achievements and successes, but it had also been marred by tragedy. In his words,

My son, between the day of his marriage and the day of his doom, had been accused of attempting to poison his wife while she was still in the weakness attendant upon childbirth. On the 17th day of February he was apprehended, and fifty-three days after, on April 13th, he was beheaded in prison. And this was my supreme, my crowning misfortune. Because of this, it was neither becoming for me to be retained in my office, nor could I justly be dismissed. I could neither continue to live in my native city with any peace, nor in security move elsewhere. I walked abroad an object of scorn; I conversed with my fellows abjectly, as one despised, and, as one of unwelcome presence, avoided my friends . . .

I am by no means unaware that these afflictions may seem meaningless to future generations, and more especially to strangers; but there is nothing, as I have said, in this mortal life except inanity, emptiness, and dream-shadows.[31]

Cardano, like Cellini, was not averse to violence. Sixteenth-century Italy, it has to be admitted, saw a massive spike in young men killing each other, so it is perhaps not surprising that he got into a few scrapes. But he survived. It is perhaps fitting therefore to end with a passage from his life that has a happier ending, even if it begins rather ominously:

> Once when I was in Venice on the birthday of the Blessed Virgin, I lost some money while gambling; on the following day I lost the rest, for I was in the house of a professional cheat. When I observed that the cards were marked, I impetuously slashed his face with my poniard, though not deeply. There were in the room two youths, the body-servants of my adversary; two lances were fastened to the beamed ceiling; the key was turned in the door. When, however, I had begun to win and had recovered all the money, his, as well as my own, and the clothes and rings which I had lost the previous day . . . I tossed a part of the money back, willing to make amends when I saw I had wounded him. Then I attacked the house-servants, but since they were unable to handle weapons, and were beseeching me to spare their lives, I let them off on the condition that they should throw open the door of the house. The master, seeing such a commotion and tumult in his household, and anxiously fearing every moment's delay, I judge, because he had defrauded me in his own house with his marked cards, after making a rapid calculation of the slight difference between what he had to gain or what to lose, ordered the door to be opened; thus I escaped.
>
> On that same day about eight o'clock in the evening, while I was doing my best to escape from the clutches of the police because I had offered violence to a Senator, and keeping meanwhile my weapons beneath my cloak, I suddenly slipped, deceived in the dark, and fell into a canal. I kept my presence of mind even as I plunged, threw out my right arm, and, grasping the gunwale of a passing boat, was rescued by the passengers. When I scrambled aboard the skiff, I discovered in it, to my surprise, the Senator with whom I had just gambled. He had the wounds on his face bound up with a dressing; yet he willingly enough brought me out a suit of garments such as sailors wear. Dressed in these clothes, I travelled with him as far as Padua.

The civilising process still had some way to go, obviously, but the individualising one was nearing completion.

'This above all – to thine own self be true,' says Polonius in Act One, Scene Three, of Shakespeare's *Hamlet*, written in or about 1600. What that 'self' was had altered beyond all recognition over the course of our period. It was not that human beings had changed in their nature: a baby from 1000 raised in 1600 would no doubt have learnt all that he or she needed to get by, and likewise one born in the late sixteenth century would probably have managed had he or she been brought up in the early eleventh. Rather it was that human nurture had evolved – with the result that the European character had changed profoundly.

By 1600, people of all ranks were mindful of what they were, not just what they did. Almost all saw themselves as free individuals, not mere functionaries. They were ready to question almost anything. Their self-awareness made them generally more reflective and better mannered and, in many cases, better behaved. At the same time, their greater self-awareness encouraged many of them to show initiative and to take risks. People presented themselves as best they could to others, displaying both their virtue and wealth wherever possible. They knew that they could improve themselves through education and personal ambition. Above all else, the umbilical cord to God had finally been cut. In Shakespeare's day, a man's or woman's individualism could be likened to a great medieval cathedral. It had been centuries under construction. It had been built by many people working together, over many years. And like a great cathedral, it was most definitely a product of the Middle Ages – and largely complete. When we say that 'Shakespeare speaks for us', we hear our medieval ancestors talking.

Envoi

A friend recently said to me in the course of conversation, 'The average schoolchild today knows more about the world than the greatest scientist in the sixteenth century.' In that one sentence, he illustrated why so many people misunderstand the distant past. There were plenty of things that even ordinary sixteenth-century people knew that we are ignorant of – from being able to recognise all the flora and fauna in their locality to knowing how to use a bread oven and how to fire a musket or tell the time from a shadow, how to ride a horse, when to sow and reap winter wheat, how to store fruit so it lasts twelve months, and so on. What was general knowledge for them has become a series of specialisms in the modern world. As for their greatest scientists – or natural philosophers, as they were called at the time – astronomers like Copernicus, Galileo, Thomas Digges and Tycho Brahe knew much more about the stars than the average schoolchild does today. Although we disregard much sixteenth-century scientific thinking as inaccurate or incomplete, they possessed a considerable body of knowledge. It is simply *different* from our knowledge – as indeed ours is different from the ways in which people will think about science in the twenty-sixth century or the thirty-sixth.

The above case highlights the fundamental problem we have in appreciating the past. We are unaware of the extent of our ignorance: we simply don't know what we don't know. We instinctively proceed to judgement on the basis of our own experiences, which are inevitably rooted in the modern world. But realising this and trying to overcome it can bring the greatest revelations. Indeed, approaching the past with this one constant in mind – the permanent questioning of received wisdom – is the prime quality necessary to be a historian. Every significant historical work is given its force and resonance by querying what we think we know. Its value does not lie in reciting what happened or discussing why things occurred as they did but in seeing the past with new eyes, recognising its meaning for people alive today, and explaining it so that present-day readers can understand it for themselves.

This hit me with great force just as I came to the end of this book, on a holiday in France. As I walked around Le Mans Cathedral, I looked up at the vaults, the arches and the stained glass. And although I had probably seen more than a hundred cathedrals over the years, I was quite overwhelmed by what I saw. The stone vaults of the transepts, which were built between 1380 and 1440, are over 100ft high. A great deal of the glass in the twelfth-century nave is original. But what captivated me was the ambulatory, built in the early thirteenth century. Its complexity is difficult to describe. I was standing in front of an arch beneath a vault looking up at a higher arch that was part of a semi-circle of arches connected by another series of vaults to an even higher semi-circle of arches which surrounded the high altar. Outside, these arches and vaults were supported by three levels of flying buttresses – each one of which was itself supported by a further pair of flying buttresses at each of the three levels. How did anyone even conceive of this design, let alone build it? How can anyone today think for even a moment that a modern schoolchild is the equal of a thirteenth-century master mason – perhaps the medieval equivalent of the 'greatest scientist' to which my friend alluded? Most of all, how can anyone today associate 'medieval' with 'backward' or 'ignorant'?

This feeling grew even stronger in me as I went on to consider all the elements of this architecture. Someone had chosen the various types of stone and arranged for the right quantities of each to be brought by cart or boat from its respective quarry, miles away, so it could be precisely shaped and assembled. But that in itself required prior knowledge as to where the most suitable stone was to be found and how easy it was to carve it, and how much it would cost to buy it and transport it to this site. Then there was the matter of the decorated carving, which would have required whole teams of sculptors. Making the glass was another reckoning. Designing the images and choosing the colours for the glass segments was yet another. Making sure the window apertures and vaults were in harmony with the glass and yet strong enough to hold it in place added another level of complexity. How did the builders work out the loads on each of the flying buttresses? They had no way of calculating the forces. And so on. I could not help but feel that anyone who associates 'medieval' with 'ignorant' is the epitome of ignorance himself.

Of course, the workers were familiar with all the necessary processes. But only to a point. Nothing like this had been possible in the early eleventh century. A cathedral in 1250 was nothing like one from 1000. Each new edifice was in some way unique and untested – an experiment in what was possible as well as what was desirable and useful.

At Beauvais Cathedral you can see a dramatic juxtaposition of the difference, where part of the old tenth-century building adjoins the massive thirteenth-century choir of an unfinished church that was meant eventually to replace it. The vaults at Beauvais are 160ft high. The contrast is not just one of scale: the earlier church is far simpler. Gradually, over the course of 250 years, cathedral builders learnt to build larger, taller and considerably more sophisticated buildings. They developed systems of construction that anyone today would find impressive. Perhaps a modern team of architects, given enough time and a large enough workforce of skilled masons, sculptors, artists and glassmakers could make a cathedral as splendid as Le Mans or Beauvais. But their systems would depend on machinery and power tools. Moreover, they would require computers, calculations, drawings and standard units of measurement. And that was what really struck me at Le Mans. The people who built all these incredible cathedrals and churches across Europe – who went from place to place, observing and undertaking new work – did not even have a standardised language, let alone fixed units of measurement. They had no drawings. The vast majority were illiterate. And yet their work has stood for hundreds of years. Our hypothetical team of modern professionals could not replicate a 100ft-high cathedral without modern systems: it is not something they are trained to do. And if they attempted it without the tools of the modern profession, you can bet the result wouldn't still be standing eight hundred years later.

This is just one example of why we should respect the Middle Ages and acknowledge that their achievements were every bit as great as our own. But as I continued to marvel at Le Mans Cathedral, I was also struck by the relevance of their work to our time. It is easy for us to think of the achievements of the past as redundant in a secular age. Some would argue that a medieval cathedral has no more relevance today than a medieval castle or a recipe for alleviating the symptoms of plague. But they would be wrong. Quite apart from the fact that these buildings still serve communities of practising Christians, they also fulfil many functions for all of us, whether we believe in God or not. They are inspirational. They are visually impressive. They are communal. Cities are proud of them as the ultimate symbols of their historical importance and identity. They provide a space in which many people can gather together for the marking of an event of widespread significance. In many cases they provide a place of retreat from the noise and pressure of the modern world. They also offer a psychological refuge from the feeling that everything is transitory. Most of all, like Shakespeare, they still speak to us. They quietly but proudly tell us about what human beings can aspire to, what we can achieve if we collaborate, and what we can hope will last of us.

What is true for the cathedrals is also true for many other aspects of medieval culture. Just before I started typing this paragraph I heard someone on the radio quoting a line from George Orwell's 1984 about the proletariat: 'Until they become conscious they will never rebel, and until after they have rebelled they cannot become conscious.' Would such a thought have been possible if it had not been for the widespread questioning of authority by peasants in the wake of the Black Death? Even if it had, it would have carried little weight. Similarly, throughout this book I have been mindful of a line by Peter Abelard: 'The beginning of wisdom is found in doubting; by doubting we come to questioning, and by seeking we may come upon the truth.' If you imagine Western philosophy as a great cathedral that has taken more than two thousand years to build – and which is still being built – it is evident that if Abelard had not said the things he did, someone else would now need to say them. If Dante had not written his *Divine Comedy* or if Shakespeare had become a glover like his father, modern society would be so much the poorer. Not only would we not have these works today, our world would not have developed as it did. The cathedrals might be one of the most obvious lasting manifestations of medieval culture but the 'cathedral' of English literature is similarly built on medieval foundations. The 'cathedral' of the English language is too. So is the 'cathedral' of Parliament. So are the 'cathedrals' of painting, music and so on. Even those metaphorical cathedrals built on much older foundations like philosophy and theology were substantially rebuilt in the Middle Ages.

Not everything created in the Middle Ages remains permanently relevant, obviously: the necessity for medieval castles came and went. Many other things have similarly become culturally redundant – interesting only to historians and their readers as examples of life in different times. But many aspects of the Middle Ages still matter today. The horizons discussed in this book show not only how profoundly life changed between the eleventh century and the sixteenth but also that this period set the parameters for how society would develop subsequently and how we can expect it to change in the future. Why do we think peace is more desirable than a perpetual state of conflict? Why do we believe in the freedom of the individual? Why do we no longer insist that everyone believe – or not believe – in God the same way that we do?

I often talk about history not being about the past but about people. But I would add that it is also about looking for the limits of our knowledge, to discover what we don't know. I hope this book has shown how we can take a metaphor like the horizon and use it as a tool to arrive at many new understandings. It is just a matter of perspective. Anyone can see that the medieval centuries have left us with cathedrals, castles and monasteries. You only need to do a little bit of research to find out that they also gave us clocks, guns, markets and banks, and new ways of dressing and cooking. You have to put in some serious effort to realise that, although medieval people were considerably more violent than we are in daily life, they also set about tackling that problem. And although they were hungrier, they rose to that challenge too. And that although they started as unfree serfs, they developed new ways of thinking about themselves. In every way imaginable, medieval people contributed to our way of living. They broadened their horizons to encompass the whole world – and, in so doing, they broadened ours too.

At the end of the day, that is the key point. The Middle Ages were not about stasis but hope, vision, effort and change. What our predecessors achieved in building higher and more beautifully – metaphorically as well as physically – speaks to us of our own spirit and ambition. Just as without Tyndale there would have been no Shakespeare, without medieval cathedrals we would not now be sending astronauts into outer space. The combination of vision, cooperation and specialist skills was essential: we could not have passed from a society of warlords and peasants to one of TV audiences watching a man walk on the moon without first building spires as high as they could go and arches as graceful as anyone could imagine. We exist on a cultural plinth that is as wide as the world and thousands of years deep. To see things otherwise – to ignore the past and be content with everything as it superficially appears, as if it had all magically come into being exactly as it is now – is to judge a film solely by its final frame. And to ignore the fact that there will be a sequel.

Notes

1. Horizons

1. This chapter is loosely based on a keynote address with the same title first delivered at Christ Church University, Canterbury, on 1 April 2016. I am grateful to Dr David Grummitt of the University of Kent at Canterbury for inviting me. • **2.** Perhaps the only exceptions are Jules Michelet and Jacob Burckhardt, who brought the cultural achievements of the Italian Renaissance to the attention of the world in the nineteenth century. • **3.** *BBC World Histories*, 8 (2018), p. 23. • **4.** David Crystal, 'The Language of Shakespeare', in Stanley Wells and Gary Taylor (eds), *The Complete Works* (Oxford, 2005), pp. xlv–lxiv, at p. lxi. • **5.** The previous St Paul's Cathedral was consumed in a fire in 1086 but it is unlikely to have been higher than 80ft. Old St Paul's stood at a height of 489ft from the late thirteenth century to 1561; 'quintupled' is almost certainly an underestimate of the increment. The tallest building in London at the time of writing is the Shard, which is 1,016ft high. Thus the increment from 1300 to now can be said to be 2.1 times. • **6.** About 45% of England had been enclosed by 1500. See J. R. Wordie, 'The Chronology of English Enclosure', *Economic History Review*, 36, 4 (1983), pp. 483–505, at pp. 494, 502. • **7.** Peter Clark, *The English Alehouse* (1983), p. 42; John Hare, 'Inns, innkeepers and the society of later medieval England, 1350–1600', *Journal of Medieval History*, 39, 4 (2013), pp. 477–97, at p. 496. • **8.** Claire Breay and Joanna Storey (eds), *Anglo-Saxon Kingdoms: Art, Word, War* (2018), p. 261. • **9.** Clare Williams, *Thomas Platter's Travels in England 1599* (1937), pp. 163–5, 171–3. • **10.** Samantha Letters, *Gazetteer of Markets and Fairs to 1516* (http://www.history.ac.uk/cmh/gaz/gazweb2.html, downloaded 19 April 2021). • **11.** The southwestern counties of Devon and Cornwall had 7.4% of the Domesday population of England within their borders but have yielded only 9 (0.4%) of the 2,451 coins or coin hoards yet found in the country for the period from 924 to 1135. See Henry Fairbairn, 'The Nature and Limits of the Money Economy in Late Anglo-Saxon and Early Norman England' (unpublished

PhD thesis, King's College London, 2013), pp. 251–3, 291. • **12.** Asa Briggs and Peter Burke, *A Social History of the Media* (2nd ed., 2005), p. 13. • **13.** The figure of 0.25% is an estimate based on the presumption that the male population was in the region of 0.8 million and that fewer than 2,000 men could read and write. For the 1500 and 1600 figures, see W. B. Stephens, 'Literacy in England, Scotland and Wales, 1500–1900', *History of Education Quarterly*, 30, 4 (1990), pp. 545–71. • **14.** If all the 4,040 books printed in the 1590s were produced in editions of 500 and had an average length of 45,000 words, this means there was an annual production in excess of 90 billion words per year in print alone. If 400,000 literate people wrote an average of just 1,000 words per month, this would have added a further 4.8 billion – hence the total word production may be conservatively reckoned at almost 100 billion per year. • **15.** Francis Bacon, *Novum Organum* (1620), Book 1, Aphorism 129. Translated as *The New Organon: Aphorisms Concerning the Interpretation of Nature and the Kingdom of Man*, collected in James Spedding, Robert Ellis and Douglas Heath (eds), *The Works of Francis Bacon* (1857), iv, p. 114. • **16.** Thomas Harriot, *A Briefe and True Report of the New Found Land of Virginia* (1590), p. 27. N.b. Harriot's spelling has been modernised • **17.** Lucien Febvre and Henri-Jean Martin, trans. David Gerard, *The Coming of the Book* (1997), p. 30. • **18.** I am indebted to Jesse Lynch for his narrative of the early uses of paper in England, which will shortly be appearing in his University of Exeter PhD thesis, 'The Spread of Paper Acceptance in Medieval England in the Long Fourteenth Century' [working title]. The detail concerning the 1275 administrative changes brought about by Edward I is in William Stubbs (ed.), *Chronicles of the Reigns of Edward I and Edward II* (2 vols, 1882), i, pp. 85–6. • **19.** F. L. Attenborough, *The Laws of the Earliest English Kings* (Cambridge, 1922), pp. 62–93. • **20.** Manuel Eisner, 'Long-term trends in violent crime', *Crime and Justice*, 30 (2003), pp. 83–142, at p. 99. The modern American figure is for the year 2019, taken from https://wonder.cdc.gov/controller/saved/D76/D99F056 (downloaded 19 April 2021). • **21.** F. G. Emmison, *Elizabethan Life: Morals and the Church Courts* (Chelmsford, 1973), p. 1. • **22.** Quoted in Roy Porter, *The Greatest Benefit to Mankind* (1997), p. 110. • **23.** Darrell W. Amundsen, 'Medieval Canon Law on Medical and Surgical Practice by the Clergy', *Bulletin of the History of Medicine*, 52, 1 (1978), pp. 22–44. • **24.** Sanjib Kumar Ghosh, 'Human cadaveric dissection: a historical account from ancient Greece to the modern era', *Anatomy & Cell Biology*, 48, 3 (2015), pp. 153–69. • **25.** Patrick Wallis, 'Exotic Drugs and English Medicine: England's Drug Trade, c. 1550–c. 1800', *Social History of Medicine*, 25, 1 (2012), pp. 20–46. • **26.** Quoted in Ralph Houlbrooke, *Death, Religion and the Family in England 1480–1750* (Oxford, 1998), pp. 18–19. • **27.** Ian Mortimer, *The Dying and the Doctors* (2009), esp. p. 63.

2. War

1. This chapter is loosely based on a keynote speech entitled 'The Meaning of War' delivered at the conference to mark the 600th anniversary of the battle of Agincourt, at the University of Southampton, 2 August 2015. I am very grateful to Professor Anne Curry for inviting me to give that paper on such an auspicious occasion. I am grateful too to David Stone and James Kidner for giving advice on that original speech. • **2.** Quoted in Thomas Asbridge, *The First Crusade* (2004), p. 316. • **3.** Quoted in Asbridge, *First Crusade*, p. 317. • **4.** Quoted in Peter Speed (ed.), *Those Who Fought: An Anthology of Medieval Sources* (New York, 1996), p. 1. • **5.** Quoted in Speed (ed.), *Those Who Fought*, pp. 1–2. • **6.** Maurice Keen, *Chivalry* (1984), p. 88. The quotation is paraphrased slightly for readability. • **7.** Keen, *Chivalry*, p. 87. • **8.** Juliet Barker, *Conquest* (2009), p. 43; *Complete Peerage*, vol. 5 (2nd ed., 1926), p. 254. • **9.** Quoted in Asbridge, *First Crusade*, p. 300. • **10.** H. T. Riley (ed.), *Chronica Monasterii S. Albani, Part 1 Thomae Walsingham Historia Anglicana* (1865), i, pp. 206–7. • **11.** E. B. Fryde, 'Parliament and the French War, 1336–40', in E. B. Fryde and E. Miller (eds), *Historical Studies of the English Parliament* (Cambridge, 1970), pp. 242–61, at p. 246. • **12.** Ian Mortimer, *1415: Henry V's Year of Glory* (2009), pp. 330–1. • **13.** Mortimer, *1415*, pp. 421–2. • **14.** Geoffrey Parker, 'The "Military Revolution," 1560–1660 – a Myth?', *Journal of Modern History*, 48, 2 (1976), pp. 195–214, at p. 206. • **15.** Steven Pinker, *The Better Angels of Our Nature* (2011, paperback ed., 2012), p. 98. • **16.** There were a few exceptions, such as George II at the battle of Dettingen (1743) and the generalship of Frederick II of Prussia and Napoleon, but after 1600, heads of state were normally kept away from the dangers of battle. • **17.** Michael Howard, *War and the Liberal Conscience* (1978, revised paperback ed., 2011), p. 5. • **18.** Quoted in Howard, *War and the Liberal Conscience*, p. 6.

3. Inequality

1. For a more detailed account of the difficulties of historical authenticity, see 'The problems of visiting the past in fact and fiction (Or why historical authenticity is every bit as difficult as historical accuracy.), A speech to the Historical Novel Society Conference, London, 2012', in Ian Mortimer, *What Isn't History?* (Rosetta Books, 2017). • **2.** I am grateful to my editor, Jörg Hensgen, for suggesting this term. • **3.** Attenborough, *Laws of the Earliest English Kings*, pp. 26–7. • **4.** Attenborough, *Laws of the Earliest English Kings*, pp. 148–51. • **5.** Marc Morris, *The Norman Conquest* (2012), p. 26. • **6.** Geoffrey Parker, *Global Crisis* (2013), pp. 17–18. • **7.** David A. E. Pelteret, *Slavery in Early*

Medieval England (Woodbridge, 1995), p. 253. • **8.** Pelteret, *Slavery*, p. 256. • **9.** J. B. Black, *The Reign of Elizabeth* (2nd ed., Oxford, 1959), p. 251. • **10.** For example, in 2008, Milanovic, Lindert and Williamson calculated a Gini coefficient for England in the year 1290 of 0.37 (Branko Milanovic, Peter H. Lindert, Jeffrey G. Williamson, 'Pre-Industrial Inequality', *Economic Journal*, vol. 121 (2011), pp. 255–72). In 2013 Bekar and Reed calculated a Gini coefficient of 0.73 for England in the year 1279 (Cliff T. Bekar and Clyde G. Reed, 'Land markets and inequality: evidence from medieval England', *European Review of Economic History*, 17, 3 (2013), pp. 294–317, at p. 306). • **11.** John Bateman, *The Great Landowners of Great Britain and Ireland* (4th ed., 1883), p. 515. • **12.** https:// www.ons.gov.uk/peoplepopulationandcommunity/housing/articles/research outputssubnationaldwellingstockbytenureestimatesengland2012to2015/2020 (downloaded 26 July 2022). • **13.** The 1086 figures are drawn from the National Archives website, with the figure for freeholders being deduced from the remainder. The 1695 figures are taken from Joan Thirsk and J. P. Cooper, *Seventeenth-Century Economic Documents* (Oxford, 1972), p. 766. The ambiguous figure for the Crown given by King is here assumed to be 1.8 million acres, not 3 million (see note 8 on p. 766). The 1873 figures are from Bateman, *Great Landowners*, p. 515. The difference of 4% in 1873 is accounted for by commercial ownership and waste land, which was not associated with any owner. • **14.** It should be noted that the 1086 figures relate to manors, not acres, and royal manors tended to be considerably larger than those of ordinary freeholders. Hence it is fair to say that William the Conqueror retained far more than 17% of the country for his personal estate. • **15.** The question of whether the Victorian pattern of land ownership reflects our modern one is difficult to answer. According to Gary Shrubsole, *Who Owns England?* (2019), the Crown Estate owns 1.4%; the Church 0.5%; the aristocracy and gentry between 30% and 47%; and homeowners 5%. That is a maximum of 54% – the possible discrepancy being due to 17% of the country having never been registered at the Land Registry (established 1862), almost all of it probably owned by the aristocracy and gentry. The rest is made up from 'new money' (17%), companies and limited liability partnerships (18%), the public sector (8.5%) and conservation charities, such as the National Trust (2%). • **16.** E. H. Phelps Brown and Sheila V. Hopkins, 'Seven Centuries of the Prices of Consumables, Compared with Builders' Wage-Rates', *Economica*, new series vol. 23, no. 92 (1956), pp. 296–314. • **17.** Stephen Broadberry, Bruce M. S. Campbell, Alexander Klein, Mark Overton and Bas van Leeuwen, *British Economic Growth, 1270–1870* (2015), p. 20. • **18.** Christopher Dyer, *Standards of Living in the Later Middle Ages: Social Change in England, 1200–1520* (revised ed., Cambridge, 1998), p. 119. • **19.** Broadberry *et al.*, *British Economic Growth*, p. 20. • **20.** Dyer, *Standards of Living*, p. 125. This figure is for the year 1292.

• **21.** Dyer, *Standards of Living*, p. 36. • **22.** Ian Mortimer, 'Equality: what is it good for?', *Englesberg Ideas* (12 May 2021). Available online at https://engels bergideas.com/essays/equality-what-is-it-good-for/ (downloaded 15 August 2022). • **23.** Ole Benedictow, *The Black Death 1346–1353: The Complete History* (Woodbridge, 2004), p. 383. • **24.** Ian Mortimer, *Centuries of Change* (2014), published in paperback as *Human Race* (2015), p. 86. • **25.** Dyer, *Standards of Living*, p. 36. • **26.** D. C. Coleman, *The Economy of England 1450–1750* (Oxford, 1977), p. 23 (meat and grain prices); Broadberry *et al.*, *British Economic Growth*, pp. 232–6 (wages). • **27.** Henrietta Leyser, *Medieval Women* (1995, paperback ed., 1996), p. 89. • **28.** G. N. Garmonsway (ed.), *The Anglo-Saxon Chronicle* (2nd ed., 1954), p. 176. • **29.** *Calendar of Patent Rolls 1408–13* (1909), pp. 389–90. • **30.** Emanuel van Meteren, *Nederlandtsche Historie* (1575), quoted in W. B. Rye, *England as Seen by Foreigners in the Days of Elizabeth and James I* (1865), p. 73. • **31.** Williams, *Thomas Platter's Travels in England*, p. 182. This section of Platter's text seems to be a quotation from the duke of Württemberg's trip. • **32.** Undated letter quoted in Seb Falk, *The Light Ages* (2020), p. 180. I am very grateful to Dr Falk for bringing this reference to my attention. • **33.** Quoted in Alden T. Vaughan and Virginia Mason Vaughan, 'Before Othello: Elizabethan Representations of Sub-Saharan Africans', in *William and Mary Quarterly*, Third Series, 53, 1 (Jan. 1997), pp. 19–44, at p. 25. • **34.** Quoted in Scott Oldenburg, 'The Riddle of Blackness in England's National Family Romance', *Journal for Early Modern Cultural Studies*, 1, 1 (2001), pp. 46–62, at p. 49. • **35.** In so doing Scot was resurrecting an old trope from the fifteenth-century mystery plays, and it is possible that this prejudice had always been lurking in the background. • **36.** Vaughan and Vaughan, 'Before Othello', p. 30. • **37.** Miranda Kaufman, 'Caspar van Senden, Sir Thomas Sherley and the "Blackamoor" Project', *Historical Research*, vol. 81, no. 212 (May 2008), pp. 366–71.

4. Comfort

1. Anthony Emery, *Dartington Hall* (Oxford, 1970), p. 268. • **2.** Nat Alcock and Dan Miles, *The Medieval Peasant House in Midland England* (Oxford, 2013), pp. 190–9. • **3.** Guy Beresford, 'Three Deserted Medieval Settlements on Dartmoor: A Report on the Late E. Marie Minter's Excavations', *Medieval Archaeology*, 23, 1 (1979), pp. 98–158, at pp. 135–6. • **4.** M. A. Havinden, *Household and Farm Inventories in Oxfordshire, 1550–1590* (1965), pp. 277–9. • **5.** Anthony Quiney, *Town Houses of Medieval Britain* (2003), pp. 96, 113. • **6.** Quiney, *Town Houses*, p. 150. • **7.** Quiney, *Town Houses*, p. 259. • **8.** D. M. Herridge (ed.), *Surrey Probate Inventories*, Surrey Record Society, vol. 39 (2005), pp. 379–81. Note, the cooking utensils are described as being in the 'buttery' in the original; the word 'kitchen' has been employed in the text for the sake of simplicity. • **9.** Margaret Case (ed.), *Devon Inventories*, Devon and Cornwall Record Society new ser. 11 (1966), p. 10. • **10.** Cornelius Walford, *The Famines of the World, Past and Present* (1879), p. 6. There was also a famine in 1050. • **11.** Walford, *Famines*, p. 7. • **12.** These were the years 1106, 1111, 1117, 1121–2, 1124–6, 1135–7 and 1141. Walford, *Famines*, p. 8. • **13.** Walford, *Famines*, p. 8. • **14.** Walford, *Famines*, p. 8. • **15.** These were 1224–5, 1226–7, 1246–7 and 1247–8. See Dyer, *Standards of Living*, p. 262. • **16.** Christopher Dyer, *Everyday Life in Medieval England* (1994, revised ed., 2000), p. 82. • **17.** Vern Bullough and Cameron Campbell, 'Female Longevity and Diet in the Middle Ages', *Speculum*, 55, 2 (1980), pp. 317–25; Don Brothwell, 'Palaeodemography and Earlier British Populations', *World Archaeology*, 4, 1 (1972), pp. 75–87. • **18.** Ann Hagen, 'Anglo-Saxon Food: Processing and Consumption' (unpublished MPhil. dissertation, UCL, 2017), p. 114. • **19.** Hagen, 'Anglo-Saxon Food', p. 235.

5. Speed

1. Michael Prestwich, 'The Royal Itinerary and Roads in England under Edward I', in Valerie Allen and Ruth Evans (eds), *Roadworks: Medieval Britain, Medieval Roads* (Manchester, 2016), pp. 177–97 (at pp. 187–8), quoting TNA: E 101/353/2. • **2.** Prestwich, 'Royal Itinerary', pp. 185–6. • **3.** Paul Hindle, *Medieval Roads and Tracks* (Princes Risborough, 1982), p. 17. • **4.** Hindle, *Medieval Roads*, p. 17. • **5.** On average, he moved nine times every month for his whole reign. A journey of 15 miles per day was usual, and one of 20 miles not unusual, although longer journeys were rare. See Prestwich, 'Royal Itinerary', pp. 178, 188. • **6.** See the itinerary in the Reading Room of the National Archives, ref 942.037. He moved to a new village or town at least 117 times in 1331, 109 times in 1332 and 106 times in 1333. His actual number of moves in each year was probably higher but his wardrobe and secretaries were often sent on ahead of him or had difficulty keeping up, and so the records do not always reveal his location. • **7.** From the itinerary in the Reading Room of the National Archives, ref 942.037. • **8.** Adam Clarke, J. Caley, J. Bayley, F. Holbrooke and J. W. Clarke (eds), *Foedera, Conventiones, Litterae, etc., or Rymer's Foedera 1066–1383* (6 vols in 4, 1816–30), ii, 2, pp. 1024–5. On 16 March he was at the Tower, on 23rd at Newcastle, on 28th at Berwick, and back at Langley on the 6th. According to an *inspeximus* of a charter, he was back at Langley by the 5th. • **9.** Norbert Ohler, trans. Caroline Hillier, *The Medieval Traveller* (Woodbridge, 1989), p. 97. • **10.** R. L. Poole, *The Early Correspondence of John* *of Salisbury* (British Academy, 1924), p. 6. • **11.** Walter Bronescombe, bishop of Exeter, set out from London on 22 June 1258 on a journey to Paris. He arrived on or before 4 July. In twelve days – or, at the most, twelve and a bit – he had covered the 72 miles to Dover, undertaken the sea crossing of about 22–27 nautical miles to Calais, then ridden the last 165 miles to Paris. The whole journey saw him ride an average of just over 20 miles per day (F. C. Hingeston-Randolph, *The Registers of Walter Bronescombe and Peter Quivil* (1889), p. 294). Thomas de Brantyngham, bishop of Exeter from 1370 to 1396, normally did the 177 miles of the route from London to Bishop's Clyst via his episcopal manors at East Horsley (Surrey) and Faringdon (Hampshire) in eight days, which is also about 20 miles per day. His successor, Edmund Stafford, took generally the same amount of time to do the same route in the fifteenth century – for example, from 20–28 May 1403 and 15–23 June 1406 (F. C. Hingeston-Randolph, *The Register of Thomas de Brantyngham* (1906), pp. 890–6; *The Register of Edmund Stafford* (1886), p. 477). • **12.** Louise Ropes Loomis, *The Council of Constance* (1961), p. 343. • **13.** C. M. Woolgar, *The Great Household in Late Medieval England* (1999), p. 188. • **14.** Woolgar, *Great Household*, p. 187. • **15.** Broadberry *et al.*, *British Economic Growth*, p. 111. • **16.** Jean Verdon, trans. George Holoch, *Travel in the Middle Ages* (Notre Dame, Indiana, 2003), p. 204. The distance by road today is less than 1,400 km but Verdon thought it between 1,700–1,800 km. • **17.** Frank Barlow, 'Becket, Thomas', *Oxford Dictionary of National Biography* (hereafter *ODNB*). Bur-le-Roi is in the vicinity of Noron-la-Poterie. • **18.** Although Cherbourg was much nearer – only 58 miles away, compared to Calais' 214 miles – it was about 90 nautical miles from the nearest English ports (Portsmouth and Chichester), which would have entailed a sea crossing in darkness for much of the voyage. Although navigators could sail by the stars if they had to, there was no guarantee of the skies being clear enough the following night when the conspirators set out. • **19.** John Gillingham, 'King John', *ODNB*. • **20.** Ohler, *Medieval Traveller*, p. 97. • **21.** W. H. Bliss (ed.), *Calendar of Entries in the Papal Registers Relating to Great Britain and Ireland, volume ii, 1305–1342* (1895), p. 498. • **22.** Verdon, *Travel*, p. 205. • **23.** Ian Mortimer, *The Perfect King* (2006), pp. 91–2. • **24.** Mortimer, *Perfect King*, pp. 132, 460. • **25.** Ian Mortimer, *Medieval Intrigue* (2010), p. 212. He may have made a dash via Portsmouth to Gloucester, apparently travelling the 102 miles between them in a single day, as royal letters recording grants at both these places were dated 10 August. However, it is possible that one was misdated. There is no other evidence of Edward managing 100 miles in a single day. • **26.** C. A. J. Armstrong, 'Some examples of the distribution and speed of news in England at the time of the Wars of the Roses', in R. W. Hunt (ed.), *Studies in Medieval History Presented to Frederick Maurice Powicke* (1948), pp. 429–54, at p. 446. • **27.** Hingeston-Randolph,

Register of Edmund Stafford, pp. 477–9. • **28.** Ohler, *Medieval Traveller*, p. 97. • **29.** The distance of a 'stage' has been much discussed. Ludwig Friedlaender proposed in 1910 that the normal operational speed of the system was 5 Roman miles per hour, including stoppages (Ludwig Friedlaender, *Darstellungen aus der Sittengeschichte Roms* (4 vols, Leipzig, 1910), ii, p. 22). That implied it normally covered 120 Roman miles (110 statute miles) on a 24-hour basis, which would imply each stage was an eighth to a fifth of this distance (15–24 Roman miles). However, what concerns us here is not how fast the system *normally* relayed information but what its maximum speed was. Some writers have argued that the usual speed of 50–60 miles per day implied that stages were about 8 miles apart (e.g. A. M. Ramsay, 'The Speed of the Roman Imperial Post', *Journal of Roman Studies*, 15 (1925), pp. 60–74; C.W. J. Eliot, 'New Evidence for the Speed of the Roman Imperial Post', *Phoenix*, 9, 2 (1955), pp. 76–80). In exceptional circumstances, according to Friedlaender, riders could convey information at speeds of up to 160 Roman miles (147 statute miles) per day. Ramsay and Eliot both mention speeds comparable with this. Procopius, however, goes further in the passage quoted in the text. His reference to horses being kept at each stage suggests each one was 25 Roman miles apart, which would imply a man might be expected to ride as much as 200 Roman miles in a day and 'hardly ever less than' 125. His text tacitly confirms this. If the speed of five to eight stages per day amounted to only 50–60 miles, his readers would not have been convinced by his claim that 'couriers were thus able to ride as long a distance in one day as would ordinarily require ten'. His readers certainly would have been able to ride more than 5–6 miles in a day. What's more, they would have known how far a stage was. Logically, it must have been one-eighth of ten times as far as someone ordinarily travelled in a day. As the usual day's travel was about 20 miles, this would equate to one-eighth of 200 miles, or 25 miles. This is the same as Procopius's distance between horse stations. It follows that Procopius's passage quoted has to be taken to mean that couriers could be asked to travel up to 200 Roman miles (192 statute miles) in twenty-four hours. • **30.** News of the event was taken by the standard bearer of the Fourth Legion to the regional commander, then stationed at Cologne, 110 Roman miles away. He arrived that evening, while the commander was still eating. If we take this to be roughly from 7 a.m. to 6 p.m., the average speed of that leg of the journey was about 10 Roman miles per hour. The news was then taken the 213 Roman miles to Rheims, from which it was despatched to Rome. This third leg was at least 879 Roman miles by the Great St Bernard Pass but the messenger probably went by the winter road built by Augustus through Montgenèvre, which was a minimum of 930 Roman miles. The news arrived on or before 10 January. Thus the whole journey of 1,253 Roman miles from Mainz via Cologne and

Rheims to Rome was covered in 210–230 hours. The time of year was the very worst for travelling at night. Nevertheless, an average time of at least 5½ Roman miles per hour including all stoppages was maintained. For details, see Ramsay, 'Speed', p. 65. N.b. Ramsay's and Friedlaender's distances for this journey are greater than those revealed by Google Maps – 1,400 Roman miles and 1,440 Roman miles respectively – allowing them to conclude that the journey was faster than estimated here. • **31.** Estimating that, after setting out from Rheims during the early hours of the 2nd, he stopped for an average of five hours each night (on the 2nd–9th) and arrived in Rome at dusk on the 10th, the journey from Cologne was accomplished in about 81 hours of daylight (9 days of 9 hours) and 85 hours of darkness or poor-quality light (5 hours on the morning of the 2nd and eight nights of 10 hours thereafter). His darkness speed was probably in the region of 4 Roman miles per hour. This is based on the average night-time speeds noted in four examples of later English couriers travelling stages at night – 3.4 mph, 2.3 mph, 6 mph and 3 mph – an average of 3.675 mph or 4 Roman miles per hour. (See Ian Cooper, 'The Speed and Efficiency of the Tudor South-West's Royal Post-Stage Service', *History*, 99, 5 (2014), pp. 754–74.) Thus the messenger would have covered 340 Roman miles in darkness or poor-quality light and 803 Roman miles in daylight, which equates to about 10 Roman miles per hour, or 130 Roman miles per day. Had such a man been riding in summer, in northern Italy, where there are approximately seventeen hours between dawn and dusk, at a speed of 10 Roman miles per hour, he should have been able to cover at least 198 Roman miles in twenty-four hours (170 in daylight, 28 after dusk). • **32.** Sir Henry Yule (ed.), *The Travels of Ser Marco Polo, Venetian* (2 vols, 1903), i, p. 435. • **33.** Yule (ed.), *Marco Polo*, i, p. 436. • **34.** This assumes the relay of light-carrying runners performed their 3-mile stints in a very relaxed 30 minutes each, so overnight the riders following the runners could have carried the message for 48 miles. As for the daytime, the riders would only have to average 11 miles per hour to hit a total of 224 miles. It should also be noted that Odoric of Pordenone claims Mongol riders carrying urgent messages would use dromedaries, which are faster than horses. 'When any matter of news arises in the empire messengers start at a great pace on horseback for the court; but if the matter be very serious and urgent they set off upon dromedaries. And when they come near those yams, hostels or stations, they blow a horn, whereupon the hosteler or the station straightaway makes another messenger get ready; and to him the rider who has arrived delivers up the letter, while he himself tarries for refreshment. And the other, taking the letter, makes haste to the next yam, and there does as did the first.' Henry Yule, *Cathay and the Way Thither, being a Collection of Medieval Notices of China* (2 vols, 1866), i, pp. 137–8. • **35.** E. D. Cuming (ed.), *Squire Osbaldeston: His*

Autobiography (1926), pp. 154–6; David Randall, *Great Sporting Eccentrics* (1985), p. 138. • **36.** Mary C. Hill, 'Jack Faukes, King's Messenger, and his journey to Avignon in 1343', *English Historical Review*, 57 (1942), pp. 19–30 at p. 26; Mary C. Hill, 'King's Messengers and Administrative Developments in the Thirteenth and Fourteenth Centuries', *English Historical Review*, 61 (1946), pp. 315–28, at p. 318. • **37.** R. W. Eyton, *Court, Household and Itinerary of Henry II* (1878), pp. 150, 153. • **38.** Michael Ray, 'Administrative efficiency in fourteenth-century England: the delivery of writs based on evidence from the register of Bishop Martival: a further contribution', esp. pp. 8 and 15, available at https://www.academia.edu/3444025/Administrative_efficiency_and_the_speed_of_government_and_church_bureaucracy_in_the_early_fourteenth-century_England_the_delivery_of_writs_based_on_evidence_from_the_register_of_Bishop_Martival._A_further_contribution, downloaded 18 July 2021. Note: the measurements of distance in this article do not seem to be accurate. For instance, he states the distance between Dunstable and Thatcham as 92 miles (rather than the 53 which is the shortest route on Google Maps), and that between Westminster and Ramsbury in Wiltshire at 86 miles (rather than 69). • **39.** Pierre Chaplais, *Piers Gaveston* (Oxford, 1994), p. 23. • **40.** The shortest route the messenger could have taken was 302 miles but it is more likely he travelled via Newcastle and then took the main highway south through York, a 350-mile journey, at a minimum of 78 miles per day. Even if he went straight to York from Burgh by Sands, this was a 323-mile trip, which amounts to at least 72 miles per day. • **41.** The National Archives: DL 10/253. • **42.** A. M. Ogilvie, 'The Rise of the English Post Office', *Economic Journal*, 3, 11 (1893), pp. 443–57, at p. 443. • **43.** Hill, 'Jack Faukes', pp. 19–30. • **44.** For example, Armstrong, 'Distribution and speed of news'. • **45.** Chris Given-Wilson (ed.), *Chronicles of the Revolution* (Manchester, 1993), p. 39. • **46.** Anne Curry, *Agincourt: A New History* (2005, paperback ed., 2006), p. 10. • **47.** Armstrong, 'Distribution and speed of news', p. 439. • **48.** This 200-mile distance was a traditional one based on an old customary mile (the statute mile was not recognised until 1593). Durham was thought to be 200 miles from London (it is actually 263 statute miles) and Berwick on Tweed was traditionally 248 miles (correctly, it is 339). • **49.** See Armstrong, 'Distribution and speed of news', *passim*. News of the murder of James I of Scotland travelled to London at more than 68 miles per day in February 1437. An account of the Battle of Wakefield moved at more than 72 miles per day to London in early January 1460, and the outcome of the Battle of Stoke-on-Trent reached York at a speed of approximately 76 miles per day in June 1487. The only possibly faster example is the news of the Battle of Barnet, which travelled at more than 65 miles per day to Cerne Abbas in Dorset. If it arrived in the morning of 15 April 1471, it would have travelled at nearer 90 miles per day, but as we do not know the times of despatch and arrival, it is impossible to be sure. • **50.** She landed at Plymouth at about 3 p.m. on 2 October. The information had reached the king by the 4th when he in turn informed the mayor of London (Armstrong, 'Distribution and speed of news', p. 453). Henry VII certainly paid for posts to the south-west in 1506, so this may have been part of a more permanent service. See Cooper, 'Speed and Efficiency', p. 762. • **51.** T. B. Lang, *An Historical Summary of the Post Office in Scotland* (1856), p. 3. • **52.** Herbert Joyce, *The History of the Post Office* (1893), pp. 1–2. • **53.** Edward Watson, *The Royal Mail to Ireland* (1917), pp. 5–6. • **54.** Cooper, 'Speed and Efficiency', p. 762. • **55.** Watson, *Royal Mail to Ireland*, pp. 13–20, esp. p. 15. • **56.** Joyce, *Post Office*, pp. 175–6. • **57.** Cooper, 'Speed and Efficiency', p. 767. • **58.** Thomas Birch (ed.), *The Works of the Honourable Robert Boyle* (new ed., 6 vols, 1772), i, p. viii. • **59.** The siege of Kinsale was defeated on 3 January 1601/2 in the Julian Calendar, then in use in England, which was 24 December in the Gregorian Calendar. Boyle thus had 85% full moonlight. See https://www.moonpage.com/. • **60.** The reasons to doubt Boyle's account are that one of the commanders at Kinsale, Sir Richard Leveson, wrote a brief note with news of the victory to Lord Nottingham, admiral of England, on the day after the battle, *Friday* 25 December (Mary Anne Everett Green (ed.), *Calendar of State Papers Domestic: Elizabeth, 1601–3 With Addenda 1547–65* (1870), p. 132). But Boyle states he set out on a *Monday* – presumably Monday 28th. It is difficult to see why he set out with such speed having waited more than two days after the first report of the outcome of the battle had been despatched to London. Dudley Carleton, who was in London, was clearly still unaware of the outcome of the battle on Tuesday 29th (Green (ed.), *Calendar*, pp. 134–5). If Boyle was simply wrong with regard to the days of the week when he undertook his journey and actually travelled on Friday and Saturday, Dudley Carleton should have heard the news by Tuesday 29th. Nevertheless, the inclusion of such a detail at such length in such a brief account of his life suggests Boyle set great store by it. • **61.** Watson, *Royal Mail to Ireland*, p. 24. • **62.** *Shakespeare's England* (Oxford, 2 vols, 1917), i, pp. 201–2. • **63.** Williams, *Thomas Platter's Travels*, p. 230. Note that Platter himself describes the journey as '44 English miles', since the postal system at this time was still using the old customary miles that had prevailed by tradition. See Joyce, *Post Office*, pp. 175–6. • **64.** Black, *Reign of Elizabeth*, p. 209n. • **65.** For example, Sir Nicholas Arnold (1507–1580), MP for Gloucestershire and Lord Deputy of Ireland, who was the most famous breeder of horses in the country.

6. Literacy

1. This chapter is loosely based on the keynote address for the twentieth anniversary conference of the International Tyndale Society, Hertford College, Oxford, 2 October 2015. The original speech was published as 'Tyndale's Legacy in English History', *Tyndale Society Journal*, 46 (Winter 2015–16), pp. 11–31. I am very grateful to Pat Whitten and Jill Maslen for their kind invitation to speak on such an occasion. • **2.** David Daniell, *William Tyndale, a biography* (1994), p. 191 says 28 October. In his *ODNB* article on Tyndale, Professor Daniell gives the date as 27 October. • **3.** Henry R. T. Summerson, 'An English Bible and other books belonging to Henry IV', *Bulletin of the John Rylands Library*, 79, 1 (1997); Anne Hudson, *The Premature Reformation: Wycliffite Texts and Lollard History* (Oxford, 1988), pp. 110–11, 115. • **4.** Daniell, *Tyndale*, p. 92. • **5.** Daniell, *Tyndale*, p. 93. • **6.** Daniell, *Tyndale*, p. 79. • **7.** Daniell, *Tyndale*, pp. 183–4. • **8.** David Daniell, 'Coverdale, Miles', *ODNB*. • **9.** For the proportions attributable to Tyndale, see Jon Nielsen and Royal Skousen, 'How Much of the King James Bible Is William Tyndale's?', *Reformation*, 3, 1 (1998), pp. 49–74. The number of words in each book of the Bible has been taken from https://holyword.church/miscellaneous-resources/how-many-words-in-each-book-of-the-bible/ (downloaded 12 August 2022). If 76% of Tyndale's Old Testament work was retained by the King James Bible committee, this equates to 257,307 words (including the Book of Jonah). 84% of the New Testament is 150,369 words. Hence the total is 407,676 (52%) of the 788,280 words in the whole Bible. • **10.** Most of this account of Tyndale's life is drawn from David Daniell's article on him in *ODNB*. The statistic about a third of Americans using the King James Bible is a combination of two other independently derived figures. According to Gallup, 72% of American citizens responded to a 2018 survey with the statement that religion played a 'very important' (51%) or 'fairly important' (21%) part in their lives. Among Christians, who form 65% of the population, the proportion was 87% (https://news.gallup.com/poll/245651/religion-considered-important-americans.aspx, downloaded 11 August 2022). Second, a 2014 survey found that 55% of American Christians relied on the King James Bible (http://www.raac.iupui.edu/files/2713/9413/8354/Bible_in_American_Life_Report_March_6_2014.pdf, downloaded 11 August 2022). If the King James Bible is regularly used by 55% of the 87% of American Christians who regard their religion as 'important', the proportion of the American population that uses it is at least 31%, not including the occasional use by Christians for whom their religion is not that important. As for alternative candidates for the most repeated words, the most likely rival is the Qur'an – but Muslims hold that to be God's words as revealed to the prophet Muhammad, who then recited them from memory. • **11.** Christopher Hill, *The English Bible and the Seventeenth-Century Revolution* (1993), p. 7. • **12.** Thomas Russell (ed.), *The Works of the English Reformers, William Tyndale and John Frith* (3 vols, 1831), i, p. 6. • **13.** Diarmid MacCulloch, *Reformation: Europe's House Divided 1490–1700* (2003), p. 203. • **14.** I am very grateful to Seb Falk for reminding me of this important point. • **15.** https://www.bl.uk/learning/timeline/item101943.html (downloaded 17 August 2022). • **16.** Hill, *English Bible*, pp. 30–1. • **17.** Henry Brinkelow, *The Lamentacyon of a Christen agaynst the Citye of London for some certayn greate vyces used therin* (Nuremberg, 1545), p. 91, quoted in E. M. Leonard, *The Early History of English Poor Relief* (Cambridge, 1900), p. 29. • **18.** Paul Slack, *The English Poor Law 1531–1782* (1995), pp. 14–15. • **19.** Quoted in Thomas Deloney, *Jack of Newbury* (2015), p. 17. • **20.** Henry Arthington, *Prouision for the Poore, now in penurie, Out of the store-house of Gods plenty* (1597). • **21.** Slack, *Poor Law*, p. 24. • **22.** UNESCO, *Progress of Literacy in Various Countries: a preliminary statistical study of available census data since 1900* (1953), p. 210. • **23.** 34 & 35 Henry VIII, cap 1. • **24.** Hill, *English Bible*, p. 18. • **25.** Stephens, 'Literacy in England, Scotland and Wales, 1500–1900', p. 555. • **26.** John Standish, *Discourse where it is debated whether it be expedient that the Scriptures should be in English for al men to read at wyll* (1554), quoted in Hill, *English Bible*, p. 16. • **27.** Paul Slack, 'Mirrors of health and treasures of poor men: the use of the vernacular medical literature of Tudor England', in Charles Webster (ed.), *Health, Medicine and Mortality in the Sixteenth Century* (Cambridge, 1979), pp. 9–60. • **28.** David Daniell, 'No Tyndale, no Shakespeare: A paper given at the Tyndale Society Kirtling Meeting, Suffolk, 16 April 2005' (http://www.tyndale.org/tsj29/daniell.htm (downloaded 11 August 2022)). Professor Daniell made the same remark in his *ODNB* article on Tyndale (2004). • **29.** David Crystal, 'King James Bible: How are the Mighty Fallen?', *History Today*, 61, 1 (January 2011). • **30.** These figures were the results of searches on the British Library catalogue. More detailed statistics are given in Ian Mortimer, *The Time Traveller's Guide to Elizabethan England* (2012), p. 104. • **31.** Russell (ed.), *Works of the English Reformers*, i, p. 244. • **32.** 'Forasmuch as our holy prelates and our ghostly religious, which ought to defend God's word, speak evil of it . . . that it causeth insurrection and teacheth the people to disobey their heads and governors and moveth them to rise against their princes; and to make all common and havock of other men's goods therefore have I made this little treatise that followeth, containing all obedience that is of God.' Russell (ed.), *Works of the English Reformers*, i, p. 197. • **33.** Russell (ed.), *Works of the English Reformers*, i, p. 201. • **34.** Karl Gunther and Ethan H. Shagan, 'Protestant Radicalism and Political Thought in the

Reign of Henry VIII', *Past & Present*, 194 (2007), pp. 35–74, at p. 60. Interestingly, the book in question has a dedication to Anne Boleyn. • **35.** Andrew Prescott, 'Ball, John (d. 1381)', *ODNB*, quoting Walsingham, *Chronicon Angliae*, 321. • **36.** Quoted in Peter Blickle, 'The Criminalization of Peasant Resistance in the Holy Roman Empire: Toward a History of the Emergence of High Treason in Germany', *Journal of Modern History*, vol. 58, Supplement: Politics and Society in the Holy Roman Empire, 1500–1806 (1986), pp. S88–S97, at p. S91. • **37.** Quoted in C. W. C. Oman, 'The German Peasants War of 1525', *English Historical Review*, 5, 17 (1890), pp. 65–94, at p. 86. • **38.** Christopher Hill, 'Tyndale and his successors', *Reformation*, 1 (1996), pp. 98–112. http://www.tyndale.org/reformj01/hill.html (downloaded 18 August 2022). • **39.** Gunther and Shagan, 'Protestant Radicalism', pp. 54–7. • **40.** Henry Broderick, *The Complaynt of Roderyck Mors* (Savoy, 1542), quoted in Gunther and Shagan, 'Protestant Radicalism', p. 57.

7. Individualism

1. This chapter was inspired by being invited to give the keynote address to the 8th Southampton Symposium of the Self and Identity, 14 July 2016. I am grateful to Dr Aiden Gregg of the Department of Psychology at the University of Southampton for inviting me and guiding me through some of the literature. • **2.** Paul J. Sylvia, 'Self-Awareness Theory', *International Encyclopaedia of the Social Sciences* (2008). • **3.** See Roy F. Baumeister, Jennifer D. Campbell, Joachim I. Krueger and Kathleen D. Vohs, 'Does High Self-Esteem Cause Better Performance, Interpersonal Success, Happiness, or Healthier Lifestyles?', *Psychological Science in the Public Interest*, vol. 4, no. 1 (May 2003), pp. 1–44. This wide survey of the literature concluded that there is little evidence for high self-esteem leading to 'better performance' or 'healthier lifestyles' but showed that high self-esteem led to 'enhanced initiative and pleasant feelings' and that high-esteem – which necessarily is dependent on self-evaluation and, before that can take place, self-awareness – 'makes people more willing to speak up in groups and to criticise the group's approach'. • **4.** This is known by the title *Rectitudines Singularum Personum*. See https://earlyenglishlaws.ac.uk/laws/texts/rect/ for the location of manuscripts and editions. • **5.** We find instances of rash behaviour throughout the Middle Ages. Even in 1278, two cases of the 145 prosecuted at a series of trials in London were for murders that had taken place following games of chess. But acts of wanton violence steadily declined. See Eisner, 'Long-term trends in violent crime' (the chess murders are noted on p. 84). • **6.** David C. Douglas and George Greenaway (eds),

English Historical Documents, ii (1953), pp. 606–7. • **7.** Colin Morris, *The Discovery of the Individual 1050–1200* (1972, Harper Torchbook ed., 1973), p. 32. • **8.** Morris, *Discovery of the Individual*, pp. 64–7. • **9.** Morris, *Discovery of the Individual*, p. 82. • **10.** From the translation by Henry Adams Bellows (1922). https://sourcebooks.fordham.edu/basis/abelard-histcal.asp, downloaded 23 August 2022. • **11.** Charles Eveleigh Woodruff, 'The Financial Aspect of the Cult of St Thomas at Canterbury', *Archaeologia Cantiana*, 44 (1932), pp. 13–32, at p. 16. • **12.** John Gillingham, 'From Civilitas to Civility: Codes of Manners in Medieval and Early Modern England', *Transactions of the Royal Historical Society*, Sixth Series, 12 (2002), pp. 267–89. • **13.** Fiona Whelan, Olivia Spenser and Francesca Petrizzo, *The Book of the Civilised Man* (2019), p. 70. • **14.** Keen, *Chivalry*, p. 30. • **15.** Helen Waddell, *Medieval Latin Lyrics* (1929, Penguin ed., 1952), pp. 182–95. Note: Waddell left the lines *Deus sit propitius / huic potatori* untranslated. • **16.** H. T. Riley (ed.), *Liber Custumarum* (2 vols, 1860), ii, pp. 2–15. • **17.** Morris, *Discovery of the Individual*, p. 44. • **18.** https://epistolae.ctl.columbia.edu/letter/25293.html, downloaded 23 August 2022, quoting J. LeClercq and H. Rochais (eds), *Sancti Bernardi Opera* (Rome, 1979), epistle 113, translated by Bruno Scott James, *The Letters of St. Bernard of Clairvaux* (1953), pp. 174–7. • **19.** Samuel N. Rosenberg, Margaret Switten and Gérard Le Vot (eds), *Songs of the Troubadours and Trouvères* (1998), p. 140. Pierre de Vic is also known as *Lo Monge de Montaudon*. • **20.** Metropolitan Museum of Art, New York: Accession no. 47.101.47. This dates from 1180–1200. It was made in Britain. • **21.** The 'bronze' used in these mirrors was really a copper alloy made with approximately 80% more tin than in normal bronze. When polished, they gave a good enough reflection for a woman to apply her makeup. See Susan La Niece, Rachel Ward, Duncan Hook and P. T. Craddock, 'Medieval Islamic Copper Alloys', *Scientific Research on Ancient Asian Metallurgy* (1990), pp. 248–54; British Museum Collection catalogue: https://www.britishmuseum.org/collection/, searched 23 August 2022. • **22.** Eva Matthews Sanford, 'Honorius, Presbyter and Scholasticus', *Speculum*, 23, 3 (1948), pp. 397–425, at p. 421. • **23.** The total value of specie in circulation in the 1150s was between £30,000 and £80,000. By 1320, it was approaching £2 million. See Martin Allen, 'The Volume of the English Currency, 1158–1470', *Economic History Review*, 54, 4 (2001), pp. 595–611, at pp. 606–7. Whereas there was hardly any credit in the 1150s, large amounts were being borrowed two hundred years later, especially in towns, where prosperous merchants financed up to three-quarters of their acquisitions by borrowing. See Pamela Nightingale, 'Monetary Contraction and Mercantile Credit in Later Medieval England', *Economic History Review*, 43, 4 (1990), pp. 560–75. • **24.** Robert C. Palmer, 'The Origins of Property in England', *Law and History Review*, 3, 1 (1985), pp. 1–50.

• **25.** Thomas Johnes (ed.), *Chronicles of England, France, Spain and the adjoining Countries by Sir John Froissart* (2 vols, 1848), i, p. 240. I have amended the wording slightly in places to make it more comprehensible. • **26.** Quoted in Paul H. Kocher, 'The Physician as Atheist', *Huntington Library Quarterly*, 10, 3 (1947), pp. 229–49; at p. 231. • **27.** Kocher, 'Physician as Atheist', p. 230. • **28.** British Library: Harley MS 6848. • **29.** As noted in Francis Meeres's *Palladis Tamia* (1598). • **30.** John Addington Symonds (trans.), *The Autobiography of Benvenuto Cellini* (New York, 1910), chapter li. Downloaded from https://gutenberg.readingroo.ms/etext03/7clln10h.htm, 14 September 2022. • **31.** Jerome Cardan, trans. Jean Stoner, *The Book of My Life* (New York, 1930), pp. 92–4.

Illustrations

'The Last Supper' from Byzantine-Campanian school frescoes, 1072–8, Basilica of Sant'Angelo in Formis, Campania, Italy (A. Dagli Orti/NPL–DeA Picture Library/Bridgeman Images).

The Last Supper by Pieter Coecke van Aelst (1502–50) (Bridgeman Images).

Rectangular map of the world, *c.* 1030, vellum (British Library Board. All Rights Reserved/Bridgeman Images).

Map of the world from the *Atlas sive cosmographicae meditationes de fabrica mundi et fabricati figura* by Gerard Mercator (1512–94), Duisburg, 1585 (Royal Geographical Society/Bridgeman Images).

'Norman cavalry attacks the English shield-wall', Bayeux Tapestry, wool embroidery on linen, *c.* 1070 (with special authorisation of the city of Bayeux/Bridgeman Images).

Siege of Maastricht (1579) by the Spanish troops under Alessandro Farnese, painting, San Lorenzo de El Escorial, Madrid, Spain (Royal Monastery of San Lorenzo de El Escorial/Bridgeman Images).

Reconstruction of a Viking-period house at Trelleborg, Denmark (Bridgeman Images).

Hardwick Hall, Derbyshire (Ian Mortimer).

Interior of a replica of a Norse longhouse at Brookpoint, Unst, Shetland Islands, Scotland (Arterra Picture Library/Alamy).

The High Great Chamber at Hardwick Hall (Bridgeman Images).

'Ploughing' from a calendar, vellum, *c.* 1030 (Bridgeman Images).

Watch with alarm by Nicholas Vaillin, made in London *c.* 1600 (Metropolitan Museum of Art, New York; gift of J. Pierpont Morgan, 1917. Accession Number 17.190.1476. Open Access).

Coconut cup made in Holland in 1533–4 (Metropolitan Museum of Art, New York; gift of J. Pierpont Morgan, 1917. Accession Number 17.190.622a, b. Open Access).

'Feminine Vanities' from *The Fall of Princes* by Giovanni Boccaccio (1313–75), vellum, 1472 (Bridgeman Images).

Portrait of a Man by Jan van Eyck, oil on oak, 1433 (Bridgeman Images).

'Studies of the Illumination of the Moon' by Leonardo da Vinci, from *Codex Leicester, c.* 1506–8, pen and ink on paper (Bridgeman Images).

Cathédrale Saint-Pierre, Beauvais, Hauts-de-France, Oise, France (Bridgeman Images).

The interior of Le Mans Cathedral (Ian Mortimer).

Index